TEEN LIFE IN EUROPE

**Recent Titles in
Teen Life around the World**

Teen Life in the Middle East
Ali Akbar Madhi, editor

Teen Life in Asia
Judith J. Slater, editor

Teen Life in Africa
Toyin Falola, editor

Teen Life in Latin America and the Caribbean
Cynthia Margarita Tompkins and Kristen Sternberg, editors

TEEN LIFE IN EUROPE

Edited by Shirley R. Steinberg

Foreword by Richard M. Lerner

Teen Life around the World
Jeffrey S. Kaplan, Series Editor

GREENWOOD PRESS
Westport, Connecticut • London

Library of Congress Cataloging-in-Publication Data

Teen life in Europe / edited by Shirley R. Steinberg; foreword by Richard M. Lerner.
    p. cm. — (Teen life around the world, ISSN 1540–4897)
  Includes bibliographical references and index.
  ISBN 0–313–32727–0 (alk. paper)
  1. Teenagers—Europe—Conduct of life. 2. Teenagers—Europe—Social conditions.
3. Teenagers—Education—Europe. 4. Self-esteem in adolescence—Europe.
I. Steinberg, Shirley R., 1952– II. Series.
HQ799.E85T44 2005
305.235'094—dc22   2005015183

British Library Cataloguing in Publication Data is available.

Library of Congress Catalog Card Number: 2005015183
ISBN: 0–313–32727–0
ISSN: 1540–4897

First published in 2005

Greenwood Press, 88 Post Road West, Westport, CT 06881
An imprint of Greenwood Publishing Group, Inc.
www.greenwood.com

Printed in the United States of America

The paper used in this book complies with the
Permanent Paper Standard issued by the National
Information Standards Organization (Z39.48–1984).

10 9 8 7 6 5 4 3 2 1

To my beloved comrades in spectacular Europe: Birgit, Erika, Françoise, Heinz-Hermann, Heinz, Jõao, Marta, Pato, Rámon, and Uwe

CONTENTS

FOREWORD: TOWARD A WORLD OF POSITIVE YOUTH DEVELOPMENT

In these early years of the twenty-first century a new vision and vocabulary for discussing young people has emerged. Propelled by the increasingly more collaborative contributions of scholars, practitioners, advocates, and policy makers, youth are viewed as resources to be developed. The new vocabulary is legitimated by scholarly efforts at advancing what are termed "developmental systems theories." These models emphasize the plasticity of human development, that is, the potential for systematic change in behavior that exists as a consequence of mutually influential relationships between the developing person and his or her biology, psychological characteristics, family, community, culture, physical and designed ecology, and historical niche.

The plasticity of development legitimizes an optimistic view of potential for promoting positive changes in human life and directs emphasis to the strengths for positive development that are present within all young people. Accordingly, concepts such as developmental assets, positive youth development, moral development, civic engagement, well-being, and thriving have been used increasingly in research and applications associated with adolescents and their world. All concepts are predicated on the ideas that *every* young person has the potential for successful, healthy development and that *all* youth possess the capacity for positive development.

This vision for and vocabulary about youth has evolved over the course of a scientifically arduous path. Complicating this new, positive conceptualization of the character of youth as resources for the healthy development of self, families, and communities was an antithetical theoretical approach to the nature and development of young people. Dating within science to, at least, the publication in 1904 of G. Stanley Hall's two volume work on adolescence, youth have been characterized by a deficit view, one that conceptualizes their behaviors as deviations from normative development. Understanding such deviations was not seen as being of direct relevance to scholarship aimed at discovering the principles of basic developmental processes. Accordingly, the characteristics of youth were regarded as issues of "only" applied concern—and thus of secondary scientific interest. Not only did this model separate basic science from application but, as well, it disembedded the adolescent from the study of normal or healthy development. It also often separated the young person from among those members of society that could be relied on to produce valued outcomes for family, community, and civic life. In short, the deficit view of youth as problems to be managed split the study of young people from the study of health and positive individual and social development.

The current scholarly and applied work that counters the historical, deficit view of adolescence, and in turn builds upon developmental systems theory to advance the new, positive vocabulary about young people and the growing research evidence for the potential of all youth to develop in positive ways, is both represented and advanced significantly by the *Teen Life around the World* series. More so than any other set of resources currently available to young people, parents, and teachers, the volumes in this series offer rich and engaging depictions about the diverse ways in which young people pursue positive lives in their families, communities, and nations. The volumes provide vivid reflections of the energy, passion, and skills that young people possess—even under challenging ecological or economic conditions—and the impressive ways in which adolescents capitalize on their strengths to pursue positive lives during their teenage years and to prepare themselves to be productive adult members of their families and communities.

Across the volumes in this series a compelling story of the common humanity of all people emerges, one that justifies a great deal of hope that, in today's adolescents, there exist the resources for a humane, peaceful, tolerant, and global civil society. To attain such a world, all people must begin by appreciating the diversity of young people and their cultures and that, through such diversity, the world possesses multiple, potentially productive paths to human well-being and accomplishment. Readers of the *Teen Life around the World* series will be rewarded with just this information.

Ultimately, we must all continue to educate ourselves about the best means available to promote enhanced life chances among all of the world's youth, but especially among those whose potential for positive contributions to civil society is most in danger of being wasted. The books in this series constitute vital assets in pursuit of this knowledge. Given the enormous, indeed historically unprecedented, challenges facing all nations, perhaps especially as they strive to raise healthy and successful young people capable of leading civil society productively, responsibly, and morally across the twenty-first century, there is no time to lose in the development of such assets. The *Teen Life around the World* series is, then, a most timely and markedly important resource.

Richard M. Lerner
Eliot-Pearson Department of Child Development
Tufts University
Medford, MA

SERIES FOREWORD

Have you ever imagined what it would be like to live in a different country? What would it be like to speak a different language? Eat different foods? Wear different clothes? Attend a different school? Listen to different music, or maybe, the same music, in a different language? How about practicing new customs? Or, better yet, a different religion? Simply, how different would your life be if you were born and raised in another region of the world? Would you be different? And if so, how?

As we begin the twenty-first century, young people around the world face enormous challenges. Those born to wealth or relative comfort enjoy technological miracles and can click a button or move a mouse and discover a world of opportunity and pleasure. Those born without means struggle just to survive.

Education, though, remains a way out of poverty and for many privileged young people it is the ultimate goal. As more and more jobs, including in the manufacturing and service sectors, require literacy, numeracy, and computer skill, brains are increasingly valued over brawn: In the United States, entry-level wages for people with only a high-school education have fallen by more than 20 percent since the 1970s. Job prospects are bleaker than ever for youths who do not continue their education after high school. And, to be sure, while there are exceptions—like the teenager who starts a basement computer business and becomes a multimillionaire—working a string of low-paying service jobs with no medical insurance is a much more common scenario for those with limited education. And this seems to be true for adolescents in most postindustrialist countries around the world.

Adolescent girls, in particular, are at a disadvantage in many nations, facing sex discrimination as an obstacle to obtaining even basic education and social skills. In the Middle East and South Asia, girls are more likely to be pulled from school at an early age, and are thus less likely to develop critical literacy skills. Across most of the world, girls face more demands for work in the home and restrictions on movement that constrain their opportunities to gain direct experience with diverse social worlds. Similarly, as rates of divorce and abandonment rise worldwide, so do the chances for young women who fail to obtain skills to function independently. And as adults, they are increasingly vulnerable to poverty and exploitation.

ADOLESCENCE AROUND THE GLOBE

Adolescent life is truly plagued by difficulties and determined by context and circumstance. Anthropologist Margaret Mead (1901–1978) may have been the first social scientist to question the universality of the adolescent experience. When Mead contrasted the experience of North American and South Pacific young people in terms of sexuality, she found their experiences and attitudes toward sexuality dramatically different (South Pacific adolescents were more tolerant), and, she contended, adolescence should be seen in the contexts in which people live and dwell. In fact, for Mead and other social scientists, the only definition that can best describe adolescence is at best, restricted to a "period of transition," in which young people are no longer considered children, but not yet considered an adult.

Adolescence is generally understood as the period between the ages of 15–19, with some scholars referring them to up to age 24. The term *young adult* is the most apt term for this age group, and without doubt, the many biological, psychological, and behavioral changes which mark this age, make this a concept that is continually dynamic and fluid in its change. Depending on region of the world, the concept of adolescence or young adult is either emerging, or already well established. Most Western European societies use legal markers to underline the passage to adulthood, commonly set at age 16, 18, or 21. Thus, from country to country, there are minimum legal ages for marriage, for consensual intercourse, and also for access to sexual and reproductive health services without parental consent.

In many developing countries, though, the concept of adolescence has either been non-existent or is relatively new in concept and understanding. Rather than define adulthood by age or biology, children become adults through well-established rites of passage—for example, religious ceremony, or marriage. In India, for example, especially in rural areas, many girls enter into arranged marriages before the onset of their first menstruation cycle, and then, have their first child at around 16 years of age. For these young Indian girls, there is no adolescence, as they shift so quickly from childhood to motherhood. Similarly, in traditional Sri Lankan society, young people— once they enter puberty—are expected to get married, or in the case of a male, wear the yellow robe of a monk. To remain single is not held in high esteem because it is considered "neither here nor there."

Yet, the world is changing. Traditional patterns of behavior for young people, and what is expected of them by the adults, are in a state of flux, and in more open societies, adolescence are emerging as a powerful force for influence and growth in Africa, Asia, and Latin America. In these regions, massive economic, institutional and social changes have been brought about by Western colonial expansion and by the move toward a global society and economy. With more young people working in non-agricultural jobs, attending school longer, delaying marriage, adolescents are holding their own ground with adults.

In Indonesia, for example, young boys in urban areas are no longer tied to the farm and have started forming peer groups, as an alternative to exclusive life spent entirely inside the immediacy of their family. Similarly, in the urban areas of India, a many girls attend single-sex schools, thus, spending more time with peer groups, eroding the traditional practice of arranged marriages at an early age. In Nigeria, young people attend school for longer periods of time, thus preparing for jobs in their now modern economy. And in many Latin American countries, where young girls were once also hurried into pre-arranged marriages, now, young girls are staying in school so, they too can prepare for non-agricultural jobs.

And yet, those without means can only fantasize about what they see of mainstream material culture. As always, money is the societal divide that cruelly demarcates and is unrelenting in its effects on social, cultural, and psychological behavior. Young people living in poverty struggle daily with the pressures of survival in a seemingly indifferent, and often dangerous world. And access to wealth, or the simple conveniences of modern society, makes a considerable difference in the development of the young people. In rural areas in Zimbabwe and Papua New Guinea, for example, simple changes such as building of a road or highway—enabling the bringing in of supplies and expertise—has had profound effects on young people's lifestyles.

When young people must leave their homes—either because of poverty, or increasingly, due to civil war, the result is often unprecedented numbers forced into bonded labor and commercial sex. For example, in the Indian cities of New Delhi, Mumbai, and Calcutta, thousands of young people take on menial jobs such as washing cars, pushing hand carts, collecting edibles from garbage dumps, or simply, begging. In Thailand, still more thousands of young girls earn their living as prostitutes. And in many countries of Eastern Europe, tens of thousands of young people are believed to be not attending school or formally employed, but instead, engaging in drug trafficking. Worldwide, the streets and temporary shelters are home to between 100 and 200 million children and adolescents, who are cut off from their parents and extended families (World Health Organization, 2000). What is it like to be them? What is it like to be young, scared, and poor?

Since the 1980s political and civil rights have improved substantially throughout the world, and 81 countries have taken significant steps in democratization, with 33 military regimes replaced by civilian governments. But of these fledgling democracies, only 47 are considered full democracies today. Only 82 countries, representing 57 percent of the world's population, are fully democratic.

Economically speaking, the proportion of the world's extremely poor fell from 29 percent in 1990 to 23 percent in 1999. Still, in 1999, 2.8 billion people lived on less than $2 a day, with 1.2 billion of them surviving on the margins of subsistence with less than $1 a day. In 2000, 1.1 billion people lacked access to safe water, and 2.4 billion did not have access to any form of improved sanitation services.

And armed conflict continue to blight the lives of millions: since 1990, 3.6 million people have died as a result of civil wars and ethnic violence, more than 16 times the number killed in wars between states. Civilians have accounted for more than 90 percent of the casualties—either injured or killed—in post–cold war conflicts. Ninety countries are affected by landmines and live explosives, with rough estimates of 15,000 to 20,000 mine victims each year.

TEEN LIFE AROUND THE WORLD—THE SERIES

The Greenwood series *Teen Life around the World* examines what life is like for teens in different regions of the world. These volumes describe in detail the lives of young people in places both familiar and unfamiliar. How do teens spend their days? What makes their lives special? What difficulties and special burdens do they bear? And what will be their future as they make their way in their world?

Each volume is devoted to a region or regions of the world. For the purpose of this series, the volumes are divided as follows:

- Teen Life in Africa
- Teen Life in the Middle East
- Teen Life in Europe
- Teen Life in Central and South America and the Caribbean
- Teen Life in Asia

Readers can see similarities and differences in areas of the world that are relatively close in proximity, customs, and practices. Comparisons can be made between various countries in a region and across regions. American teens will perhaps be struck by the influence of American pop culture—music, fashion, food—around the world.

All volumes follow the same general format. The standardized format highlights information that all young people would most like to know. Each volume has up to fifteen chapters that describe teen life in a specific country in that region of the world. The countries chosen generally are representative of that region, and attempts were made to write about countries that young people would be most curious to learn more about.

Each chapter begins with a profile of the particular country. Basic political, economic, social, and cultural issues are discussed and a brief history of the country is provided. After this brief introduction to the specific country, an overview of teen life in that country is given, with a discussion of a teenager's typical day, family life, traditional and non-traditional foods, schooling, social life, recreation, entertainment, and religious practices and cultural practices. Finally, each chapter concludes with a list of resources that will help readers learn more about this country. These resources include nonfiction and fiction, web sites, other sources to find information on the country, such as embassies, and pen pal addresses.

Although these chapters cannot tell the complete story of what it means to be a teenager in that region of the world and recognizing that perhaps there is no one typical lifestyle in any country, they provide a good starting point for insight into others' lives.

The contributors to this series present an informative and engaging look at the life of young people around the world and write in a straightforward manner. The volumes are edited by noted experts. They have an intimate understanding of their chosen region of the world—having either lived there, and/or they have devoted their professional lives to studying, teaching about, and researching the place. Also, an attempt was made to have each chapter written by an expert on teen life in that country. Above all, what these authors reveal is that young people everywhere—no matter where they live—have much in common. Although they might observe different social customs, rituals, and habits, they still long for the same basic things—security, respect, and love. They still live in that state where they half child/half adult, as they wait anxiously to become fully functioning members of their society.

As series editor, it is my hope that these volumes, which are unique in publishing in both content and style, will increase your knowledge of teen life around the world.

Jeffrey S. Kaplan
Series Editor

REFERENCES

Baru, R. "The Social Milieu of the Adolescent Girl." In *Adolescent Girl in India: An Indian Perspective*, ed. S. Mehra. Saket, New Delhi: MAMTA, Health Institute for Mother and Child, 1995.

Caldwell, J. C., P. Caldwell, and B. K. Caldwell. "The Construction of Adolescence in a Changing World: Implications for Sexuality, Reproduction, and Marriage." *Studies in Family Planning* 29, no. 2 (1998): 137–53.

Dehne, K. L., and G. Reidner. "Adolescence: A Dynamic Concept." *Reproductive Health Matters* 9, no. 17 (2001): 11–16.

Deutsche Gesellschaft fur Technische Zusammenarbeit. *Youth in Development Cooperation: Approaches and Prospects in the Multisectoral Planning Group "Youth."* Eschborn: GTZ, 1997.1998.

Goswami, P. K. "Adolescent Girl and MCH Programme in India." In *Adolescent Girl in India: An Indian Perspective*, ed. S. Mehra. Saket, New Delhi: MAMTA, Health Institute for Mother and Child, 1995.

Larson, Reed. "The Future of Adolescence: Lengthening the Ladders to Adulthood." *The Futurist* 36, no. 6 (2002): 16–21.

McCauley, A. P., and C. Salter. "Meeting the Needs of Young Adults." *Population Report*, Series J, no. 41 (1995): 1–39.

UNAIDS. *Sex and Youth: Contextual Factors Affecting Risk for HIV/AIDS*. Geneva: UNAIDS, 1999.

UN Development Report. 2002.

World Health Organization. 2000.

INTRODUCTION: WHAT MAKES TEEN LIFE SO UNIQUE?

Shirley R. Steinberg

Many teachers, parents, psychologists, and researchers have claimed that it is nearly impossible to know what makes a teenager so unique. Adolescence is relatively new in the historical discussion of the development of human beings. Before the twentieth century babies grew quickly into men and women. Childhood was very short; many children were working by the age of 9 or 10. Children joined the daily workforce with their parents at young ages, married young, and died early as adults compared to the life cycle in the twenty-first century. Naturally, since so many people over 10 years old were treated as adults, there was never a time to consider the unique needs and state of being we know as the teenage years.

During the end of the nineteenth century and beginning of the twentieth century, citizens started to acknowledge that childhood was indeed an entirely different state of being than adulthood. Teenagers over 13 or 14 were still treated as adults. School was not required for teenagers; many married young and became adults at a very young age. It wasn't until boys and girls were required to attend school that adults started to view those in their teen years as not quite adults, as people who were between childhood and adulthood. Consequently, in the last hundred years, childhood and adolescence have become new social constructions, new social states. It is the social and chronological state of the teenage years that this book addresses.

Why read this volume? If the reader is not from a European country, then he or she can compare and contrast the similarities and differences. If the reader is from Europe, he or she can enjoy looking at the differences that appear between teens that literally live only a few kilometers from one another. There are definitely themes that flow through this book. One can make generalizations about school, sports, parents, and family life. The differences begin to appear as climate, geographical location, history, religion, economics, and parental/governmental involvement are considered.

As society changes, so changes adolescence. As cultural revolutions occur, Western teenagers are the first to reflect new ways of seeing the world, living their lives, and creating new ethics and standards. Because adolescence is so biologically shaped (in that being a teenager contains very complex physical changes), issues involving gender identity, sexual identity, and physical appearance are very important—perhaps the most important things about being a teenager.

While childhood is considered endearing, sweet, innocent, and constantly in need of supervision and care, adolescence is a state where teens can be looked at as obstinate, worldly know-it-alls, constantly in need of control and demanding of independence. Teen music, clothing, social life, language, and attitudes reflect the conflicts between what adults want of and see in teens and what teens want of and see in themselves. Maybe that is why studying the life of teens around the world is so very important. If the reader is a teenager, then this book can serve to share the lives of teens in Europe; if the reader is an adult, then this book can serve to exemplify the social position and identity that teens demand throughout the world.

Had this book been written 20 years ago, it would have been much different. The importance of the Internet, video games, and cell phones to teenagers are new additions to those aged 12–20. European countries boast advanced technologies that bring the Internet into many homes, video games to cafés and pubs, and a cell phone in many of the pockets of hip-hop-styled pants or low-waisted jeans. These technologies have allowed teens to explore their own environment as well as surf for knowledge and relationships around the world. This new global adolescence creates freedom for teen surfers and also brings the world closer to youth. Cell phones allow youth to contact one another quickly, and also create a way for parents to keep in close contact with their teens. Along with the influences of technology comes the amount of time spent by teens engaged in its use. New addictions have been formed for video-game playing, Internet surfing, and cell phone use. Researchers are interested in how much time is spent by youth on these activities and if this time is detrimental to the health and development of teenagers.

Music is the constant that has always defined teenage years. While each country in Europe has unique musical roots, teenagers have seemed to find common ground as they share music from each others' countries and North America. One listening to youth-centered radio stations in

European countries may find it difficult to name the country where the program originates due to the global fusion of artists from the West. While ABBA is a Swedish group, music of this group airs daily over the radio in every European country. The Canadian group Barenaked Ladies can be heard in the cafés of Amsterdam and the pizza restaurants of downtown Naples, and hip-hop artists have lent their influence in dress, language, and music to teens on the beaches of Nice. Music for teenagers is an international language, and teen knowledge of popular culture and music allows them to identify with teens in many other countries.

In adolescence, as goes music, so goes style. Teenagers express their musical tastes through hairstyles, makeup, dress, slang, and dance. Generally speaking, many teens choose their look because of the music they listen to. Sports also contributes to assisting teens in creating personas. Young European men and women often wear sports clothing as casual dress, and look to sports players as role models.

Because adolescence ushers in the need for romantic relationships, physical looks become one of the most important aspects of being a teenager. National origin doesn't seem to make a difference in this particular aspect of being a teen. The enjoyment of music and sports lends to the socialization of young men and women, as do schooling and after-school activities. The teenage years contain the most volatile emotions, and along with these emotions comes the awkward need to be accepted and part of a larger social group. There is not an expert nor a teenager anywhere that can deny that being an adolescent is incredibly hard and emotional, and yet can be the best years of one's life. Being "not quite a man" or "not quite a woman" creates a classification of social beings called teenagers, and boys and girls from ages 12–20 in European nations can identify with kids from around the globe at this unique age.

The authors in this volume each allude to popular culture as a feature of teen life in each country. It would be difficult to list all the particular movies, TV shows, comics, books, and artists that teenagers in each country like. However, it is important to acknowledge the influence and importance of popular culture to European teens. By definition, popular culture is the culture of the moment, the fad of attention, the trend that is being set, the current "thing." Popular culture changes rapidly; what is considered "in" one week can be old by the next. Teenagers are acutely aware of popular culture, and in many ways teens are the people who decide what is popular. Entire groups of teens revolve around certain types of popular culture. Role-playing games, sports, foods, drinks, and entertainment create the current culture of each country. Knowledge of popular culture is also important to teens that wish to participate as peers.

Along with the desire to have a peer group, teens are often influenced by other teens. The authors in this volume take up the difficult discussion of the use of drugs and alcohol by European teenagers. Unlike teens from the United States, European teens can legally drink alcohol at a young age. Some countries allow the consumption of wine and beer by teens at 15. Ironically, the degree of teen alcoholism in Europe is much lower than that of the United States, causing one to consider if keeping youth from drinking until 21 is both unrealistic and punitive, and that the laws themselves may be an indirect cause of addiction.

Drug use is also discussed in this book. In several countries, the use of marijuana, Ecstasy, magic mushrooms, and hashish is legal and used in public. This is in strict contrast to American youth, who know that the use of any of the mentioned drugs would result in arrest and possible conviction. The topic of drug use is especially sensitive, and it is important to note that this book neither endorses nor condemns the legal use of drugs in different European countries. The important word here is *legal,* and this editor cautions all youth who read this book to make sure of all laws and ordinances relating to drugs and alcohol in each individual country.

The other sensitive discussion that appears throughout this book is that of youth and sexuality. The countries of Europe differ greatly in how adolescents view sexual development and activity before legal marriage. While some countries are described as sexually liberated, others are very traditional in dating and physical relationships. Each country's author discusses the development, changes, and ramifications that result from sexual decisions that youth make in each country. Youth pregnancy and sexually transmitted diseases are also discussed, as is the widespread encouragement of safe (protected) sex. Again, this book neither condemns nor endorses any country's sexual lifestyles, but encourages the readers to compare and contrast each country with his or her own, and, most importantly, to make decisions based on his or her own ethics and beliefs.

Why are teenagers unique? Because the years between 12 and 20 bring in the most changes, the most challenges, the most fears, and the most discoveries of one's life. This book attempts to share a glimpse of European teenage years with the reader in the desire to further global understanding and education.

ADDITIONAL READING

Kinderculture: The Corporate Construction of Childhood. (2004). Steinberg, Shirley R., and Joe Kincheloe (Eds.), Boulder, Colo.: Westview Press.

Chapter 1

DENMARK

Gitte Stald

INTRODUCTION

Everyday life for Danish teenagers is characterized by well-known daily routines, duties, obligations, and pleasures. Usually adolescent living is thought of as divided into school and leisure time, just as many adults would think of everyday life as framed by work and time off work. Every now and then or over periods of time the well-known patterns of everyday life are challenged by special experiences and events, both good ones and bad ones. Falling in love, traveling, going to a special party, moving home, finishing secondary school, starting a new education—or breaking up with the sweetheart, having troubles with best friends or in the family, being ill: these are a few examples of ups and downs of life that on different levels influence the life world of the individual and the perspective in which everyday life is seen.

In this respect, Danish teenagers are probably quite like many other teenagers around the globe, at least in Western societies. Still, differences in our ways of living can be distinguished when we look at political systems and national economy as well as individual economic resources, social security, access to education, work, material goods, infrastructure, and media—just to mention some major essential areas. In the following, everyday life for teenagers in Denmark is described with a focus on what is typical for the majority of young Danes. However, the chapter also attempts to demonstrate areas where patterns of conditions and of social and cultural practices might be recognized in an international context—be it from a Western point of departure or put in a global perspective.

Geographically, Denmark is a small country in Scandinavia. It is surrounded by sea except for the rather short line of land to the south where the peninsula Jutland borders on Germany. In addition to Jutland, Denmark consists of two large islands, Zeeland and Funen, and more than 400 smaller islands. The capital, Copenhagen, is situated in north Zeeland; other large cities are Aarhus and Aalborg in Jutland and Odense in Funen. Denmark's neighbors are England to the west, Sweden and Norway to the north, and the Baltic countries (Estonia, Latvia, and Lithuania) to the east. Both Greenland and the Faeroe Islands, far away in the North Atlantic, are part of the Danish national community, as they have so far remained under the Danish Crown while retaining extensive self-government under home rule. This chapter, however, does not describe aspects of teenagers living in these two countries, as there are some differences between mainland Denmark, Greenland, and the Faeroe Islands regarding everyday life due to geography, climate, history, and culture.

Denmark is situated in the temperate zone of the Northern Hemisphere and has an oceanic climate. Therefore Danes experience four very different seasons, and the summers are not very warm, nor are the winters very cold. Except for single days or short periods of, for example, stormy weather or heavy rain or snow, the climate does not influence the general state of society and its activities. Denmark's population is 5.37 million inhabitants, of which about 10 percent are teenagers between 13 and 19. Life expectancy for men is 74.3 years, for women 79.0 years.

Denmark has been a member of the European Union since 1972, but has not adopted the euro, so the Danish currency is still the krone (crown) as of 2005. Within the European Union traveling has become easier, and, for example, working and living in another membership country is much less restricted compared to staying in a non-EU country. Young people can quite easily conduct part of their education and training in another EU-membership country. The goal is to encourage a cross-cultural exchange within Europe and to encourage young people to consider themselves Europeans as well as national citizens.

The official language is Danish, with English as the first foreign language, mandatory in school at all levels starting in third or fourth grade. German and French are optional in secondary school, as they are at the high school level, along with Russian, Spanish, or Italian. Danish is spoken by a small number of people and only understood—more or less easily—by Swedes and Norwegians and vice versa. However, understanding a language is not being able to speak it. Therefore English is an important tool in Danes' communication across national borders. It is also a cultural marker, as a large number of cultural products in Denmark, in particular in a youth-cultural context, have an Anglo-American origin. English is used increasingly often in companies and within academia as the lingua franca of communication.

Young Danes with an ethnic-minority background have to master three or more languages: their mother tongue at home and in their ethnic cultural communities; Danish at school, with friends, and in society contexts; and English across communities and contexts, especially in relation to media uses and international, often computer communication.

Distances between parts of Denmark are very short, but it is still possible to distinguish local dialects, even if they are not as pronounced as they used to be with previous generations. Media use and geographical mobility contribute to equalizing the local typical vocabulary and tone. Besides more or less pronounced use of dialect, most young Danes sometimes change between different "sociolects" and perhaps "ethnolects," dependent on social context and situation. Depending on whom you are with and what you are doing, you more or less consciously and consistently modulate your language to fit the common discourse in the situation.

Historically, Denmark as a nation is very old, and it is the oldest monarchy in the world. But Denmark is also a modern society with an ambition of being forward in the world regarding industry, research, political influence, and culture, even if it is a small country. The government is a representative democracy, lead by the Folketing (meaning "people's council," and equivalent to a parliament), headed by the prime minister and his ministers. The Danish welfare model is ruled by the solidarity principle; that is, everyone pays taxes to the community according to income and receives due to needs. Education, health care, old-age pensions, and infrastructure are free to all, but the principles of the welfare systems have been challenged from the 1980s onward. An increasing privatization of the health system and educational system make it possible, for example, to pay for quicker treatment or more choices of schools.

There are still substantial social differences in the Danish community, even if the differences are not as marked as in some parts of the world, and although the system prides itself on taking care of everybody who needs to—and wants to—be taken care of. A small group of Danes are very wealthy. Then there is a large group of middle-class people and skilled workers who earn good salaries. A second relatively large group are the unskilled workers who earn less, and finally there is the group of longtime unemployed people together with people on social security and new immigrants, who receive only the necessary means to pay rent and have something to eat. Geographical distances are short in Denmark, but in spite of the solidarity welfare model, social and cultural distances are distinguishable. This means among other things that teenagers with the same background tend to choose certain schools, clothing, and leisure-time activities, and teenagers from rich families obviously have better opportunities to live in nice places, have a number of good things, travel, and so forth, while in comparison children of single parents on social aid are restricted in their possibilities. Young people easily identify social and cultural differences in appearance and language. The Danish prime minister has launched the liberal vision of young people, who break what he calls "the negative social inheritance," getting good educations and positions in society—and many do strive to do so, but have to fight the realities of social inheritance. The majority of young people, however, have both opportunities and family support to get an education and/or a job.

In spite of the inequalities, the level of unemployment in some fields, and the level of violence and insecurity in society, Danes in general tend to think of Denmark as the best place in the world to live—even when the exciting and sometimes exotic globe allures. Both collectively as a nation and as individuals, however, Denmark and the Danes tend to be split between on the one hand being very proud of Denmark and any possible achievements by Danes and on the other hand being influenced by the "law of Jante's"—"Who do you think you are?"—introduced by the Danish-Norwegian poet Aksel Sandemose in the 1933 novel *A Refugee Crosses His Tracks*. Yet young Danes tend to combine a positive individual and national self-esteem with a global outlook that tones down the influence of the social laws for modesty and knowing one's position in a restrictive way.

TYPICAL DAY

Depending of course on distance to school or work and on individual class schedules, the average day begins at 6:30 or 7 A.M., as school usually starts at 8 A.M. Most days both in secondary school and senior high school have between five and seven classes, that is, school ends between 1 P.M. and 3 P.M. In comparison, the workday for workers and trainees within the trade or health sectors might start at 7 A.M. Employees within other areas of service sectors might start between 6 and 9 A.M. A week is between 25 and 30 classes at school or 37 working hours.

In families with children and young people mornings are generally busy—everybody wanting to use the bathroom, getting dressed, making lunch packets, remembering all the last-minute things, and making arrangements for the day. Some families probably still try to get together around the breakfast table in good time, but most commonly mornings are sort of the family rush hour. The Danish health sector is worried because too many teenagers do not take time to eat a proper meal in the morning and hence lack mental and physical energy during the day and are perhaps tempted to eat something unwholesome instead on their way to or in school. When breakfast is on the schedule it usually consists of either cereal, yogurt with fruit jam, or plain yogurt with muesli. White or rye bread or rolls with jam, cheese, honey, or chocolate (or more seldom ham or salami) follow this. Most teenagers prefer tea to coffee or have juice or milk. Sometimes fresh fruit is also on the menu. Oatmeal porridge and rye-bread-and-beer soup with cream are traditional dishes but not often on the morning table in modern Denmark. Quite often breakfast is just something grabbed from the table in the passing.

Depending on the distance to school and work, the teens take off by foot, bike, motorbike, bus, or train, or get a lift in their parents' car. Only a few teenagers have their own car, even if some get a driver's license when they are 18 (the required age). Taxes make cars and gas very expensive, so only the wealthiest families would have cars for their oldest teenagers. Teens with full-time jobs who make it a priority might have their own car—most likely an old model. In addition, distances are, at least in town areas, short, and the infrastructure and transportation system are well developed and functional. Biking is popular because it makes the teenager independent of other transportation and timetables, it is cheap, and there are special biking paths along a large number of Danish roads to make biking safer and quicker.

Lunch usually consists of a lunch packet, eaten at school or at work, or there are canteens where the students or employees can buy and eat their lunch. The traditional lunch packet holds a number of open sandwiches on rye bread with pâté, salami, cold ham, sausage, meatballs, or meat, all wrapped in paper, along with perhaps vegetables and a piece of fruit. As patterns of food and eating are changing, lunch packets are changing as well. Today sandwiches, salads, pasta, and lots of fruit and greens are more common. Canteens usually sell sandwiches, pizza slices, pita bread with filling, hunks of rye bread, buns, fruit, greens, pastry, milk, and juice. Larger canteens often have warm meals available as well. In some cities and towns the students choose to buy lunch at nearby pizzerias, burger bars, or delis. Lunch breaks are usually 20–30 minutes, so there is no time for going home or for having a siesta.

After school in the afternoon and evening many teenagers have a part-time job, engage in sports, get together with friends, relax with one or more media (TV, music, the Internet), or do their homework for school.

Teens with jobs might not work every day or even in the afternoons, but will on weekends. Only children over 13 years of age are allowed to work. Typical jobs would include shop assistant, babysitter, cleaner, newspaper or circular distributor, messenger, or baker's shop assistant. Laws regulate the pay for young people, but some work under rates, without the security and regulation of labor legislation. Young people almost always work to get money for clothing, makeup, mobile phone bills, partying, music, and other interests. Only very few have to contribute to the family by working. Some save up money for larger planned purchases, travels, driver's licenses, and so on, but young Danes do in general have quite a lot of money to spend on leisure-time activities.

Evenings are divided between obligatory tasks, such as homework, and social or cultural activities. Some teenagers go to youth clubs in the evening to be with friends, listen to or play music, play computer games, or practice drama. Others take care of their sports training. Many hours, however, are spent in the company of friends and/or media in the bedroom, especially in the winter. In the summer, evenings are more frequently spent outdoors, playing basketball or soccer; groupings in squares and parks, sports areas, or beaches; or walking in the streets. Some like to frequent outdoor cafés.

In most families parents gradually stop controlling bedtime and activities in the evening when the children become teenagers and get near the end of secondary school. So it is difficult to estimate a general approximate hour for the end of the day. No doubt lots of homework is done, and a lot of movies are watched, computer games played, and books read after the parents have said goodnight—probably more than earlier generations, reading with a flashlight under the duvet. Up until the mid-1980s the daily activities were framed by well-known patterns of media use—the morning, midday, and evening radio news; the morning newspaper; and the monopoly Danish national television in the evening, which ended around 11 P.M. Today the vast choice of media—news and information as well as entertainment—is accessible around the clock, and there is no natural closing of the days when one of the screens turns black. So it is a daily balancing between the attraction of media and the sensible bedtime, which would be around 11 or 11:30 P.M. This is both a liberty and a stress factor to the young people, whose lives are ruled by considerations of obligations and expectations on the one hand, and the individual adolescent's need to be entertained and engage in pleasurable, interest-driven activities on the other. And needs for pleasure and entertainment can be satisfied in many ways from the time school or work ends until it starts again.

Danish teenagers are busy. They may not go to school or work for as many hours as some adolescents do in other countries, but as they in general have ambitions for their future life, they try to deal with school and other activities that will prepare them for the adult life. At the same time, they want to exploit all their possibilities for being part of active cultural and social networks and for having fun and enjoying time. Leisure time culture in modern society costs money, so many teenagers have jobs to be able to be part of the consumer culture. In short, many teenagers have to time-manage their days in order to manage all their obligations, interests, and networks, and this combined with serious considerations about future possibilities regarding education, job, family, and perhaps political and societal matters might cause a more or less strong sense of stress. Even if it may look like it from an outside position, the life of Danish adolescents is not a "take-it-easy"—rather, a "life-is-too-short"—culture, depending of course on who you are and what the conditions of your life world are. Furthermore, this is not a typical Danish phenomenon but an international, Western-world phenomenon.

FAMILY LIFE

The idea of the typical nuclear family is Mom, Dad, and (two) children. Most Danish families still follow this pattern—with varying numbers of children, of course. One or two children are the norm, but increasingly often families have three or more children, sometimes with shifting partners. Very few families have more than four children. Many experience broken families, resulting in a single parent living with one child or more, or new families with children of different marriages and maybe new siblings—"my children, yours and ours." By January 1, 2001, there were 652,630 families with children in Denmark, which is just under 25 percent of all families (or households, as half of all "families" are singles living alone). Nineteen percent of families with children have a single parent, 63 percent are married couples with children, and 18 percent are other couples with children. There are 2.7 divorces per 1,000 inhabitants each year—a number that has been practically unchanged during the past 25 years (Statistics Denmark 2002). It has become popular again to marry, but still many couples live together without registration. It is possible to have joint custody over children. There are no moral or normative reactions against living together, except in exclusively religious communities. Socially, divorce is not as devastating as it was decades ago, since it is a quite common phenomenon and since women are not socially or economically dependent on their husbands. Often parents claim that they have a "good" divorce, in consideration of their children among other things. Nevertheless, divorces obviously have an impact on the life on children and young people, both emotionally and socially.

When parents remarry, the children have to adjust to more sets of norms, conditions, and personal relationships. This may be difficult for teenagers in particular, who are struggling in general to find their own values and norms—to a large degree actually based on those they have been brought up with.

In most Danish families both parents work, which means that both fathers and mothers contribute to the economic basis for the family's existence. Eighty-one percent of all men and 74 percent of all women between ages 16 and 66 are employed; 4.1 percent on average are unemployed. Women are educated equally as men, but spend more years to reach the average levels of income and position—primarily due to giving birth, child care, and to some degree and for some women, due to priorities that do not enhance promotions. Substantially fewer women than men hold top positions within industry, institutions, public administration, academia, and political life. It is then obvious that there is not an optimal equation in Denmark, even if we come relatively close. Young people struggle with the definition of their own gendered position, personally as well as in society, and quite often opposing signals and realities confuse the picture. Young Danish girls in general seem to be self-consciously aware of their of potential and strive to achieve a good education and good positions in society. On the other hand, they still fight stereotypical ideas of what women can do and should be. And teenage boys fight to find their masculinity and simultaneously be the modern, all-around responsible and sensitive men. It is not easy to form one's psychological, cultural, and social identity in the context of modern society.

It is not common in Denmark to live with more than two generations in the same household. That is, very few families with children live with the older generations. One reason is that economic resources make it possible to live in separated households. As young people often leave the parental home at an early age and later establish their own family, there is no practical reason for living together. Many grandparents of both sexes are still active in the labor force, and even when they retire they are usually busy with interests, friends, and activities of their own. Many young families probably prefer to live alone without the interference of grandparents—and many grandparents presumably also like their independent everyday life. Nevertheless, grandparents often help out with child care and practical tasks, and many families are close, including all generations—brothers, sisters, cousins, aunts, and uncles—and it is a tradition to spend time together at feasts, holidays, and family celebrations. But young people almost never grow up in a large family, with many relatives across generations. Tradition and the family story are hence inherited only through the parents' way of living and bringing up their children, and through the occasional meetings with other relatives.

Some families, but relatively few, live in what could be described as alternative or experimental environments, for example, in collectives/communities, on boats, in the famous free city of Christiania in Copenhagen, or on little farms trying to live ecologically from their own production.

Women still take on the large part of cooking and cleaning in Denmark, but since the 1960s it has become increasingly common for men to cook and do the shopping and housekeeping as well—and take responsibility for the daily upbringing of their children. The youngest teenagers—boys and girls together—learn housekeeping and cooking at school (sixth and seventh grade) and are usually more or less part of a family collective, cooking, cleaning, and so forth. This is necessary since both parents in most families work outside the home. Only the wealthiest families can afford to employ a maid or cook. Some middle-class families pay to have their house cleaned once a week, but many teenagers are obliged to participate in the housekeeping. On the other hand, many teenagers are somewhat spoiled because they have such a busy everyday life and are at home very few hours. Subsequently, their cooking and cleaning make up a minimum of activity. Some Danish parents find it easier to do the jobs themselves than discuss it with their sulking teenager, or they hold the opinion that young people should take care of their school and enjoy life. In most families, however, it is likely a balance between teenagers taking care of their domestic duties and enjoying their rather privileged position. In principle there are no gender-related differences in which duties girls and boys are expected to take care of, which is a direct result of the fight for equality between the sexes that was up-front in the 1970s and after. However, old patterns are difficult to wipe out, so variations of the "equality in the home" occur. This is also supported by the fact that equal rights between men and women are not totally integrated in all areas of the working field or institutionally, even if legislation and democratic principles prompt this. It is also interesting that during the past decade an enhanced pedagogical, societal, and, following this, individually oriented interest has occurred in supporting what is considered to be the characteristic biologically or culturally arisen differences between sexes. Therefore it is okay or perhaps even expected to demonstrate and even underline female or masculine trends in appearance and behavior. This is obviously important to teenagers, who are in the middle of the challenging process of finding and developing an individual as well as social and cultural identity. What is important is that the demonstration of gender aspects does not automatically bring adolescents back to the patterns of their grandparents as they integrate the historical experiments and achievements of earlier generations.

Most teenagers who live with their parents have their own bedroom supplied with various media such as a stereo, television, and computer, and, increasingly often, Internet access. Furthermore, most teenagers have a mobile phone of their own. Due to the hours of activity outside the home and the standards of bedrooms, media, and means of communication, teenagers can live a life rather secluded from the rest of the family. Subsequently it is commonly a matter of choice to be with the family in various activities or hours of *hygge*.

The fact that many teenagers, as mentioned above, have a relatively large amount of money for their own use also supports this pattern of the teenagers' life with his or her family and vice versa. Allowances; salaries for trainee, after-school, or full-time jobs; unemployment or social security benefits; and, for those over 18, state-financed study grants supply the average teenager with money for clothing, entertainment, communication (mobile phone and Internet use is rather expensive), additional meals, drinks, and so forth. Most Danish teenagers live with their parents at least until they reach the age of majority at 18 or end high school, and some stay for more years due to the difficulties of finding a cheap apartment, college residence hall, student hostel, shared house or flat, or commune in the larger cities and towns. An increasing number choose to attend a lower secondary boarding school for 14–17-year-olds for one or two years to end their secondary school. Afterward they usually move back home and continue their education, finding a job or a position as trainee, if possible.

Adolescence has a reputation of being the "difficult age"—a challenge to all parents (and to most teenagers as well). Physical changes combined with changing social and cultural options and expectations and a growing degree of expected responsibility, determination, and exploitation of possibilities make this age very demanding both physically and psychologically. In spite of the "difficult age" syndrome, however, there is an extensive tradition, especially within northern European countries, that regards children and young people as independent, reasonable, and rational beings who have a right to opinions and a voice in decision making in the home (yet not formally at a political level until they reach the age of 18). This in many cases fosters a mutual respect, or at least mutual acceptance, between children/young people and parents that promotes communication and peaceful coexistence. It does not extinguish conflicts, shouting, slammed doors, or parents' sleepless nights. It might also at a certain level promote teenagers' immediate confusion and feeling of being rootless, because traditional patterns of authority, expectations, and choices can be challenged. Many young Danes work very hard to live up to the expectations—both the real ones and the imagined ones—but find it difficult to fulfill these ambitions. In spite of these general frustrations, it is obvious that young people to a degree do reproduce some of the cultural and social patterns and listen much more to their parents than the parents would believe, or the adolescents would realize or care to admit.

Family patterns and traditions of the many families belonging to an ethnic minority may differ from the description above. Immigrants and their descendants make up 7.4 percent of the population. Many teenagers whose cultural family background is not Danish have dual cultural identities, as they often attempt to honor family cultural values and perhaps religious beliefs, yet at the same time live alongside other young Danes with different norms and values. Integration of ethnic minorities into Danish society and culture is an ambition, but the ideas of which means and goals should be prioritized are not agreed upon. Conflicts between groups of Danes with an immigrant background and ethnic Danes do flare up occasionally because of marked ideological positions, but a number of the origins of the conflicts are not rooted in cultural difference but in social problems, as relatively more immigrants are unemployed, without education, and bound to live in ghetto-like areas where integration into Danish culture is difficult, as it is largely absent. Many young immigrants do get good educations and jobs, and hopefully equality also reaches this area as Danish society becomes accustomed to being a (more) multicultural society.

FOOD

There are no standard breaks in the afternoon like the British tea, but employees usually have a coffee break. As school and most other types of education usually end early, no additional long breaks are needed. There are short breaks between classes to have something to drink, fruit, or a cigarette, for those who have chosen to smoke. Danish pastries, cookies, or buns traditionally accompany coffee or tea, but young people would probably prefer a soda and a chocolate bar, or perhaps juice and fruit.

In the evening most families still value the common dinner, even if it may be difficult to get the family together every day around the table and even if some families are very small—for example, the single-parent family with one or two kids. Dinner is traditionally warm and is served between 6 and 8 P.M., which is later than it used to be a few generations ago.

Traditional Danish dishes are meatballs with potatoes and gravy, cooked ham, roast pork with red cabbage, fried sausage, minced beefsteaks, cutlets, fried chicken, stuffed cabbage leaves, roast beef, fried herring or plaice, cooked trout, and meat or chicken soup. Danish kitchens used to depend on the foods in season, but today all sorts of typical or exotic foods are imported and can be purchased throughout the year. Danish meals usually include a lot of meat and milk products as well as fish, as Denmark is an old agricultural and fishing society. Potatoes and cabbage are traditional basic foods, but potatoes are increasingly exchanged for pasta or rice, while cabbage has become rather infrequent on Danish dinner tables. Boiled peas, carrots, leeks and beans, and fresh tomatoes and cucumbers are traditional greens, now often supplemented with mushrooms, peppers, squash, eggplant, and various salads. Traditional desserts are red stewed fruit with cream (*rødgrød med fløde*—the popular test for the ability to pronounce the difficult Danish language), and pudding, cold soufflé, or ice cream. During the second part of the twentieth century various rice and pasta types; exotic spices like curry, paprika, chili, and garlic; imported vegetables and salads; and new ways of preparing meat were introduced and have become common. Even if some families still prefer rather traditional cooking, the Danes' kitchens at home and in restaurants are often inspired by international cuisines such as French, Italian, Greek, Asian, Arab, and perhaps American. The changes have come through a combination of international trading, Danes' increasing travel outside their own part of the world, and, since the 1970s, a relatively large immigration of new citizens from countries outside northern Europe. Greengrocers with exotic vegetables, fruit, and spices as well as little ethnic restaurants enter urban areas with colors and scents that have become familiar to the young generations. This development has happened rather late in Denmark, compared to, for example, America.

Patterns of eating and food preferences are still characterized by social diversity. It is, for example, more expensive to buy organic foods and the best greens and meat. On the one hand, there is a strong focus on healthy living and good nutrition among young people in Denmark. On the other hand, fast food and frozen, ready-made foods have become more common because they are easier and available close to school or work, and because young people have the money for buying their lunch, dinner, or snack on the street.

Food is important to most young Danes—for better and for worse. Usually breakfast and dinner, and all meals on weekends, are eaten in the home with the family, although this pattern is changing. Many families, especially with older children and teenagers, have busy everyday lives and instead eat something quick when the timetable allows, order something from a fast-food shop (be it burgers, pizzas, or *shawarmas*), or go out to a cheap restaurant if money allows it. But large meals are also important when family and friends get together on weekends, for celebrations or the traditional feasts.

To many teenagers food is more than meals and nutrition. Food, snacks, candy, fruit, and drink can also be comforts or rewards, or simply indispensable elements. New research show that more than 15 percent of Danish teenagers are overweight due to eating the wrong foods, overeating, and getting too little physical activity. The diverse situations are also well known: teenagers who suffer from serious eating disorders and either overeat uncontrollably or starve themselves beyond imagination. In these cases food is used as a tool for control, and the disturbed eating patterns reflect deep psychological problems. "Ordinary" weight problems due to eating disorders are becoming increasingly common in the Western world, according to some experts because of the frustrations of adolescent life in modern society mixed with the impact of societal, parental, and their own demands regarding education, job, family life, and looks. The focus on the perfect body enforces the troubled self-image produced by a number of young people. The impact of the body-culture is underlined by the fact that an increasing number of young men suffer from eating disorders and that it has become rather common to have plastic surgery at a very young age to correct or "upgrade" the bodily physical appearance. One form of reaction is the trend of body decoration among teenagers, especially by getting pierced or tattooed. By doing so, the individual demonstrates both bodily consciousness and attempts to appear special, with an individual look.

The National Health Service is conducting continual campaigns on various levels regarding nutrition—for example, the "six a day" slogan, meaning that all individuals should eat six pieces of fruit and vegetable each day in order to get vitamins and fibers and satisfy the need for nourishment in a healthy way. "Six a day" is also used in a campaign to use food as a preventative against cancer and various lifestyle diseases, and has been especially directed toward children and young people to give them healthy eating habits. It should be underlined, however, that the majority of young Danes live healthy lives, with what could be described as sound souls in sound bodies.

SCHOOLING

The majority of Danish children attend preschool classes at around the age of six. All children have to attend the *folkeskole* (primary and lower secondary school for 7- to 16-year-olds) for nine years. According to the Danish Ministry of Education, 82.5 percent of young Danes between 15 and 19 attend school (senior high school, trading high school, basic vocational schools) or other kinds of education; teens between 13 and 14 are not included in the survey because they attend secondary school with only very few exceptions). The rest (a little less than 2 out of 10) leave school after 9th or 10th grade when they are between 15 and 17 and get a job where no education is required, perhaps while considering in which direction they shall go on. Some of these choose some kind of education or training. School fatigue is relatively common among teens, and the perspective of earning a (relatively) proper salary can be attractive. A small minority leave school and do nothing related to education or work. School and education are considered to be of basic importance, and most young people acknowledge the need to acquire some sort of education and training after the basic nine years at school. In fact, a former president of the University of Copenhagen stated that well-educated youth is the sole raw material to be found in Denmark, and therefore the prosperity and wealth of both the Danish society and the individual citizen builds on education.

Education is free of cost at all levels, and the majority attend public schools, but it is possible to get an education at private schools where a fee is paid along with expenses for books and other material. The standards and educational level of public schooling, however, is generally very high, and therefore the choice of private schools is often determined by the predominant pedagogical principles, special focuses, or religious foundations of the particular school. Education at universities and other institutions of higher education is free of cost, but the student must pay expenses for books and various activities. Some young people and adults decide to acquire an education while having a job and may attend "open university" or evening classes at the high school level where they have to pay a fee. Only a few teenagers, however, have started higher education, as they traditionally finish high school between the ages of 18 and 20.

Danish schools are not divided by gender, except for a few schools where a religious basis prescribes separation of girls and boys—or in schools that experiment with separation in order to encourage the "quiet" girls to be active and the "wild" boys to achieve focus. So generally boys and girls are educated together at all levels of education.

Likewise, students are not divided by qualifications, but attend what is described as the comprehensive school. A few decades ago students were divided into three different levels after the seventh grade—the common line, the academic line, and the technical line. This, however, was considered to enforce a predestination of future choices and a preservation of social patterns, and so the comprehensive school was established.

Schooling for teens in Denmark is a balance between fulfilling the obligatory curricula and trying out new ways of preparing adolescents for their adult life, both professionally and personally. Schools take on a certain responsibility for their students' well-being in relation to education but also socially and emotionally, by acting as adviser and supporter, primarily in collaboration with but sometimes instead of parents. In eighth and ninth grade students have three opportunities to experience a week's job experience in order to get closer to possible choices of education and career. Each school also has a placement counselor who advises students their choices and follows their steps some years after they leave school.

SOCIAL LIFE, RECREATION, AND ENTERTAINMENT

When you ask a young Dane when he or she has a really good time and is happy, the answer is almost always "When I am with friends" or (less so) "When I am with my family." Friends are the pivotal point for social life; they form the basis of networks and communities, which are important in the process of identity formation and socialization. Most adolescents have a few really good, intimate friends whom they trust in all matters. Besides these, they also have a number of friends with whom they share interests and meet in various communities. Finally, young people usually have countless ephemeral encounters with other people in relation to the networking functions of youth culture and social practices—often established through friends or via computer. Most of these relationships are left instantly and with no regret, while a few develop over time into lasting relationships.

Most young people engage in a number of youth groups either institutionally or with their peer groups—that is, groups formed in relation to school, youth clubs, sports clubs, and so on, but also in the more or less loosely defined groups of interest, such as fan cultures, gaming cultures, music cultures, or simply groups of peers who enjoy doing things together and share interests in the local as well as in the larger context. Some also engage in political organizations or movements in relation to, for example, peace organizations, humanitarian organizations, or environmental-protection groups.

Actors from the Hans Christian Andersen parade in Lotzes Have, Odense, Denmark, 2004. Courtesy of Stefanie Grabbert.

Generally groups are the basis for the establishment of communities where meetings of common understanding, needs, expectations, experiences, attitudes, and frustrations are possible. Through these communities young people seek both stability and continuity in a confused, unstable world, and they find companions in their fight to avoid feeling alone and being bored. The proximity also provides the possibility of feeling the closeness of belonging with other people while at the same time liberating them from the family. Groups gain importance at different levels, but all are more or less essential to individual and collective socialization and identity formation. The group is often the forum where the members can mirror themselves in the other group members, and in the group the adolescents find the basis for feeling special in relation to others.

Media play an important role in young Danes' cultural and social practices. Films, TV shows, sports programs, and music channels are platforms for common references where entertainment, experience, and attitudes can be exchanged. Video nights are a common phenomenon among young teenagers—a group meets privately and watches three or more films together, in sleeping bags and with lots of chips, candy, and soda. Despite the cheap and widely available access to movies on TV or video, it is also very popular to go to the cinema with one or more friends and share the intimate and intensive total experience of a popular movie. Music accompanies many activities where young Danes are together, both as background and as focus for shared attention and discussion or at concerts or music festivals where thousands of young people enjoy the live performances while being with many other like-minded people.

Communication media are also very essential in Danish youth culture. The mobile phone is an important tool for keeping in touch, primarily on a local basis. The use of SMS (short message system, or text messages) and icons and symbols together with the more expensive normal talk create a system of keeping in touch and, not least, feeling included in the network of friends. Instant messaging and e-mails are also used, though e-mail not as extensively among friends. Chat programs are used primarily in groups of similar interests and in random searches for new meetings. Sometimes virtual and physical meetings cross in certain activities, for example, online multiplayer computer games, where many choose to visit an Internet café with friends while playing the game online with people both locally and globally situated.

Danish teenagers usually plan their social activities themselves, but there are obviously different rules in different families regarding curfews, when they are expected to spend time with the family, when they are expected to call, and so on. The mobile phone is an effective means of control on both sides but is also a channel for security—to be able to get in touch and call for parental assistance if needed. This has probably influenced the level of individual freedom for many teenagers—and has calmed parents' anxieties in many situations.

Young people benefit profoundly and positively from their social relations in a number of ways. But peers and groups also play a role in the adaptation of habits that are not very healthy or sensible, as in most other cultures. The majority of young Danes are aware of the potential dangers of any kind of stimulant and of the potential joys and negative experiences related to sex, and they act thereafter without abandoning either. Information campaigns in schools and diverse public-relations campaigns as well as parental norms and guidance do heighten young peoples' attention and influence their behavior. Still, problems are not entirely avoided.

A recent survey on young Danes' lifestyles shows that 24 percent of Danish adolescents between 16 and 20 smoke every day, while 65 percent never smoke. The rest are "party smokers." More than a third of young smokers want to quit but find it very difficult. There are no simple explanations for why young Danes start to smoke. No young Dane can be unaware of the harmful effects of smoking. National health campaigns, a general focus on the relationship between lifestyle and health, and restrictions and public opinion against smoking have been intensified during the past decades. Furthermore, it is expensive to smoke, as there is a heavy tax on tobacco. One explanation could be that smoking is part of a lifestyle—"live and let die"—and they don't worry about the consequences. The young smoker demonstrates the individual's right to like to smoke. But most young people start to smoke because some of their tough "in" friends show the way, and from there a rather simple physical need to have the nicotine level balanced is easy to work up. Or parents smoke and hence have troubles prohibiting their teenagers from smoking with convincing arguments.

Smoking quite often goes together with drinking, and it is a sad fact that Danes are among the heaviest young drinkers in Europe. The survey shows that 78 percent of boys between 16 and 20 and 71 percent of girls have drunk alcohol within the last week—even if many of these have not drunk much—and 13 percent of boys and 6 percent of girls have been drunk more than six times within the last month. Almost all drink only on weekends at parties. There are, of course, great differences in the patterns of drinking—some have their first drink very early, while others don't like alcohol or being drunk. One of the explanations for the level of drinking among young Danes is that it is possible, meaning that adolescents have a relatively large amount of freedom and money, and many shops sell alcohol like "alco-pops" or little bottles of vodka or cheap beer especially directed toward young people. Furthermore, drinking is, in Denmark as in most other Western countries, a social phenomenon. Being together often includes having a drink. Besides, adolescent Danes' drinking patterns mirror those of adult Danes. Finally, a motivation for drinking is the potential release of stress, tensions, and (not least) individual restraints in personal relationships, especially with the opposite sex. Most young Danes manage to engage in casual drinking, while some choose not to drink at all. And a small group have serious problems that are bound to grow with age. In the past few years national information campaigns and an increased public focus on the potential dangers of young Danes' drinking habits have provided the first steps for a more critical and selective use of alcohol among adolescents. The full effect, however, needs the same effort among adults who drink too much.

All drugs (except tobacco and alcohol) are illegal in Denmark, but nevertheless they have become more common in Danish youth culture, as in most other Western countries. Hash is the most commonly used drug, followed by amphetamines, mushrooms, and Ecstasy. The survey of young Danes' lifestyles shows that 37 percent of the boys and 29 percent of the girls have tried hash—while 13 percent of the boys and 6 percent of the girls have used it within the past month. Extensive use of hash is often related to the use of other stimulants, such as smoking and alcohol. Most young people who have tried an illegal drug do not continue to do so, but of course some suffer from use in the form of addiction, poisoning, depression, or psychosis. The attitudes toward a number of drugs have changed as certain drugs have become more common in young people's party culture. Drugs are no longer limited to certain subcultures but are used across social and cultural borders. A new phenomenon has occurred: the weekend addicts who throw away all restraints and party all weekend with drugs and alcohol and live their ordinary lives as students or employees during the week—as long as it works. There is, also in this area, a sharpened public attention to the problems of drugs in youth cultures, and again information campaigns paired with different actions and efforts are used in the fight to bring down the use of drugs among young people and in the population in general, and most young people are very much aware of the potential harmful effects of drugs.

No young Danes have to break the law (by stealing or likewise) in order to survive, and the number of young criminals is low. Crime among adolescents is usually related to alcohol and/or social problems. The minimum age for criminal prosecution is 15 in Denmark. Offenders under this age are taken care of by social services, depending on the extent of the criminal action. Young people have to break the law more than once to be taken away from home and detained by social services. For offenders over 15 but under 18, the punishment would usually be a combination of social care and confinement to a youth detention center for rehabilitation and, for example, job training. Teenagers are almost never imprisoned with adult criminals.

Adolescence is also the time for trying out relations with the opposite sex, and a lot of time is spent experimenting with gender identity, self-presentation, and, following this, intimate relations with boyfriends or girlfriends. It is not uncommon in Denmark for boys and girls to be friends. These relationships give adolescents the freedom of getting close to the opposite sex with the built-in tension of play with gendered identity, but without having to live up to any sexual expectations. Generally, both girls and boys become sexually active at age 15 or later. Some, especially girls and in some cases more vulnerable individuals, have their first sexual experiences much earlier. Teenagers' sex lives are in principle, but usually also in practice, not surrounded by strong parental and societal morality; that is, it is accepted that teenagers have sexual relations. Many older teenagers can spend the night in their bedroom with their loved one with their parents' acceptance and do not have to find secret places to be together. Insecurity about being able to live up to their own and others' imaginations about sex, and the fact that it is not that easy to get a boyfriend or girlfriend whom you can actually imagine having intimate relations with, is probably the main reason why the average age of sexual activity is relatively high in spite of the social and moral liberty. Fear of venereal diseases, especially AIDS, and of pregnancy may also to some degree restrain the young girls' and boys' sexual activities despite sex education in schools and information on and easy access to various forms of contraception. Information campaigns do work: even if many older teenagers have frequent sex with their partners, there are relatively few abortions and few births among teenage girls. When teenagers have unplanned and unprotected sex, it is often under the influence of alcohol. Another factor that probably influences the patterns of young peoples' sexual behavior is a sort of new morality, developed within youth cultural groups among the very young: a girl who sleeps with more partners over a short period of time risks being considered cheap, while her mother at the same age was probably seen as exploring personal needs and identity. Finally, a new group of adolescents who are supposed to refrain from sex until marriage are the Muslim girls whose families live by traditional rules. All in all, any changes in attitudes toward adolescents' sexual behavior almost all relate to girls. Still, compared to other countries, young Danes have much freedom to explore their sexuality. It is just a question of how to use and administrate this freedom.

Recreation time for Danish teenagers is connected to leisure time in the afternoon and on weekends and holidays. It is best described as a combination of physical and mental training and relaxation—but is very much dependent on the individual's efforts, interests, and opportunities. In the Western world recreation is often related to the consumption of either goods or cultural products, such as having something nice to eat, shopping, going to the cinema, having some new music CDs or computer games, or watching a movie or TV show—or, on a larger scale, being able to buy a nice holiday or giving a party. Most teenagers, however, have multiple interests regarding physical and cultural activities, and adjust them depending on the situation and context.

In the afternoon or early evening many young Danes do some kind of sport. According to the lifestyle survey from 2002 (Statistics Denmark), 65 percent of 16–20-year-old boys and 54 percent of girls are physically active during leisure-time activities at least three hours per week. A third of boys and a quarter of girls exercise more than six hours per week. A fifth of boys and girls are not physically active at a moderate level.

Activity level decreases with age, and it can be presumed that teens between 13 and 15 are even more active than older teenagers. All in all, the majority of young Danes are quite healthy and fit, but an increasing percentage are unhealthier now compared to a few years ago. A number of reasons connected to lifestyle are listed, such as sedentary work at school or work, increased media use in front of a screen, and less physical means of transportation like walking or biking, but it is difficult to point to one explanation rather than to a complex combination of causal connection. Lack of motivation, family tradition, and peer-group inspiration or support should probably be added—nonphysical living can become self-perpetuating.

Many teenagers engage in organized sports clubs. Soccer is the most popular among boys, but an increasing number of girls also choose this sport. Handball, tennis, badminton, swimming, and basketball are other popular sports for both sexes—with gender-divided teams. Besides, the majority of Danish teenagers are physically active in a more casual way—they, for example, play street basketball, play soccer in parks, or swim at the beach or in a pool. And some pay to work out in a fitness center. All in all, the physical training itself is an important motivation—often in order to appear fit and in shape—but so are competition and the social aspect of doing sports.

Other recreational activities during the week usually include either being with friends, watching television, listening to music, playing computer games, going to the cinema, or practicing, for example, music in a group or alone. Most adolescent Danes have access to a broad variety of media and TV channels, so the patterns of use vary somewhat according to interests, age, and gender. In general, media preferences are predominated by Anglo-American products, but Danish films, music, and TV shows have triggered new interest among young Danes during the past few years as standards have either matched internationally produced entertainment or have enhanced a combination of what is conceived of as international-quality with typical Danish qualities, such as humor, satire, well-known settings, and recognition of Danish themes and problems.

Weekends usually last from Friday afternoon until Monday morning and are primarily spent with friends—or occasionally with the family. Sleeping late, relaxing with media, and playing computer games for many hours in a row are obvious ways of spending time. Besides, partying is an important activity, and even a limited get-together can be transformed into a party by the participants, because partying represent the quintessence of becoming adult, being independent of parents, relaxing and letting go, and, not least, exploring social relationships and love affairs.

"Cirkus Charlie" is a small travelling circus in the Northern part of Denmark, summer 2003. Courtesy of Bo Hansen.

However, many do also find time and energy during weekends to enjoy sports either as spectators or participants, explore nature, or, for example, play live role-playing games in one of the public forests or other sites that have been opened to these activities.

Each summer from the end of June to early August schools close for six or seven weeks. Adolescents who are employed full-time or as trainees have five weeks of vacation time, and many use three of these during the summer. Summer vacations at higher-education institutions start by the end of June and end September 1. Some students work all through or part of their summer vacations, but many spend time with friends or family on vacations abroad or in Denmark, often at the seaside, in a summerhouse, or at a campsite. Danes in general travel a lot—often to southern Europe or to more exotic destinations with warmer climates, deep blue seas, and interesting food and drink—or they spend their vacations hiking or camping in other parts of Scandinavia. Young Danes can buy a cheap Interrail ticket on which they can travel by train all over Europe for a period of time. Older teenagers (generally aged 17 or 18, although some are younger) often travel with a few friends or girlfriends/boyfriends as backpackers, where they experience the world on their own. They have usually traveled with their parents and like to explore other geographical and cultural surroundings. It is a freedom to many young Danes to be able to save up money and travel on their own. Some young Danes do not have the opportunity or inclination to travel—often prohibited by money or because they have never traveled as children and are not inspired to do so. In the summer many teenagers love to go to the beach—and many live close or relatively close to the coastline—or to other places in the countryside.

Schools close for one week in October for the traditional potato-harvest holiday, which is now simply a week off. At Christmas most have the days between December 23 and January 3 off. These days are traditionally spent with family. In February schools usually close for one week for the winter holidays, when some go skiing in northern Scandinavia, Austria, or France. Most, however, stay at home and enjoy a week without school. Employees do not automatically have a winter holiday. Other short holidays include Easter, when many schools close for a week and employees usually have five days off, and Store Bededag (a Danish public holiday), Whitsunday, and Constitution Day, each with one day off. All these short holidays are usually spent with family, friends, or at work.

Recreation is more than just getting ready to work more, at school or the job. It can also be considered an experience of mind and body that has an impact on development, intellect, and identity. Therefore, recreational activities are very important, especially in adolescents' everyday life.

RELIGIOUS PRACTICES AND CULTURAL CEREMONIES

Approximately 85 percent of all Danish citizens belong to the Danish National Evangelical Lutheran Church, but the percentage of active members is much smaller. Danes are born members of this church, and you have to actively resign your membership if you do not want to support the church. Other Christian churches as well as religious groups are allowed, the Muslim group being the second-largest after the Christian communities. The church and religion are not influential in Danish society and everyday life, and young Danes are not in general actively practicing a religion, even if most celebrate the traditional feasts. These are primarily seen as opportunities to be with the family, have something good to eat, and *hygge sig* (a Danish word for a combination of being cozy and homey and having a good time). Religion, however, does maintain its importance in everyday life to a small number of young Danes. One example is those young people with an immigrant background where culture, religion, and social life are closely connected and where religion supports the forming and maintaining of an identity. Another example relates to a number of diverse young people in a confused, material, demanding world, search for a spiritual dimension to the understanding of life and death and our position on Earth.

CONCLUSION

Young Danes are globally orientated but locally rooted. That is, they are interested in what is going on in the world and informed about it by media, education, and self-experience, for example, obtained on travels abroad. Many Danish teenagers play with the idea of spending time in another country. Some dream of staying in another European country, others imagine more exotic destinations like Asia or South America, and some have thought of going to the United States, the fellow Western country that seems to be very well known through so many media representations and yet can be a rather dangerous and challenging place to stay. Pictures of and information on the world do support a number of young Danes' longing to go out, but almost all claim that they are surely going to return to Denmark after a year or six months. Teenagers have reached the age when a greater understanding of others and the world is mixed with the continued need to find one's footing, self-identity, and understanding of one's own position in the world and in relation to others. The world is experienced as exciting and full of possibilities, and the idea of leaving the local parish is intriguing. At the same time, the world is conceived of as full of threats, fear, and insecurity. Every now and then the conception of the world as a dangerous place and of Denmark as a safe and stable haven is reinforced by terrorism, warfare, and the threat of globally spread diseases or natural catastrophes around the globe. But when the first shockwave of the actual events and the media coverage, public alert, and educational focus in school have died down, the balance between the fascination of the foreign and the apparent safety of the local is reestablished.

Young Danes meet the world in many ways in their everyday life. On a local basis, ethnic Danes meet peers of other ethnic backgrounds in school or other places and get to know other cultures, norms, and values than those that are considered typically Danish. Even immigrants who have stayed in Denmark for two or three generations almost all have connections in their family's homeland and a family history that can inform ethnic Danes about other cultures and living conditions. On a global scale, young Danes have multiple sources of information on foreign places and cultures. Young Danes have almost all traveled in Europe or to more distant parts of the world, and they evaluate personal experience as important for their knowledge and impressions of other cultures. Media are constantly updated, and all around are channels of facts, information, experience, and personal accounts that add fragments to the picture of the global realm. The world is also represented in numerous forms of media entertainment, from films to music to games to literature. The orientation toward Anglo-American, primarily commercially produced culture products, norms, and values is strong, and the pleasurable enjoyment of cultural products and phenomena is immediate. At the same time, however, the internationally produced platforms for experience are transformed into local usefulness with certain reflexive considerations of meaning and impact. Digital media, especially the Internet, provide adolescents with numerous ways of meeting people, establishing relationships, creating communities, and thereby exchanging experience and attitudes toward what is going on globally as well as locally. Many do explore these possibilities, often established through communication in relation to groups of interest such as fan communities, computer games, sports sites, and so on. Many young Danes engage in large networks of relationships and communities, yet consider their locally based groups of friendship and interest to be most valuable and important.

Teenagers in Denmark of all possible backgrounds have an idea of what Danish culture and the Danish way of living is. Some see impressions and inspiration from other cultures as challenges or perhaps even threats to what is considered Danish culture and use the foreign to frame the well known or use the Danish to frame their ethnic cultural background. But the fact is that culture changes in a symbiotic process under the influence of elements from other cultures. Typical Danish culture today is different from what it was 10, 20, or 30 years ago. Young Danes try at the same time to maintain a basis of understanding of values and norms that can supply a solid platform in everyday life and for the future perspective, but they are also, more or less consciously, challenging these values and norms both in the very local context and at the level of society. Very few young Danes would reject the fundamental idea of democracy, but they might question whether democratic principles are always enforced optimally; few would be against integration of immigrants into the Danish society and against the rights of other cultures to maintain relationships with their motherland culture, but they might question the way it is done today; and few would disagree with the principles of the welfare society, but they might disagree—both with established Denmark and internally with other adolescents—about how to maintain and administrate the relationship between public rights and individual responsibility.

One of the fundamental conditions that young Danes benefit from is the level of personal and political freedom. Democracy and a general belief that young people are rational beings enhance their possibilities of influencing and forming their own life and future. A number of standards enforce this, such as the level of free education, living standards, health care, social care, campaigns, and cooperation across institutions to prevent and heal social or personal problems. Danish society has the surplus wealth to worry about young people as a group that makes up the future basis of society and as individuals who are entitled to a good life and good prospects for the future. Young Danes are generally well informed, well educated, and reflexive about their own life and way of living as well as about what is going on in society and around the globe. The majority feel that they have a good life, but at the same time they tend to be concerned about both the future for a troubled world and their own abilities and possibilities to make a good future life in a society where demands for and the value of skills shift so rapidly. Some parents claim, with the best intentions of giving freedom and trust, that "we do not care what you choose to do as long as you are happy," which is a liberating freedom to young people but also a demarcation of the independence and great responsibility that rest on young Danes' shoulders exactly because they have more choices and are supposed to make an extra effort to form their own future. Young Danes are accustomed to the fact that the world as they know it is characterized by constantly shifting trends, ideas, sources of information, ways of communication, and so forth, and they are in general masters of exploring new potentials and adapting to new situations. All in all, Danish culture and norms of Danish-ness may change over time, but the essence is that whatever it is to be Danish and to be young in Denmark, it is generally considered to be quite OK.

RESOURCE GUIDE
Nonfiction

Information on Denmark and additional factual papers and books about Danish history, culture, political structure, social structure, and so forth can be ordered by institutions (for example, school libraries) or via the Danish

embassy in Washington, D.C. Web site: http://www.denmarkemb.org/;
  e-mail: wasamb@wasamb.um.dk.
http://search.eb.com/search?query=denmark&ct=eb&x=8&y=7 (*Encyclopedia Britannica*)

Fiction

Check out especially (among authors of fiction in general) Benny Andersen,
  Hans Christian Andersen, Martin Andersen Nexø, Herman Bang, Steen
  Steensen Blicher, Inger Christensen, Peter Høeg, Ib Michael, and Hans
  Scherfig, and (among authors of children's/teenage fiction) Cecil Bødker
  and Bjarne Reuter.
Bjarne Reuter: "7.a," "Buster's World," "The Boys from St. Petri," Peter Hoegh,
  (Litteraturnet.dk)
http://www.childbooks.dk/childbooks/html/litnet/sprogvalg/engelsk/index_
  engelsk.html
http://www.danlit.dk/gbindex.html

Web Sites

http://www.denmark.dk/
http://www.denmarkemb.org/
http://www.dst.dk/dst/dstframeset_800_en.asp (Statistics Denmark)
http://www.kulturministeriet.dk/sw1356.asp (Ministry of Cultural Affairs)
http://www.mic.dk/db.cgi?db=en&uid=default&view_records_
  forside=1&ID=1002
http://www.socialministeriet.dk/eng/ministeriet/index.html (Ministry of Social
  Affairs)
http://www.statsministeriet.dk/ (Prime Minister's Department)
http://www.visitdenmark.com/portal/

More Information

http://www.ciriusonline.dk/eng/?Id=421
http://www.duf.dk/DUF/site.nsf/framesets/frameset/
http://www.youropa.dk/visiting_en/

Pen Pal Information

http://www.foreningen-ming.dk/ven.htm
http://groups.yahoo.com/subscribe.cgi/penpalsmail4you/
http://www.opendiary.com/diarylist.asp?list=6&start=1&countrycode=DK&
  countryname=Denmark

Chapter 2

ENGLAND

Michael Watts

INTRODUCTION

Oscar Wilde, in his short story "The Canterville Ghost," wrote of the English that "we have really everything in common with America nowadays, except, of course, language." Although written by an Irishman back in 1887, and although written with a large helping of irony, there is a fair amount of truth in this: teenagers in the cities of London or Manchester are likely to have much in common with teenagers in, say, New York or Los Angeles; and teenagers from the rural areas of England, such as East Anglia or the Cotswolds, probably have much in common with teenagers in the Midwest. However, this does not excuse anyone from the short history and politics lessons that follow.

The best starting point is an explanation of the difference between England, Great Britain, and the United Kingdom. England is one of four countries making up the United Kingdom (or the United Kingdom of Great Britain and Northern Ireland, as it is properly known). The other countries are Wales, Scotland, and Northern Ireland—which should not be confused with the Republic of Ireland. Although these four countries-within-a-country have their own histories, identities, and traditions, they are represented on the world stage by the United Kingdom. Their shared histories go back more than a thousand years through trade, treaties, and wars, but the political union that we have today began over 700 years ago when England basically annexed Wales in 1301. Some 300 years later, in 1606, Scotland joined England and Wales to make Great Britain. Then, in 1801, Ireland (which at the time was one country) joined Great Britain (that's England, Wales, and Scotland), and the United Kingdom was born. However, in 1921 Ireland split in two, with the Republic of Ireland becoming a separate and independent country and Northern Ireland remaining within the UK. There are several reasons why people confuse England, Britain, and the United Kingdom. It was England that started the process of building up the UK by taking on the other countries. History has seen several radical and often fairly violent attempts to make the other countries more English, including the suppression of other languages in favor of English (although this is a very simplified—and short—version of history). However, this means that the capital of England, Britain, and the UK has always been London. As the capital, London has always been the seat of government as well as the financial capital and, historically at least, the cultural capital. Also, England is the largest of the four countries (the UK has a total population of about 59 million, and 49 million—about 84 percent—of them are in England). The reason this explanation is a good starting point is that the Welsh, Scots, and (Northern) Irish get annoyed when people speak of England when they mean Britain or the UK, because it implies that they are also English. It happens a lot.

England has a reasonable claim to being the oldest parliamentary democracy in the world (King Canute is said to have held meetings on the current site of the Houses of Parliament in the early eleventh century), but it took a long time to establish today's modern form of government. Parliament might meet in more or less the same place today, but much else has changed. Government in England (as part of the UK) is made up of the monarch, the House of Commons, and the House of Lords. A useful (but limited) comparison can be made with the president, the House of Representatives, and the Senate. The monarch, currently Queen Elizabeth II, is head of state. Unlike in the United States, however, this is a hereditary position (the queen is a direct descendent of King Egbert, who united England under his rule in 829), and she has no real powers. It is the prime minister who has the real power to govern, but unlike the U.S. president, he or she cannot block legislation passed by the government. Also, the prime minister is not elected separately, but is the leader of the largest political party in the democratically elected House of Commons. This is where the prime minister gets his or her power, and it is extremely unusual for a prime minister to be in a situation where his or her party does not provide enough support for that party's agenda. However, this does not mean that the government, or the governing political party for that matter, is blindly obedient to the prime minister. The prime minister can serve any number of terms in office, but several have left sooner than they would have liked because their own party did not like the political direction they were taking: the prime minister is only the political leader of the UK and not the head of state, and so disloyalty to the prime minister is not seen as disloyalty to the country. The House of Commons is where most of the day-to-day business of government takes place, with MPs (members of Parliament) debating and passing laws, imposing taxation, and so on. The House of Lords, most people now agree, is a rather stranger institution. It is something of a historical leftover, and its current role is basically to advise Parliament. Like the Senate, the idea is that a collection of the "great and the good" can bring their expertise and wisdom to bear on the government; and, on the whole, people agree that this is a good idea. The problem is deciding who the "great and good" are; and, unlike the Senate, the House of Lords is currently unelected. It is being reformed but still remains a mixture of the hereditary nobility, retired MPs, and friends of the party politicians.

The main political parties in England are Labour (with policies similar to those of the U.S. Democratic Party), Conservative (similar to the Republican Party), and the Liberal Democrats (a more liberal version of the Democrats than Labour). In addition to these parties, in the rest of the UK Scotland and Wales also have their own nationalist parties, and in Northern Ireland the political contest is between various loyalist parties (wanting to maintain the union with Britain) and nationalists (seeking unification with the Republic of Ireland). All four countries—England, Wales, Scotland, and Northern Ireland—are represented in the House of Commons, with MPs being elected from some 650 constituencies across the country (although some Northern Ireland republican MPs refuse to take their seats because they want a united Ireland). The very end of the twentieth century saw limited political powers being handed over to the Scottish Parliament and the Welsh Assembly (the situation in Northern Ireland has not been fully settled because of ongoing concerns for the peace process). Interestingly, though, England does not have its own parliament.

On the world stage, England (as well as the rest of the UK) has played a very big part for such a small country. There is the language, of course, and writers from William Shakespeare to J.K. Rowling (of Harry Potter fame) have made good use of it. Sir Isaac Newton "discovered" gravity and the basic laws of physics, Charles Darwin introduced evolutionary theory with *The Origin of Species*, and Crick and Watson (an Anglo-American team) first unraveled the secrets of DNA. And then there was the British Empire. History is never straightforward and understanding it is never easy, but England (as part of Great Britain and then the UK) ruled over much of the rest of the world at one time—from Australia to Zimbabwe. The 13 states of the eastern seaboard that are represented by the red and white stripes of the U.S. flag were once British colonies. While America gained independence, so many other countries came under direct British rule or indirect British influence that it was said that the sun never set on the British Empire. By the 1970s most of these countries had achieved independence—and it is interesting to note that many of the founding fathers who pressed for independence (founding mothers are rarely recognized by history) were educated or trained in Britain. Terrible things were done in the name of the British Empire (terrible things are done in the name of all empires), but today most countries that had once been under British rule now work together as equals through the Commonwealth.

At the beginning of the twenty-first century, the UK still exerts considerable influence around the world. The UK sits alongside the United States as one of the five permanent members of the United Nations Security Council (the other permanent members are China, France, and Russia), and both countries are members of the military-focused NATO (the North Atlantic Treaty Organization) and the Group of Eight most economically powerful nations (or G8, as it is usually known). The UK is also a member of the European Union (although, unlike most other members, it has not yet adopted the euro as the common European currency) and the Commonwealth. However, like any other country with sufficient resources, the UK is not above using economic or military force as an alternative to diplomacy.

In spite of this, the English have created a national characteristic of fair play—"supporting the underdog," as it is sometimes known. This may seem a strange characteristic for a country that once ruled over much of the world, but perhaps it is a self-defensive justification for the loss of power. Then again, it may also be a self-defensive justification for the fact that English sporting teams do not perform as well in the world as they would like to. Yet there is an element of fair play in the welfare state that provides free health care and free education (until the university level, when it is heavily subsidized).

However, rampant capitalism and privatization are taking their toll. The welfare state is now chronically underfunded, and many people live in poverty. The vulnerable, including the young and teenagers, fear crime, and media reports of increasing violent crime may be exaggerated, but they feed into this fear (there is relatively little gun crime, though, as private guns are more or less completely banned throughout the UK). People also fear for their jobs, and in a climate of economic concern discrimination rears its ugly head: newly arrived refugees fleeing persecution in their own lands are frequently persecuted in the popular press. English teenagers from nonwhite ethnic minorities are likely to experience discrimination. And then there is the whole class issue—which is a lot more than just how much money one's parents make or what jobs they have. Social class is breaking up and becoming a lot more complex than it ever used to be, but people are still socialized and influenced by their surroundings. It might seem obvious, and it might seem unfair, but it can have major consequences: a middle-class teenager with at least one parent who went to college, for example, is more likely to grow up wanting to go to college, and going to college generally gives one more opportunities in life.

Sixteen is the pivotal age for teenagers in England (although most other teenagers are likely to say that whatever age they are is the most important age). Being 16 means that one can legally leave school, have sex, and buy cigarettes. At 16, a teenager can also get married with parents' consent (otherwise they must be 18). English teenagers have to wait until they are 17 before they can get a driver's license. At 18 they can vote and legally buy alcohol. Buying alcohol is usually more popular.

TYPICAL DAY

For most teenagers in England, the day revolves around some form of education. Schooling is compulsory up until the age of 16 (although plenty of teenagers take unauthorized time off), and then about 8 out of 10 17-year-olds and 6 out of 10 18-year-olds go on to some form of education or training. So the typical weekday (Monday through to Friday) starts with more or (usually) less enthusiastic preparations for school. The school day starts around 8:45 A.M. and ends at about 3:30 P.M. (although there are some small variations between schools). These times vary for those teenagers in postcompulsory education and depend on the type of institution they are studying at. Some teenagers, especially those living in more rural areas, may spend an hour or more traveling to secondary/high school or, for the older teens in postcompulsory education, college.

Some teenagers may have early-morning jobs (such as delivering newspapers) and others may have chores to do at home (for example, making sure that pets or younger siblings are fed and looked after). Islamic teenagers may get up earlier for morning prayers. Most teenagers, though, try to maintain the balance between staying in bed as long as possible and getting ready for school—just in time. Breakfast is becoming increasingly uncommon for teenagers: either they don't want it or they don't have time (although the mother may pack something to eat on the way to school). For older teenagers, this pattern is repeated with preparations for either postcompulsory schooling at college (which may allow more time in bed) or for work.

There is usually homework to be done once school is over, and for those teenagers who actually do their homework, the amount increases as schooling progresses. Weekday evenings are likely to also include time spent in front of the television or computer and socializing. For older teens there may also be part-time evening work. All these activities mean that there is less time for family life, and family meals, traditionally a time when families got together, typically become less important the older teenagers get.

Take away school or work, and one pretty much has the weekend routine. Although many older teenagers still in school may have part-time weekend jobs (and those who are interested in their studies may well spend some time catching up on homework as well), a lot of the weekend is spent catching up on the week—which means that a lot of teenagers will spend time in front of the television or computer or catching up on their social lives. If families do get together for one special meal a week, it is likely to be Sunday lunch. Historically and traditionally, England is a Christian country, but it is an increasingly multicultural society, and religious observance for teenage Muslims will revolve around Friday mosque (although attendance will depend upon school times) and for teenage Jews it will revolve around Saturday synagogue. On the whole, though, religion does not play a great part in most teenagers' lives. For teenagers of all faiths, Sunday night is often spent doing last-minute homework and getting ready for school on Monday morning.

FAMILY LIFE

Although many English teenagers like the idea of leaving home as soon as they can, the increased cost of living means that this is not always possible, and college is often the first opportunity many have to live away from home. However, living at home is not quite the same as living with one's family. Teenagers tend not to help out around the home too much, unless they are asked, but they are becoming increasingly self-sufficient. For example, while they may not cater to others, it is quite common for teenagers to prepare their own meals. This contributes to the fracturing of the family, with different family members, particularly teenagers and young adults, increasingly eating separate meals at separate times. As in the United States, more and more teenagers in England have phones, televisions, stereos, and computers in their bedrooms, and this has the effect of creating a home-within-the-home.

At the same time (and, again, as in the United States), the structure of the family is becoming increasingly complicated, with high divorce rates and more and more single-parent families. Traditional extended families are becoming less important (except, perhaps, in some ethnic minority families), but divorced, separated, and single parents will have partners who may well have children of their own, and this is creating a new kind of extended family. Single or separated parents may also turn to grandparents for help, especially with children and younger teenagers. Such "broken families" (as many people still call them) are common, and this means that children and teenagers are no longer made to feel different if they don't live with both their parents.

Although the mother may stay at home for younger children, and some families may have child minders, it is not uncommon for older children and teenagers to come home to an empty house or find themselves looking after younger siblings until their parents return from work. If both parents are working, it is usually the mother who will have the sort of job that allows her to spend more time in the home. Although there is supposed to be employment equality, men are the typical breadwinners and women typically fill many of the lower-paying jobs such as secretarial work. There is a greater sense of gender equality in the middle-class professions (such as teaching and accounting) and less so in the more manual and lower-status jobs. Go to a gas station or supermarket and one might find men or women serving behind the counters, but one is no more likely to find a male secretary than a female plumber in England.

It is much the same in the home. Typically, there is a greater move toward gender equality in the middle-class homes than in less affluent homes. Many middle-class families employ some form of home help and divide the remaining work between them. However, it is more likely that the mother will take on the less pleasant parenting responsibilities, leaving middle-class fathers to help out with household chores they can attach some remnant of machismo to—such as washing the car or cooking. In less affluent homes it is not unusual for the mother to do the "double shift"—coming home from work to take on all the household chores. This means that although England's teenagers are growing up in a world where there is supposed to be greater gender equality, there is still an awful lot of gender inequality going on in the home.

This can affect the type of relationship that teenagers have with their parents. English teenagers do talk to their parents, but they have different interests in and different interpretations of what is happening around them. So teenagers and their parents might find themselves talking at cross-purposes (and for the children of immigrants, there is the very real likelihood that they may not have a common language that extends beyond the basics). For all of this, though, social values are changing rapidly, and teenagers are able to talk about, and parents are more willing to listen to, important issues. Although Mom is more likely to be there to listen to emotional problems while Dad is more likely to find himself explaining (or trying to explain) how to fix the car, the old social structures are crumbling, and these parental roles might easily be reversed. However, just as teenagers and their parents find themselves able to talk to each other if they want, there are fewer reasons for teenagers to turn to the family for advice on the more important issues in life.

Parents are not always the best people to talk to, and the widespread failure of parents to talk to their children about sex, for example, is one of many complex reasons attributed to the high rate of teenage pregnancies in England. In response to this, most teenagers now have sex education classes in school, and the schools, recognizing that many teenagers will have sex anyway, place age-appropriate emphasis on consent and safe sex. Parents can withdraw their children from these classes. Schools are increasingly being given such responsibilities and give lessons on a wide variety of subjects that could be grouped under the heading of life skills. There are also other services outside schools that offer advice on subjects from debt management to homelessness and relationships. These government-funded services mean that there is less reason than ever for teenagers to turn to their parents for advice—unless they want to.

Access to such advice and information means that English teenagers are able to take greater control of their lives. This is an important factor in family relationships because teenagers do not need to turn to their parents for help, and this means that they are likely to reject unlooked-for advice. However, while English teenagers are becoming more independent in this sense, the high cost of living in England means that they might need to rely on their parents, and stay at home, longer than they would like. It can be a tricky balancing act, particularly as traditional patterns of family life are also changing. Family meals symbolize family unity, but attempts to have mealtime conversations often founder in front of the television. Scenes from *The Simpsons* with the family gathered silently around the television to eat are not unusual (although it is to be hoped that the manners are a little better). The world is rapidly changing, and young people are subject to pressures that were unknown to previous generations. At the same time, the traditional source of stability, the family itself, is typically becoming more dysfunctional. It has never been easy being a teenager, but on the whole English teenagers are coping fairly well—sometimes with and sometimes in spite of their families.

FOOD

Forget rumors about English food—a recent survey found that the country's most popular dish is chicken tikka masala. This is a rather strange favorite food, because it is an English adaptation of an Indian dish (basically it has been made less spicy). Traditional food has gone the way of the traditional family meal—and for much the same reason: there is less time for anyone to prepare it and fewer people prepared to sit down and eat it. Instead of the traditional "meat and two veg" there is now a greater emphasis on convenience food (which may well be a microwave-ready pack of "meat and two veg"). As for teenagers, they might simply add a jar of pre-prepared pasta sauce to a pan of pasta and take pride in their ability to cook. Or they may just defrost a frozen pizza.

The French slang for the English is *rosbif* (it makes sense when one says it out loud), and there was a time when the traditional English dinner was roast beef and roast potatoes. However, beef has always been fairly expensive, and the deregulation of food standards in pursuit of cheaper meat led to the outbreak of a very unpleasant disease called BSE in the country's cattle stock in the early 1990s. As this basically rotted the cattle's brains and was transferable to humans, this tended to deter people from eating beef. Chicken, always a cheaper meat, became even more popular, but it never attained the status of "traditional" English food—until the tikka masala was added. Roast turkey has always been a traditional Christmas meal, but there are no other special occasions in the English calendar that have their own particular foods.

The problem is that traditional dishes all take time. With more parents working (and working longer hours) and the useful freezer/microwave combination, the emphasis is on convenience. An American teenager would not feel altogether out of place in a typical English supermarket—although there is not yet the same huge choice of cheap, almost-ready-to-eat meals. Frozen this, microwave that, and packet the other make up increasingly larger proportions of the typical family's shopping. For those who do not want even this much trouble, there are the take-aways. The traditional English take-away has always been the fish 'n' chip shop. The fish is usually coated in batter and deep fried (remember that *chips* in England are the American *french fries*—with the important difference that English chips are usually cut directly from the potatoes rather than powdered and then put neatly back together again). Fish 'n' chip shops have tried to keep up with the times and people's tastes by diversifying. One can now order curry sauce with one's chips in most places, and, if a person tries hard enough, he or she can find other places that will deep-fry battered chocolate bars. Other popular take-aways offer Indian and Chinese food (although, in deference to English tastes, most will also fry up some fish 'n' chips). However, the food phenomenon of the past 25 years has been the huge increase in American and American-style fast-food outlets. The big names in England are KFC, Burger King, and the ubiquitous McDonald's. McDonald's in particular has wormed its way into the lives of England's teenagers: flashy advertising, cheap food, quick service, and a whole series of gimmicks designed to make it attractive have taken their cultural toll. And, of course, it works. After all, fast food is more appealing to most teenagers than, say, fresh vegetables. There is increasing consumption of junk food among English teenagers; and this, together with social lives geared more toward inactivity, is impacting upon their health. Obesity is becoming a big problem for English youth. This, though, is typically a class-based phenomenon. Cheap food is poor-quality food in England as much as it is in the United States, and preparing properly balanced, healthy meals takes time and costs money.

An increasing number of teenagers, though, are rejecting the superficial appeal of fast food and becoming more sophisticated in their eating habits. Various food scares, including BSE and the ongoing refusal to accept that genetically modified foods are as safe as the manufacturers claim they are, have encouraged this. Many teenagers are vegetarians, and while this may once have been little more than an excuse to live on a diet of coleslaw and chips, now it is often a response to the growing realization that meat production is cruel and inhumane. It is also a lot easier to be a vegetarian now, and most supermarkets stock an increasingly wide range of nonmeat substitutes.

SCHOOLING

Few English teenagers would claim to actually like school, but, as in America, school plays an important part in their social lives. As with many (if not most) aspects of English life, social class makes a difference. There are clear links between educational aspirations, achievement, and social class. Teenagers from professional, middle-class families are more likely to have grown up recognizing the importance of school, stay in school, study more academic-focused subjects, and enter traditional forms of higher education (that is, full-time, university-based academic courses). However, this situation is changing, and, particularly in an increasingly competitive capitalist society, there is an increasing acknowledgment that education and the exam results education produces are important because of the extra opportunities they offer. Of course, there will always be those who do well in life, but a better education and better exam results do give more options in England.

Most students in England go to state-maintained schools, or what are called public schools in America. However, public schools in England are very different, because they are the fee-paying, private schools (or independent schools, as they call themselves). Only about seven percent of secondary/high school students go to these fee-paying independent schools. Many people see them as socially divisive because they allow people with money to buy their children's education, and this goes against the desire to provide the best possible education for all. As in America, the "better" fee-paying schools offer entry to elite social circles, with all the unfair advantages these have, and they are seen to provide a more direct route to the high-status universities, particularly the ancient universities of Oxford and Cambridge (where only half the British students are from state schools).

There used to be two kinds of state schools in England: grammar and secondary modern or technical schools. The grammar schools were selective (that is, one had to pass through tests and interviews to be admitted) and had a very strong academic focus. They were often modeled on the public schools. The secondary moderns/technical schools were where everyone else went to be less academic. However, in the 1960s there was a move toward making schools comprehensive—that is, they served the local area and included everyone, without distinction. English schools are also comprehensive in a socially important way, and there is a greater move toward social inclusion in schools. This means that most students with disabilities or learning problems are now taught in mainstream (as opposed to special) schools. This has led to a greater understanding and acceptance of England as a more inclusive society. Although successive Conservative (and now Labour) governments have tried to undermine the comprehensive ideal of equality, this is still the term that many people still use. Nearly all the secondary moderns have gone, and there are less than a few hundred grammar schools left across the country. But with general paranoia about falling academic standards in many Western countries, places for grammar schools are keenly fought for, and the comprehensive system is under attack. There are still many church-based schools in England that require at least a nod toward religious observance and a small number of Muslim schools in cities with high minority populations. There are very few boarding schools (schools where one lives as well as studies), and most of these are the fee-paying schools. Home schooling is very unusual in England.

Schools in England tend to focus on the more academic subjects, especially the core subjects of English, math, ICT (information and communication technologies), and science. However, there is a growing realization that an academic focus is not for everyone, and changes are underway to include more practical and vocational work. One recent change has been the introduction of citizenship classes. This is not just the civics classes that are taught in American schools (although that is part of this new curriculum) but an attempt to educate young people to become responsible citizens who will actively participate in society. Such classes are often used to tackle wider social issues and encourage alternative and responsible views on matters such as racism and bullying. Schools are also used to introduce students to sex and drugs education. One problem with the new citizenship classes is that this is not a subject that students are tested on (as yet), and so they do not always take it seriously. After all, many students, especially those who want to do well in school, feel that there is little point in studying a subject that will not give one an exam grade that one can show one's future university or employer. This is a reflection of the unfortunate reality that English schools are about the most exam-oriented in the whole of Europe, and this means that too much attention is given to passing exams and not enough to making school as interesting as it can possibly be. Despite this, there are no repeat years in England: students progress automatically to the next year.

Schooling is compulsory until the age of 16, and so, in theory, everyone goes to school. The reality is rather different, and a survey carried out in 2002 found that a quarter of 11–16-year-olds admitted to having played truant for at least one whole day. The main reasons for this were being bored by the classes, not getting along with teachers, and wanting to do something better than stay in school. Relatively few students do this on a regular basis, although there is a hard core of truants. Particularly in less well-off families, truanting may be something that young people do with parental consent or even encouragement.

Beyond 16, about 7 in every 10 teenagers stay in some form of education; just over half of these continue to study the more traditional academic-focused subjects, while the rest will be studying for more vocational qualifications. There is still a bias toward academic subjects, but there are increasing attempts to raise the status of vocational courses (often by including some academic-based content). The government is trying to get more and more young people into higher education because it is seen as a way of generating national wealth—university graduates typically earn more money when they work. Until fairly recently, entry into a university required a collection of academic exam results, but the drive to widen participation and the rapid increase of nontraditional degrees means that it is now much easier to get into college with nonacademic qualifications (including, in some cases, work experience). The transition to college typically takes place at 18, and some 40 percent of young people eventually enter higher education. However, more and more teenagers from families with no tradition of going to college are now doing so, and they may well prefer to start at a later age (perhaps after time spent working and realizing that a degree offers better employment opportunities). Although the government continues to meet most of the cost of going to college, recently introduced fees and the ever-present living costs are increasing, and nowadays it is not unusual for students to leave college with £10,000 (about $16,000) of debt to pay off.

The usual school day in England starts at around 8:45 A.M. and goes through to 3:30 P.M. (although actual times may vary from school to school). Typically there are four 45-minute classes in the morning, with a break in the middle, and three more after lunch. Once in school, classes are relatively small—there should be no more than 30 students in a class, and often, particularly with some subjects, there are far less. At the beginning of secondary/high school, students are likely to remain in the same form groups for all subjects, but most schools still place students in classes of differing ability as they progress toward the important national exams. In school, these are typically taken at the age of 16, but some students will repeat the exams later if they need better results. These class sizes (similar to American schools but relatively small compared to those in some other countries) mean that there is less focus on book work (in the sense of rote learning and lecturing) and more emphasis on student-centered learning and problem solving. Such learning will involve interaction with other students as well as with the teacher. It is also resource-intensive. This means that it is expensive (the simple fact is that providing a wider range of learning materials costs more), and it is not unusual for schools to try and raise their own money for resources, particularly computers. Computers are everywhere in England's schools, and all students must learn at least basic IT (information technology) skills. However, the days of "cut and pasting" homework assignments from Encarta or the Internet seem to be over. Most teenagers (even those who admit to liking school) will complain that there is too much homework—up to several hours a night the older one becomes—and the pressures of school and exams often interfere with the other activities of young people in England.

SOCIAL LIFE, RECREATION, AND ENTERTAINMENT

Many teenagers see home as a place where adults are in control, so they spend more time in the bedroom (the home-within-the-home) or outside

the home, often on the streets. The older teenagers get, the more important it is to have a sense of their own space. This is particularly important
when it comes to socializing. Opportunities for teenagers to socialize and
meet other teenagers depend on where they live. In urban and suburban
areas it is relatively easy to meet up with friends, and there is a greater
range of things to do. In more rural areas there is a greater dependence on
transportation (which often means a greater dependence on parents—at
least until driving age) and there are fewer things to do. It can be difficult
to meet up with friends, let alone meet new ones; a young teenager living
in a rural area must rely on parents to drive them. Seventeen, the age at
which a teenager can start to drive in England, is therefore a magic age for
teenagers, and it is not unusual to find at least some driving lessons among
the 17th-birthday presents.

English teenagers of all ages are asserting more independence, and they
are more likely to negotiate rights with their parents or other adults. This
becomes increasingly important as teenagers get older, and if negotiations
fail they may well reject the values that others try to impose on them.
Ironically, although there are now these greater freedoms, peer pressure
plays a greater part in monitoring teenage behavior than parental control
can ever hope to. Lifestyles are closely associated with friendship status,
and this means conformity in such things as clothes, musical tastes, material possessions such as mobile phones, and, when old enough, cars. Other
associations that might keep teenagers in or out of particular peer groups
might include drinking, smoking, drugs, and sex.

There are few social restrictions on friendships in England, and those
that exist reflect the values of the local community. Even social class has
less of an impact on friendship groups now, as schooling and leisure activities cut across the class system. Teenagers, especially female teenagers,
from ethnic minority groups may have restrictions placed on their social
lives (although these are likely to decrease as families move up the social
ladder and into more mixed areas or simply become more "English"). The
drive for greater inclusion in schools means that disabled teenagers are
more likely to be integrated into local communities and, as a result, have
a wider circle of both disabled and able-bodied friends.

School and college play important roles in the social lives of England's
teenagers, providing opportunities to make and meet friends of both sexes.
School can also provide an opportunity to meet teenagers from different
backgrounds (although where there is a wider choice of local schools,
mainly in high-population urban areas, school populations tend to reflect
social divisions). Most schools are mixed. The fee-paying independent
schools are more likely to be single-sex than state-maintained schools. In

Young jugglers start to juggle with flaming items at Picadilly Circus, London, October 2001. Courtesy of Peter Zelei.

the state sector, grammar schools are typically single-sex (although there are far fewer grammar schools than there used to be), and there may be some single-sex comprehensive schools in the cities, where there is room for them to exist alongside other schools. Single-sex schools in the state sector usually have "brother" or "sister" schools catering to the other sex. Formal social events, such as those often held in American high schools, are unusual in England. The nearest equivalent is the school disco, which few people can look back on without at least a shudder of embarrassment (teachers trying to socialize with their students and act cool never did work and never will). However, English schools do increasingly have the formal Leavers' Ball.

Few English teenagers need such formal occasions to begin the dating game—they just informally get on with it. The greater sense of independence enjoyed by most teenagers means that there are few restrictions on dating. Girls are becoming more assertive and are just as likely to make the first move now as the boys. School is often where the dating game is first played out, but many younger female teenagers will put off having boyfriends to avoid being pressured into having sex too early. Of course, others don't, and England still has a very high rate of teenage pregnancy and unmarried teenage mothers. Among teenagers (if not older generations) the two taboos of gay/lesbian and interethnic dating are not only more common, but may even have special kudos. However, gays (not so much lesbians) might still encounter homophobia and risk gay-bashing.

At the end of the school day, many teenagers will just hang around—although in many rural areas, where there are problems with pubic transportation, they are bused home. Many schools provide a range of after-school activities (which might depend on the interests of the teachers running these groups) and sports clubs. Youth clubs are quite popular, and many have been set up to keep teenagers out of trouble (which doesn't always work—particularly when there are a lot of potentially bored teenagers all together). Schools, after-school clubs, and youth groups are where most younger teenagers meet their friends and peers. Beyond school, work may be a way to meet other teenagers, but it is college that has the big social draw—all those other teenagers living away from home for the first time and all those activities aimed at giving you, the student, a good time. As in America, alcoholism is a big problem in many of England's universities. The club scene is important to older teens (where *older* really means looking old enough to get in), and, except in the more rural areas of the country, most places have some sort of club. Pubs are also popular with those teenagers who are (or who look) old enough to get served alcohol. The legal age for drinking in pubs is 18—although most teenagers will know which pubs are not too fussy about checking.

Most English teenagers would laugh at the idea of formal dances, although some of the more posh schools may teach ballroom dancing. Clubbing, though, is very different: low lighting and a big dance floor, strobe and flash lighting, loud music (dance, trance, dance versions of chart music), most people drinking, drugs probably available somewhere (dope, Ecstasy, speed, with coke becoming more popular but still quite expensive), bouncers at the door, and maybe a police presence outside. However, most people go for fun, and any trouble is quickly stamped out. Like many other elements of English social life, clubbing cuts across social class, so rich and poor are more likely to mingle. Of course, there are other social activities that cost a lot more than others, and so there are still some distinctions.

Styles of dress vary and are influenced by the many subcultures and cross-cultures determined by the media, musical preference, and lifestyle choices. They are similar to American dress styles and just as important to English teenagers because no one wants to look like a "minger" (pronounced with a hard *g* and generally meaning uncool, ugly, and socially inept). So having the right clothes is very important (and, again, this can cost): brand names are more important for the boys, just looking good for the girls. However, there is a growing reaction against brand names. For some older and more politically aware teenagers this might be a rejection of the appalling working practices employed in many sweatshops in the developing world that the brands use, but for most it is just the realization that if everyone has the same brand name, it's no longer cool. Although the majority of English schools have some sort of uniform, the blazer is increasingly a thing of the past, and the uniform may be little more than a sweatshirt worn over other clothes. This means that school uniforms are capable of considerable variety. Fashion and style are therefore important in schools. Dress styles vary greatly, but it would be a very confident (or very lonely) teenager who did not pay attention to whatever his or her peers were wearing. In school, a failure to conform to socially accepted dress codes can lead to social exclusion and even bullying, because they immediately highlight and signify difference. Most schools will try to ban most body piercings except for earrings (although a clear nose stud, for example, can look remarkably like teenage acne).

Social class and affluence determine a lot of what teenagers do for recreation and entertainment. Middle-class teenagers are more likely to spend time reading books, doing various hobbies, or going to concerts. By way of contrast, those from lower socioeconomic backgrounds tend to read magazines and comics, hang around "doing nothing," and go clubbing. Whatever their social class, English teenagers spend a lot of their free time in front of the television, with friends, and listening to music. Although many younger teenagers belong to youth clubs, few of them attend them on a regular basis. After-school activities remain popular. A lot of time is spent just hanging around the streets, although as teenagers grow older this loses its appeal as a meeting place, and many gravitate toward fast-food restaurants (and McDonald's in particular) because they provide somewhere to sit at the relatively cheap cost of a meal. Sleepovers and cinemas are popular with older teenagers, and by the age of 16 many are trying to get into clubs and pubs. By now, many of these teenagers may be experimenting with sex, alcohol, cigarettes, and soft drugs. Such experimentation is something that cuts across social classes as well as both rural and urban areas. About a third of English teenagers aged 16 and over balance part-time work with their ongoing education. Jobs depend on the local area, but they are usually in the service industry, provide no training, and offer low rates of pay. Typical jobs for teenagers remaining in school include waiting tables, kitchen work, and assisting in a shop. Other teenagers will have left school at 16 and have entered, or are trying to enter, the workforce. Seventeen is the minimum driving age in the UK, and learning to drive takes up a lot of these older teenagers' time. Those who pass their driving test and own, or get to use, a car go on to spend a lot of time ferrying their friends around. At 18 it becomes legal to drink alcohol (although, particularly in the cities, many pubs and clubs have a minimum age limit of 21). Eighteen is also the age at which British teenagers get the vote—but this never seems as popular an option.

Television is central to most teenagers' entertainment; and an increasing number of young people in England have televisions, videos, and computers in their bedrooms. On average, younger teenagers spend up to 24 hours a week (one whole day out of every seven) watching television. Homework is often done with the television on. Cable, digital, and satellite television are all becoming more common in England, but English teenagers do not have access to the same number of channels as their American counterparts. However, the programming is similar: soap operas (especially from Australia), chat shows, music, films, sports, and lifestyle shows. Teenagers are increasingly involved in the development of programs targeting them as an audience, so they are less patronizing, less geared toward a middle-class ideal of what young people should be, and more diverse than they used to be. A number of American shows make it across the Atlantic, and *Friends* and *The Simpsons* are probably the most popular U.S. programs in England (Homer was voted the most popular TV character in one recent poll). For all these similarities, there is one significant difference between English and American television: Americans turn on black, white, or, increasingly, Latino programs, but English television, while still predominantly white, is more multicultural within the actual programs.

English cinema is dominated by Hollywood, although the country's sizable Bangladeshi, Indian, Pakistani, and Tamil communities mean that Bollywood is becoming a force to be reckoned with (Bollywood is located in Bombay, the old name for modern Mumbai in India). English films produced with one eye on the international audience, such as *Notting Hill or Shakespeare in Love*, tend to find leading roles for American actors, and even Bridget Jones, a favorite with teenage girls, was played by an

A teenage girl watching the "telly," London, England. Courtesy of P&PB Photos.

American (although some might say this makes up for the old injustice of Vivien Leigh playing Scarlett O'Hara in *Gone with the Wind*). Older teenagers, particularly those in college, may develop an interest in what is commonly seen as the more sophisticated British film industry with its all-British cast lists (and which is usually doomed to failure on the international stage).

The charts are mostly filled with British artists, although Americans from Britney Spears to Marilyn Manson are popular with English teenagers. Hip-hop is a big American influence on the English music scene. As in America, it rapidly moved out of areas of black deprivation to find a more mainstream audience, and Eminem enjoys the same controversy on both sides of the Atlantic. World music is becoming more and more popular in England.

Teenagers in England are becoming more politically aware, but this is usually an interest in local, grassroots, and single-issue politics such as animal rights, antiracism, and the environment. Apart from this, traditional party politics bore most teenagers, and they feel that they are ignored by mainstream politics and politicians—until they get to vote at 18, when they will usually receive a standard letter from their local MP (whose name they probably do not even recognize). There is also a strong tradition among older teenagers of volunteering, although the motivation for this is usually balanced between genuine interest and the need for something to add to the CV (the curriculum vitae or résumé).

Sporting activities are another useful addition to the CV. Football (soccer) is the most popular sport across in England (as it is across much of the world), and most teenagers, girls as well as boys, will find themselves playing football at some time. Rugby is also very popular, although more as a spectator sport than one to play. Cricket is a very English game and is particularly popular among English teenagers of Indian, Pakistani, and Sri Lankan descent. Many teenagers enjoy watching wrestling (of the WWF variety), and older teens might watch Formula One racing.

Nearly all teenagers participate in some sporting activity up until the age of 16, when compulsory schooling, together with compulsory PE (physical education) classes, ends. Boys and girls tend to take part in the same activities—badminton, basketball, hockey, football (soccer), gymnastics, swimming, table tennis, and tennis are all common—but not always at the same time. Boys might also get to play cricket and rugby, while the girls might play netball and rounders (baseball lite).

Teenagers playing football in London, England. Courtesy of P&PB Photos.

There have been attempts to move away from sporting competition to encourage greater participation by the less athletic, but these attempts have largely failed, and those students who are good at their sport usually have more kudos than those who are good at their classes. However, many teenagers see participating in sports as uncool, particularly when it is linked to school PE. At the same time, though, more teenagers are now joining sports clubs or taking part in competitive sports, and older teenagers tend to recognize the advantages of physical activity: girls because it makes them look good and lose weight, boys because it is healthy.

RELIGIOUS PRACTICES AND CULTURAL CEREMONIES

All students in England's schools are supposed to learn about the world's six major religions: Christianity, Judaism, Islam, Buddhism, Hinduism, and Sikhism. Historically, England is a Christian country, but church attendance is in a state of decline, and although the two big Christian festivals of Christmas and Easter are still celebrated, they have lost much of their religious significance and are now hugely commercialized. However, in an increasingly multicultural society, other religions, particularly Islam, are growing, and the festivals of this and other religions may be observed in schools where there are high concentrations of students practicing them. A small but growing number of teenagers are showing interest in alternative religions, including spirituality and paganism. In general, though, it is not cool to be religious in England.

Instead, other nonreligious occasions are becoming more important—although some, such as the Queen's golden jubilee in 2002 and the funeral of Princess Diana a few years earlier, still have religious overtones. Most royal events also involve military tradition. English teenagers have grown up far away from war (even the Northern Ireland conflict is slowly settling down into peace), but there has been a renewed interest in the annual Remembrance Day (held on the nearest Sunday to November 11—the day the First World War ended), when everyone from the youngest children to the oldest pensioners wear symbolic red poppies to remember those who died in war. Since September 11, 2001, representatives of New York's fire and police services have also been invited to participate. Another annual event is Red Nose Day, when there is a nationwide drive to raise money for projects in Africa and the UK through the charity Comic Relief. Some £37 million (about $62 million) was raised in 2003, and much of this came from teenagers. Schools, colleges, and universities as well as workplaces all organize special events, and teenagers (along with the rest of the country) can pay to make fools of themselves and others for charity.

Such occasions are significant because they are an opportunity for all sorts of people, whatever their class or color, to come together in a common cause. Major sporting events do the same—although there may be more rivalries. The 2002 World Cup (remember that outside the United States, the World Cup means football—or soccer) was held in Japan and South Korea, and this meant that games were broadcast live in England in the morning. Most schools opened early to allow students the chance to watch them.

The biggest names in English football are David Beckham (currently playing for Manchester United) and Michael Owen (of Liverpool). They are part of the cult of celebrity that reflects current popularity—and is just as strange in England as it is in the United States. It includes the typical range of pop and rock musicians, rap artists, TV personalities, and film stars. But there are also some very strange members of this cult, and they can have very strange effects. Reality TV turns unknown, ordinary people into celebrities overnight—although many of them are trashed in the media soon after. Harry Potter made glasses, always considered uncool by younger teens, more popular. And then, of course, there is the only slightly more real Ozzy.

CONCLUSION

As the English cult of celebrity suggests, the world can be a funny place. It can also be a very difficult place for teenagers to grow up in. George Bush Sr. once complained that families in the United States were more like *The Simpsons* than *The Waltons*. It can be like that in England, too—dysfunctional kids in dysfunctional families trying to cope with the dysfunctional world around them. English teenagers are struggling to balance the old and the new, and struggling to balance newfound responsibilities with newfound opportunities. There are good and bad things about being an English teenager, and all in all, most of them will be familiar to American teens. However, this does not mean that it is a waste of time learning about the lives of English teenagers. It is important to recognize that teenagers around the world share many things in common and that for all the diversity there is in the world, different cultures only mask a deeper and more significant common (teenage) humanity. It is easy to spot the similarities between American and English teenagers, and this should be used as an opportunity to look for other similarities with teenagers in other countries.

But there is another reason why looking at the lives of English teenagers might be important. Unfortunately, society is not always good, and governments do not always do what is right. However, wherever one is in the world, it can be very difficult to take a good, hard look at one's own society and one's own country, because few people want to seem disloyal or unpatriotic. Yet many things that are wrong in the world happen because people did not speak out against them. Often, people did not even think there was anything wrong. Looking at a country as similar as England, and looking at the bad as well as the good, might just help everyone to recognize where every society can be improved.

RESOURCE GUIDE
Nonfiction

Some of the best history books for younger teenagers are the *Horrible Histories*, which can be accessed on the *Horrible Histories* Web site (http://www. horrible-histories.co.uk). The following is a brief selection of other (and more grown-up) books on English and British history, culture, and society.

Peter Ackroyd, *Albion: The Origins of the English Imagination* (2002, Reading, UK: Chatto & Windus).

Niall Ferguson, *Empire: How Britain Made the Modern World* (2003, UK: Allen Lane/Penguin Press).

Adam Hart-Davis, *What the Victorians Did for Us* (2001, London: Headline Book Publishing Ltd.).

Nigel Nicolson, *The Queen and Us: the Second Elizabethan Age* (2003, London: Wiedenfeld & Nicholson).

Jeremy Paxman, *The English: A Portrait of a People* (1999, London: Penguin).

Mike Phillips & Trevor Phillips, *Windrush: The Irresistible Rise of Multi-Racial Britain* (1998, London: HarperCollins).

Liza Picard, *Dr. Johnson's London: Everyday Life in London in the Mid-18th Century* (2002, London: Wiedenfeld & Nicholson).

Simon Schama, *A History of Britain III: the Fate of Empire 1776–2001* (2002, London: BBC Consumer Publishing).

Jacqueline Simpson & Steve Roud, *A Dictionary of English Folklore* (2001, Oxford: Oxford University Press).

Rozina Visram, *Asians in Britain: 400 Years of History* (2002, London: Pluto Press).

Fiction

England has a healthy tradition of writing about contemporary issues in teenage fiction. The following books offer a cross section of those issues.

Melvin Burgess, *Junk* (1997, Puffin). The title has it—drug addiction.

Gillian Cross, *Tightrope* (1999, Oxford University Press). The complexities of becoming involved in minor delinquency to escape the drudgery of everyday life.

Bel Mooney, *Joining the Rainbow* (1997, Mammoth). Discusses environmental protest.

Beverley Naidoo, *The Other Side of Truth* (2000, Puffin). Political asylum, racism, free speech, and bullying are all explored as a family of Nigerian refugees tries to settle in England.

Louise Rennison, *Angus, Thongs and Full-Frontal Snogging* (1999, Piccadilly Press). Teenage angst as a young Bridget Jones deals with problems from how to dress for fancy dress and what to do when the boys don't fancy you.

Robert Swindells, *Smash!* (1998, Puffin). A powerful exploration of youthful racism and its impact upon society.

Robert Westall, *Falling into Glory* (1993, Methuen). The angst of falling in teenage love—but this time it is a boy falling in love with his teacher.

Jacqueline Wilson, *Girls under Pressure* (1999, Corgi). Three teenage girls struggle with their friendship and the pressure of conforming to media stereotypes.

Benjamin Zephaniah, *Face* (1999, Bloomsbury). Racism and antiracism, exclusion and inclusion in the East End of London.

Benjamin Zephaniah, *School's Out: Poems Not for School* (1997, AK Press). Something different—the title says it all.

Web Sites

http://www.bbc.co.uk/

The home page of the British Broadcasting Corporation does more than just tell one what is on the TV in England: it has pages for teenagers (fashion, advice, music charts—the lot, really) and up-to-date worldwide news (in 43 different languages!). One of the best Web sites going. Two links that might be of particular interest follow.

http://www.bbc.co.uk/schools/

This will give one an insight into English schools—particularly if one wants to know more about the subjects that are studied. Conveniently, it also has revision hints (although these work best for UK-based exams).

http://news.bbc.co.uk/sport/

The direct link to the BBC's sports roundup has up-to-date sporting news from England—as well as the rest of the UK and the world.

http://www.britainusa.com/

The official Web site of the British government in the United States. This is the virtual British embassy and includes the sort of information on Britain that a U.S. audience wants and a regularly updated review of the British newspapers.

http://www.britcoun.org/

The British Council represents Britain (and England) around the world. Good for culture and a good source of official information.

http://www.nationaltrust.org.uk/

The National Trust was established to preserve the country's natural and built heritage. The Web site is full of photos and information.

http://www.royal.gov.uk/

This is the official site of the monarchy and includes current news, historical information, and photographs (including some of the places in the palaces one would not be able to see in real life).

http://www.shakespeare.org.uk/

England's most famous writer deserves his own home page—and this is the best of them.

http://www.visitbritain.com/

The official tourist site. Its purpose is to encourage people to visit England (and the rest of Britain), so there is lots of information and plenty of pictures.

http://www.young.gov.uk/

As government can be a bit dull for teenagers and young adults, this site has been designed with them in mind. It has links around England and the rest of the UK and is (supposed to be) teenager-friendly.

Pen Pal Information

http://www.opendiary.com/diarylist.asp?list=6&start=1&countrycode=UK&countryname=United+Kingdom

Chapter 3

FRANCE

Françoise Bodone

The French constitute the most brilliant and the most dangerous nation in Europe and the best qualified in turn to become an object of admiration, hatred, pity or terror, but never indifference.

—*Alexis de Tocqueville*

INTRODUCTION

From *Salut les Copains*[1] to McSolaar[2]

France is located in the western part of Europe and borders seven other countries: Belgium, Luxembourg, Germany, Switzerland, Italy, Spain, and Andorra. France counts about 59 million people living on 549,192 square kilometers. The country is divided into 22 *régions*, each subdivided into *départements*. There are 96 *départements* in the *métropole* (France mainland), 4 overseas (Départements d'Outre Mer—DOM, Martinique, Guadeloupe, French Guiana, and La Réunion) as well as overseas territories (TOM—French Polynesia, New Caledonia) and the *collectivités territoriales* of Mayotte and St.-Pierre-et-Miquelon.[3]

Centralization has been a traditional feature of French society. Paris (called Lutetia over 2,000 years ago) hosts all government bodies (the French Assembly, the Senate, and the president's quarters at the Hotel Matignon) and is a renowned capital for its history, culinary tradition, museums, fashion, and an effervescent world-music scene and production. Since the 1980s decentralization efforts have allowed regional and departmental authorities (*conseil régionaux*) to assert their local power.

Populations migrated out of Paris and its vicinity to booming provincial cities such as Lyon or Lille. French regions are reclaiming and affirming their cultural identities and traditions, reviving their local *artisanat* (craftsmanship) and languages such as Provençal, Breton, Alsatian, Catalan, Corsican, Basque, and Créole.[4]

Since 1958, France has been under the dictates of the Fifth Republic. The *président de la république* (currently Jacques Chirac) is elected through a direct universal vote with an absolute majority and governs the nation in partnership with a ministerial cabinet for a seven-year renewable mandate. He appoints the *premier ministre* (prime minister), who heads the cabinet and a team of ministers (in education, agriculture, sports, and so on). Each Wednesday morning, the entire cabinet meets with the president to discuss current issues, projects, and initiatives that will be proposed to the French Assembly (l'Assemblée Nationale). The current government is an untraditionally younger group (between 45 and 55)[5] and has women in key positions (for example, head of the armies). The *députés* (elected and representative of each region) sit at the French Assembly and ratify government proposals, together with the members of the Sénat (French Senate).

French *syndicats* (workers' unions) are a strong political force and often the organizers of massive national strikes whenever they feel the government infringes upon workers' rights or, in contemporary economics, favors European interests over French ones. French people make vocal critiques of their government and like to take to the streets, often mobilizing and immobilizing the entire country: you may recall thousands of truck drivers blocking major highways, or French airlines and trains stopping their services, or hundreds of thousands of students and educators demonstrating on the streets of major cities in 1986 and 1998 against the state of education (see the education section).

Up until the end of World War II, France was an agricultural nation; 60 percent of the land is still used for agricultural purposes, and with its temperate climate and the diversity of its soil, it remains a farming paradise (Corbett, 1994). The second half of the twentieth century witnessed a tremendous economic reconversion, with alternating trends between strong state intervention/state-owned industries, and privatization and economic liberalism (Hughes & Reader, 1998).

France's industry is the most dynamic sector of the economy. The country is particularly strong in the air industry (Airbus in Toulouse is Boeing's main competitor), pharmaceutical products, perfumery, and cars. France is Europe's second largest producer of agricultural goods and still the world's biggest wine exporter: 3.35 percent of the land is planted with vines, and 6 million people work in the wine industry, primarily in the southeastern and southwestern regions. Luxury products in fashion and fine foods (for example, foie gras) are also a growing sector. Finally, France is the world's most visited country: as of 2002, it had the largest number of visitors yearly, ahead of the United States, Spain, and Italy (INSEE, 2002). However, it is an ailing economy faced with increasing market pressures imposed by the EEC (European Market). The unemployment rate is one of the highest in Europe (11.9 percent in 1999), especially among young people (15–24 years old) (INCA, 2002). Much like in other developed countries, France faces harsher competitive markets, economic recessions, and the consequences of globalization, with particular groups being more affected than others, such as minorities and young people.

France (known as La Gaule a long time ago)[6] shares tight and long historical connections with its European neighbors[7] as well as countries on the African continent that were colonized in the earlier part of last century.[8] The French Revolution (1789), with its celebrated motto of liberté, égalité, fraternité (taken up by the U.S. founding fathers) ended centuries of monarchy in favor of a democratic/republican regime up until the Napoleonic years (1804–73), which saw a succession of three self-proclaimed emperors (the best known is Napoléon I) whose imperialistic visions initiated French colonial projects. (For more details, see Appiah & Gates, 1999.) Colonized nations in Africa and Southeast Asia gained independence in the early 1960s, at times violently—for example, Vietnam (with the battle of Dien Bien Phu in 1954) and the Algerian War (1962). The latter one "left deep scars in the French psyche ... And a profound ambivalence towards Algerian Muslims" (Hughes & Reader, 1998, p. 299). The last 40 years have seen important waves of immigrations as part of the decolonization process (again, see Appiah & Gates, 1999) from North Africa (Morocco, Algeria, and Tunisia) and Southeast Asia (Vietnam): in 2000, 13 percent of the total population was of foreign origin (Caldwell, 2000). France is also a terre d'asile, an asylum for political refugees from around the world or les gens du voyage (Romani people, or gypsies) who establish temporary homes on the outskirts of cities and villages across the country.

Religiously, France is also diversifying. It has traditionally been a Roman Catholic country: before the Vatican in Rome, the pope resided in Avignon, where vestiges of his palace are still great tourist attractions, and France "was known for centuries as fille ainée de l'Eglise, elder daughter of the church ... because for thirteen hundred years (until 1790) Catholicism was the 'religion of the nation and an essential

element of its identity'" (Rémond, 1987, in Corbett, 1994). (For insightful details on this time of history, read *In the Name of the Rose*, by Umberto
Eco, or watch the movie version featuring Sean Connery.) Islam has
become France's second religion, with "about four million Muslims, two
million of them French citizens" (Caldwell, 2000), followed by Judaism,
Protestantism, and Buddhism.

Racism, both individual and institutionalized, has worked its way
through French society parallel to the massive influx of new people. It
is heightened during times of economic recession, where immigrants are
usually accused of "stealing French people's jobs." Poverty affects primarily non-European immigrant populations who reside in the *banlieues* or
cités (suburbs) and where youth is most exposed to violence, drugs, and
other societal ills (see Hargreaves, 1991), much like in U.S. inner cities.
Young people often react violently to these conditions in which they and
their parents exist. One particular group, the *beurs*[9] (second-generation
immigrants of North African origin born in France who feel neither
fully French nor fully Arab) have become the symbols of a new French
generation (*génération beur*) that has success stories like Zinedine Zidane
(Zizou—the victorious captain of the French soccer team, 1998 world
champions) and various artists, for example, rappers, writers, and cineas-
tes, who tell their stories of integration, rebellion, or survival between
cultures, as well more tragic stories filled with violence, gang life, drugs,
and despair. The lives and experiences of these immigrant youth impact
all aspects of French society and are a reminder of France's intricate,
ambivalent, and complex connections with peoples who share different
cultures and religions and who have chosen France as their *terre d'asile*.
For example, with Muslim populations, the problem of racism is exac-
erbated "because differences of religion are involved. Islam envisions
an Islamic State in the world. This creates constant conflicts between
a state based on the Rights of Man [and the separation of church and
state, French *laïcité*][10] and a religion that, strictly interpreted, holds that
all legitimate political power flows from the Koran" (Caldwell, 2001).
France is learning to be heterogeneous and faces the challenges as well
as opportunities of the cultural, religious, and linguistic diversity that is
changing its identity yet again.[11]

TYPICAL DAY

Much like most of their peers around the world, the life of teens in
France revolves around school. A typical day starts early in the morning
(between 6 and 7:30 A.M.) with a quick breakfast. Parents usually take

their teens to school, or they use public transportation or walk to school if they are lucky to live near by. However, many opt to ride their bikes or *mobylettes* (little mopeds or Vespas). After school, teens participate in different activities: they play sports, hang out with their friends at the local café, or head home to do their homework (typically a heavy load), help out with dinner preparation, or play with their home computers. School is in itself a full-time activity that does not leave much room for a part-time job, except on weekends. However, weekends are typically spent with friends and family and playing sports (see the social life and recreation sections) as well as catching up on homework and helping out around the house.

Schooling may be a common set of experiences for teenagers; however, what they do before and after school differs depending on where they live (urban, suburban, or rural environments), their socioeconomic situations, and their cultural and religious beliefs. For example, a Muslim youth may have to devote time to prayers daily before and after school, or a youth in a single-parent family has to take care of his/her siblings after school rather than hanging out with his/her friends.

FAMILY LIFE

Since the 1970s people have tended to marry later in life or not marry at all, preferring to live in *unions libres* (free unions). By the mid-1990s, the rate of marriages in France was Europe's lowest. However, the matrimonial institution is regaining ground, with more Saturday afternoons loud with honking cars rolling down main streets, celebrating the newlyweds. In addition, women have been able to control their sexuality (through contraception and abortion) and have also dramatically increased their numbers in universities and in the workforce (Rodgers, 1999).

La famille remains a strong component of French society, a tradition: "The French put family first. It is the social cement and a specific duty for each individual involved. Outside are public life, philosophy, politics, art and cuisine. Inside is family" (Adamson Taylor, 1996, p. 135). Typically, families are nuclear (father, mother, and the children) and the number of children varies. Large families are less commonplace as people moved to urban environments and both parents worked.[12] The last 20 years have also seen an increase in single-parent families (Rodgers, 1999). People in France are rather sedentary and like to establish their families close to one another (if they can), as a way to sustain the emotional and economic benefits of the extended family, such as grandparents picking up their grandchildren after school or babysitting. Sundays are still sacred

family days where people gather around a table for a good meal, take an
outdoor trip together, or simply visit with each other.

In the last 30 years, women have joined men in working full-time jobs.
They have received considerable support from the government (envied
in many other developed countries), such as financial aid (*allocation
familiale*), long paid maternity leaves, child care, free nursery schools,
and numerous after-school programs to take care of their *chérubins* (little
ones) while still working full time. If gender roles have been slightly
modified (such as fathers helping out in the kitchen or changing diapers;
see Kidd & Reynolds, 2000), the responsibilities of each member of the
family are still strong and well defined. Early on, children are taught
about their place and role in the familial environment. They each have
their share of personal (for example, making your own bed, tidying up
your room) and communal (helping out with cooking, grocery shopping,
taking care of younger siblings) chores. They also know better than to
be disrespectful to their parents, or any older member of the family for
that matter. Reprimands, verbal or physical, are not uncommon whether
privately or publicly. It is not considered abuse (as it may often be in the
United States), but a demonstration of a firm hand and actual caring
attitude. One French saying actually applies here: "Qui aime bien,
châtie bien" (Who loves well, disciplines well). Parents are an authority, there to provide insights and guidance, but not to baby sit. Children
are encouraged to be responsible for their actions early on in life and to
solve problems among themselves with little to no adult intervention.

At age 16, youth can be served alcohol at bars and cafés. However, in
the private realm, parents decide when the appropriate drinking age is.
(Drinking wine at the dinner table is a national tradition. For teens it
often symbolizes a rite of passage into young adulthood when wine is finally
served to them.) At 18, adolescents are able to vote and drive. The *permis
de conduire* (driver's license) is generally the next best thing on a teen's list
of priorities after high school. The permit requires a mandatory number
of driving lessons (*leçons de conduite*) at official driving schools that are
extremely costly. Young people often take summer or after-school jobs to
cover the cost, or parents help out: *les leçons de conduite* are often a deserved
high school graduation present. The driving test is a grueling experience,
and passing it is cause for much celebration. Inexpensive secondhand cars
are usually preferred for the first years of driving, especially as auto-insurance
premiums are at their highest until the youth turns 25.[13]

During adolescence, French parents usually trust their children. They
relax the rules around them and support their independence and desire
for freedom and experimentation as long as rules of conduct are respected

in the family home (such as no offensive language, showing up at dinner time, or helping out—*les bonnes manières*). However, the increasingly violent societal environments in which youth grows (especially in urban and suburban areas) and their subsequent attitudinal changes are eroding parents' trust as well as their parenting expertise. A recent survey (IFOP—a French Poll Organization) indicates that 74 percent of people (young and old) believe parents are not doing their job well and need help. Educators offer insights; so do popular rappers like NTM: "Laisse pas traîner to fils à l'aube de l'an 2000. Laisse pas traîner ton fils si tu ne veux pas qu'il glisse, qu'il te ramène du vice" ("Don't let your son hang out in the street on the eve of 2000. Don't let him hang out if you don't want him to slip and come back filled with vice") (Remy, Chartier, & Orgé, 2003).

It seems like in the last 10 years, the government has been paying closer attention to youth issues, be it at the educational, social, or cultural levels (see initiatives taken by the Ministries of Culture, of Education, and of Youth and Sports—see the resources section), partly because the youth is finding a stronger voice, positively, via political demonstrations (see education section), artistic venues such as music or literature, and, more negatively, increased violent responses to an enduring and endemic institutionalized racism that still characterizes parts of French society. French and other European governments are listening to their youth, or at least providing forums for discussions on matters that interest/concern them. For example, after two years of European consultation, a new policy has been adopted that aims at dealing with the questions posed by youth (15–25 years old) about education, employment, social integration, autonomy, and so on. Youths are encouraged to fill out online questionnaires. Their responses inform current European policies and help governments understand societal ills from a youth perspective. It is a work in progress that may or may not solve all problems, but at least recognizes the weight and influence of youth in contemporary and future societies.

FOOD

French people take their food very seriously, and eating is a central social activity to their daily lives. For example, lunchtime is sacred. During the week, most shops close (until about 2 P.M.), phones stop ringing, and people take an hour minimum break to eat their sandwich (a winner is *jambon-beurre*—ham and butter on a baguette), go to the local restaurant (for a steak frites and french fries or menu du jour) or head home if located in the proximity. Dinners, usually around 7:30 P.M., bring the family together to discuss everyone's day and family or other matters. On weekends, people gather with friends and families for serious food, namely copious lunches or dinners that can last hours as people eat, drink, argue ... and eat some more.

Much like other customs and ways of life in France, food is a regional tradition. For example, the southeastern regions share commonalties of ingredients and food preparation with neighboring Italy. Olive oil is central to most dishes; so are pasta and cheese, as well as variety of meats (for example, raw ham and all kinds of sausages, cooked and raw—*saucissons* is a favorite). Closer to the Mediterranean Sea and the Atlantic Ocean, people eat fish and other sea products. Inland, in the southwest corner, a hunters' stronghold, people eat foie gras and other game products, and usually a high-fat, succulent cuisine. On the northeastern front, Alsace-Lorraine offers its quiche lorraine and other dishes influenced by German food traditions heavy on cabbage and sausages (for example, choucroute). The spices of Tunisian and Moroccan cuisines on one hand, and Southeast Asian (Vietnam, Thailand) on the other, add to the local diversity in increasing and interestingly tasteful ways. In downtown Marseille, viewed by many as the Algiers of France, one finds every item needed to complete a traditional Algerian dish in streets busy with open markets where Arabic is more often heard than French. Common staples at the dinner table are wine, bread, and cheese: France has about 360 different sorts of cheese, and each wine region is proud to offer a distinctive regional taste. One can't go wrong with that.

At home, women typically prepare food, although men and children have become accustomed to helping (with more women out at work). French streets abound with food stores of all kinds, specializing in meats (*boucherie/charcuterie*), pastries (*patisserie*), breads (*boulangerie*), pastas, and spices, among others. However, big food chain stores like Carrefour or Intermarché are the most popular, offering lower prices and a wider range of products, all in one place—a more practical solution for busy, full-time working families. Open markets are still one of France's best places for quality, fresh, and organic foods and are daily occurrences in most towns and villages: Le Marché des Halles in Paris is world-renowned, a place where famed chefs come to select their ingredients. (In the United States, San Francisco's Fisherman's Wharf or New Orleans's French Corner are comparable sites.)

Fast-food chains, such as McDonald's or Burger King, have grown popular over the years, especially among young people, who often eat a MacDo (hamburger) and fries. The typical characteristics of fast, cheap food (as found in the United States) do not really apply, though: a hamburger costs about two dollars, and people tend to stick around as they would in another restaurant, for hours.

SCHOOLING

Historically, education was a church matter, up until the 1880s, when Jules Ferry (a reformer) gave "every town, village a state primary school for boys and girls where schooling was free, compulsory and non-religious between 6 and 13." Currently, education is still a right for every child or young person regardless of his/her socioeconomic, cultural, or geographical background. It is virtually free for everyone and financed by the government: public-sector institutions provide schooling for about 86 percent of children in primary level education (age 6–11) and 79 percent of those in secondary education (12–18) (INCA, 2002). Compulsory education now ends at 16 (upon completion of the first year of upper secondary education).

The Ministry of Education decides on school curriculum, the training of teachers, and other schooling regulatory processes. It prescribes the skills to be acquired in the course of each cycle of compulsory education but does not prescribe specific teaching strategies or materials. Teachers are free to make that decision within the administrative regulations of their own school. The ministry's curricula usually encompass French, mathematics, science, history/geography, civics, technology, modern foreign languages, physical education, and art (including music) (INCA, 2002). The educational system consists of four phases:

1. Precompulsory education (3–5 years old) gives every child the opportunity to attend a free nursery school (*école maternelle*) from 7:30 to 4:30 P.M., allowing full-time careers for both parents (this is often where the close extended family comes in handy, as they pick up the little ones after school): "Overall, 98 percent of children between three and five are in school in France, compared to 50 percent in the United States ... The focus is on socialization through play and manual activities designed to stimulate the intelligence of pupils" (Corbett, 1994, p. 99).

2. Primary/elementary education (6–10 years old) is when things become serious for French children. They learn basic knowledge and tools in oral and written expression (focus on French grammar and reading skills) and mathematics. Primary schoolers go to school for six hours every day, except Wednesdays and weekends, and become familiar with homework: "French elementary schoolchildren have the longest workweek in Europe: twenty-seven contact hours, that is, six hours per day from Monday through Saturday except Wednesday, which is free" (Corbett, 1994, p. 104).

3. Lower secondary education (*collège*) is from 11 to 14 years old. It is an important and symbolic step in the educative life of French children: the entrance in *sixième*, the first level of lower secondary, is the entrance to the big school (often already attended by an older brother or sister), and students take it very seriously. Lower secondary reinforces the basic skills learned in primary school, with a focus on numeracy and literacy skills and classes to be taken in both arts and sciences. In *collège*, students are exposed to their first foreign language (English is favored, although German has its aficionados). Latin and Greek are also optional choices, and usually good bases to learn German and other Romance languages such as Italian or Spanish. At the completion of ninth grade (the end of lower secondary), French students can earn a diploma, the *brevet de collège* (or BEPC) by earning satisfactory course grades in academic courses and performing well on examinations. The BEPC is optional and does not affect one's chances with the *baccalauréat*. However, it gauges students' performance mid-secondary and is a good barometer of their academic preparation and subsequent success in the upper secondary division.

4. Upper secondary students are streamed either into a professional high school for vocational training or into a combined year (*la seconde*) during which they are oriented either to a *baccalauréat* "général (the traditional academic system intended to lead to university);[14] or the bac technologique (based on technological skills, leading to a shorter post-secondary training)" (Kidd & Reynolds, 2000). In vocational high schools, students can continue on to a *bac professionel* (focusing on special skills and work experience). The general *baccalauréat* is the hot item, the ticket to college, and offers a more rigorous academic curriculum. Students (or rather their parents) choose between scientific (Bac S—the hardest and most prestigious, which provides access to engineering or medical schools, computer sciences, and so on), literary (Bac L—the intellectual option, which is a bit more limiting career-wise but still filled with exciting opportunities; your author opted for that one), and economic studies (Bac ES). In all three options, students are expected to take on another foreign language and to test in French literature, history, geography, and philosophy (the latter academic focus is now taught for every *baccalauréat* preparation during the last school year, in *terminale*).

Life in high school (*lycée*) is no fun—*galère*, in the words of high schoolers. Students work from 8 to 5 P.M., with a recess at midmorning when they step outside, share a cigarette, and a gossip. Lunch lasts about an hour (either inside or outside the premises—at parental discretion). Classes continue all afternoon until 5 P.M. The focus is on academics (with a heavy load of homework) and leaves little time for socializing, and barely any physical activity (two to three hours of PE instruction per week, as your author sadly remembers) for that matter. The preparation for the *baccalauréat* and the actual examinations are a grueling process that is emotionally and psychologically draining for students. The written part tests your acquired knowledge and analytical abilities, and the oral section, one-on-one with an examiner, checks your ability to present information and your oral skills. The tests are distributed nationally on the same day and at the same time (usually the end of June), and last about two days (between all the subject areas). Results are published in the official newspapers (and probably online these days) within two weeks.

French education faces numerous crises such as increasing violence, high dropout rates and absenteeism, academic results that are declining and showing strong inequities between socioeconomic groups (Allègre, 2002), and increasing illiteracy rate: 1 French person out of 10 between 17 and 25 years old does not know how to read or write correctly (Simonnet, 2002). The system has been accused of elitism for many years through its tracking system at the *baccalauréat* level and an ethnocentric curriculum that ultimately favors students from higher socioeconomic classes and who come from the dominant French culture. Over the years, however, immigrant families have placed a high value on education, pushed their children to work hard, and seen the fruitful results of their children's economic and social success (see Kidd & Reynolds, 2000, pp. 62–65, for case studies).

To respond to the increasing violence in school and lower achievement in impoverished areas, the government designated certain schools as ZEP (*zone d'education prioritaire*—education priority zone) so that they could receive additional funding to improve teaching, the school premises, and other needy areas. The flipside of this "priority zone" labeling is that the schools quickly became the undesirable places of the educational system, the at-risk areas where children of non-European immigrant families are segregated (see Jolly, 2003) and given little chance to succeed, except for a few who manage to get out of the ZEPs or outsmart the odds. Confrontations between students and teachers and among students occur regularly, and schools have become violent sites. Much like in schools in the United States, it is not rare to find concealed weapons or witness students' rebellious attitudes against teachers (students questioning violently the content of their courses), who are ready to give up and go (Haget and Saubaber, 2003).

In general, students are changing and are more vocal about what they expect to learn and how they want to learn. They interact with the Internet every day, learn about global issues from a variety of perspectives, are exposed to different histories and realities that are often ignored in their curriculum, and question. (The teaching of philosophy helps to foster those critical minds.) Following the example of their elders, half a million students from all walks of life (black, white, and *beurs* all together) took to the streets of major French cities in the fall of 1998 to demand changes in school and to counter a law aimed at raising college fees and imposing further tracking, thereby reducing access. The youth spirit was in the right place: "Yes, it's pretty good here, but we're doing this in solidarity with others who are worse off" (Noveck, 1998). The government paid attention and started reform efforts to respond to the students' demands. In addition, the Ministry of Education sent out a survey to 3 million students and educators, "Le questionnaire lycéen," to take stock of current schooling practices and their effects. Here is a sample of questions and answers:

> What would you like to learn in high school that you have not been taught yet? To be able to deal with daily problems and be able to use my hands.
> What would you suggest could make high school a place of individual success? Give us reasons to learn. Stop elitism and remain conscious that we are only humans. Too much work, too heavy schedule, and stop obsessing about the bac.

In some schools, 30% of the student population talked about teachers' lack of respect towards them: "They always say that we're the ones who are violent, but this violence is provoked." (de Léotard, 1998).

Reforms are underway. Luc Ferry's (the new minister of education) agenda focuses on youth, diversity, prevention of violence, intergenerational dialogue, and improvement of teacher education programs.

Students who earn any form of the *baccalauréat* can attend all universities. Generally speaking, they choose degree programs that match their *bac* concentration. For example, a Bac S holder will likely choose a degree in biology, or computer sciences. In the late 1990s, 46 percent of French people between 18 and 22 attended a university. In contrast to the United States, life in French universities is cheap: student fees run about $100–200/year, tuition is free (thanks to other peoples' taxes and government or state subsidies), insurance is inexpensive, and through the CROUS (state-run network of university canteens), students can eat three meals a day for about $3. (Kidd & Reynolds, 2000). The first couple of years in college are often lived as "freedom" years, post-high-school-stress, a time to catch up on social skills (for example, partying and exploring new things) rather than seriously studying. It is not uncommon to see students repeating their freshman year or changing to another specialty. The low costs allow for that flexibility. Funding for public higher education has not matched the increasing number of students attending: the buildings are old, the equipment outdated, and the quality of instruction often undesirable depending on university attended. This results in a high dropout rate after the first year and students who often leave a four-year degree with little to no qualifications (Cook & Davie, 1999). Another route that students can take after their *baccalauréat* is that of the Grandes Ecoles (such as prestigious business schools, or the ENA, the French National School of Administration), after an additional grueling and highly competitive two years of preparation. The Grandes Ecoles almost guarantee successful careers in business management or politics, the continuation of the French elite. They are under great scrutiny for their selective or filtering access practices that favor youth from upper-middle-class milieus and have been pressed to accept larger and more diversified crowds (Cook & Davie, 1999). A recent move from the Sciences Po in Paris (a private Parisian institute in political science that does not require the two years of prep) to offer seats to *baccalauréat* graduates from ZEPs started a heated debate among sociologists and other intellectuals (Chartier, 2001).

SOCIAL LIFE, ENTERTAINMENT, AND RECREATION

French people in general love to sit at cafés, either indoors or outdoors, daily, if they can. It is not so much about drinking coffee as it is a social moment, to watch the world and literally the crowd go by, discuss political issues or other matters of serious concern, play cards, or simply gossip about life. French youth follows the tradition as they crowd cafés, especially on weekends, during lunch breaks, or after school. McDonald's and other fast-food places have also become popular spots, but still have not supplanted the café culture.

Youth usually hang out in large groups of friends, or *bandes de copains*, who have known each other for years as neighbors or schoolmates. Schools do not have social events such as the prom nights or graduation ceremonies found in the United States, but students get to know each other quite well when they follow the same academic tracks for years. Boys and girls go to school together, play sports together, and learn to appreciate their differences in a variety of contexts. A recent survey of French students showed that French students strongly supported coeducation. A young man commented that "knowing the girls already at school and learning about them help to ease up the dating process, la drague" (Durand, 1999).

Premarital sex is more commonly accepted in France, a traditionally Catholic country. Rather than judging youth's sexual behaviors, parents, educators, and the government take proactive measures through early information (especially about sexually transmissible diseases [STDs] such as AIDS), distribution of contraceptives in schools (even the morning-after pill), and a supportive attitude. Sex is not taboo in France. You can read about it and see it publicly portrayed on post signs (as advertisements for the Minitel Service) or openly discussed in private or public places, on TV, on the radio, and in books and magazines. However, families with strong religious beliefs, be they Catholic, Muslim, or Jewish, may not regard this sexual liberation in such supportive ways and prevent their children from engaging in premarital sex.

Youth fashion varies, although is greatly influenced by the U.S. import of hip-hop culture. You can see a lot of large, baggy pants and reversed caps that bear the initials of U.S. sports teams, or the X of Malcolm X. Styles from the 1970s are also in, with flared-up jeans and corduroy pants, flowery shirts, hip-huggers, thick-soled shoes, and bare belly buttons. Other youth prefer the Rasta style of tie-dye shirts and dreadlocks, or all-black outfits (with safety pins and piercings all over). Youth from strong religious families, especially girls, will be seen wearing the chador on top of more Western-looking outfits. Designer clothing (Gucci, Chanel) is also popular with older youth that can afford it, and usually in larger cities.

Other popular items with youth are cellular phones (almost everyone has one), portable video games, and at 18, a car (a Renault Clio or Volkswagen Golf) loaded up with heavy, loud speakers and rap music blasting, so that everyone can enjoy the hip-hop sounds of Missy Elliott, Eminem, the Nubians, or McSolaar . . . sound familiar?

What do young people do for fun? Sports are embedded in the French lifestyle. According to the French embassy Web site, "two third of men and half the women in France take part in a sporting activity and nearly a quarter of the French now belong to sports federations, three times more than in 1970." Football (soccer), rugby, cycling, basketball, and tennis are the most popular sports in the *métropole* and hold regular national and transnational championships that draw huge crowds and millions of TV viewers. The Tour de France remains one of France's most followed sporting events, with people lining up by the roadsides to support the athletes. The national and European soccer cups rank highest in popularity, followed by the French Open at Rolland-Garros in tennis, the Tournoi des Cinq Nations (involving France, Scotland, Ireland, England, and Wales) in rugby, and the basketball championships (Many nondrafted NBA players move to France, Italy, or Spain to play).

As families, French people often take trips to the mountains or the sea, where they hike (there are 25,000 miles of hiking paths spread out through the country), ski (alpine, cross-country, snowboarding), sail, surf, and more. Multiple national sports federations offer services all year round to parents and children alike. (For more information, see the embassy Web site.)

France counts about 2 million licensed footballers and 1.3 million tennis players (who belong to sports associations and federations) as well as millions of walkers, joggers, and swimmers who practice independently (like the brother of your author) (Kidd & Reynolds, 2000). Young people have a multitude of opportunities to participate in sports, organized or not. Towns all over the country have publicly subsidized sports clubs that teach youngsters martial arts (France has been world champion in judo many times), sailing, tennis, soccer, and rugby, among others. These are usually after-school or Saturday activities, facilitated by licensed instructors/ coaches. During the winter and summer vacations, millions of students attend sports camps all over the country, where they improve their athletic abilities and learn to live together. A great number of camps are subsidized by the government or private companies where parents work.

So how do young people let off steam? Sports is one healthy way. Schools do not really offer sports, besides a couple hours of PE instruction. There is no such thing as the NCAA championships in college, as there are no organized team sports except for intramural types of activities. So youth look outside the school, either in clubs or through neighborhood initiatives. For example, in many *banlieues*, young people enjoy street football and basketball (Kidd & Reynolds, 2000), much like in U.S. inner cities, proudly wearing number 23 on their shoulders. Besides sports, and in between cafés and socializing on the street, young people often hang out in video arcades for hours, spending at times entire afternoons shooting virtual enemies or driving virtual race cars. Internet cafés are also growing in popularity, where youths that do not own a home computer can connect with the rest of the world. Finally, another source of expression worth noting is tagging, the most basic form of graffiti, which usually consists of a word, usually a gang signature. Tagging is on the rise. It started as a hip-hop expression in primarily urban contexts and has now invaded every empty surface around the country and in other parts of Europe, regardless of whether the surface is a historical monument or a simple wall.

French people enjoy up to five weeks of vacation a year, most of it spent as family, and since 2000, they work 25 hours/week for the same salary and benefits as a 40 hour work week, preferring more leisure time over money in their pockets. France has 11 public holidays per year, the highest rate in Europe, celebrating the ends of World War I and II, the birth of France as a *république* (July 14), and workers (May 1). Often, if a holiday falls, for example, on a Tuesday, people will not hesitate to take an extra day off to connect with the weekend (commonly referred to as *faire le pont,* or even the *viaduc,* when people literally bridge days to make a long vacation).

France is a country of many festivals, either national, local, or regional, that draw huge crowds of aficionados. The list is long, from the International Film Festival in Cannes (a two-week annual event in May that brings together the best in the movie industry from around the world) and Festival d'Avignon (a theater festival in July) to the numerous jazz festivals of Antibes or Nice Cimiez that have brought such stars as Miles Davis, Ella Fitzgerald, and Lionel Hampton every year, or the Festival des Saintes-Maries de la Mer (in the Camargue region) that brings hundreds of thousands of gypsies annually to celebrate their culture together. The government is a proud sponsor of many of these cultural events. For example, La Fête de la Musique (instigated in 1982) celebrates the summer solstice (on June 21) with uninterrupted music and dances in the streets of cities and villages all over the country. The festival has now spread beyond the borders of France into other European cities.

Young people all take part in these various festivities. They also like going to the movies, which remains one of the best dates. Surveys conducted between 1990 and 1995 showed that "by far the most popular outing for the 12–25 age group in 1994 was to the cinema (90%), while other favorites were fun fairs (60%), night clubs (57%), and amusement parks (41%)" (Hughes & Reader, 1998, pp. 570–571). In terms of music, young people listen to a wide range of genres, with hip-hop and world music probably stealing first place. Since the 1980s, with the arrival and influence of North and West African musicians, France has become the capital of world music with the talent of Youssou N'Dour, Angélique Kidjo, Salif Keita, Manu Dibango, and Touré Kounda, as well as Gipsy Kings, Kassav, and Cheb Mami and Khaled, among many others, one of the many "articulation[s] of

French post-colonial identities" (Warne, 1997, p. 136) to be seen as part of a larger movement. The sounds of American hip-hop and rap music have long filled the airwaves and found French voices with NTM, Doc Gynéco, IAM, and McSolaar, again among many others, and a large audience: 28 percent of 15–19 years old listen to rap music (Mucchielli, 1999), which makes France the second-largest market for hip-hop music. These rappers gave voice to their African origins and their experiences as non-European immigrants in France. French hip-hop, in contrast to its American counterpart, gathers people from a variety of cultures and histories (*beurs*, West Africans, whites) who share the *banlieues*, their poverty, and harsh conditions, as their sites of creativity and resistance. As a musical genre, French hip-hop is reaching audiences far beyond the *banlieues* into mainstream culture (Cannon, 1997), similar to the United States.

Musical events, rock and hip-hop concerts, and raves draw, every summer, hundreds of thousands of young people. French people have long danced in the streets since the days of the *bals populaires* (in the 1930s). Young people continue the tradition, be it on July 14, or during *la fête de la musique*, while listening to the beat of McSolaar and Youssou N'Dour.

RELIGIOUS PRACTICES AND CULTURAL CEREMONIES

Catholicism in France is declining. Consider the numbers: in the late 1950s, 90 percent of French people declared themselves Catholic, a figure that dropped down to less than 70 percent in the 1990s (Davie, 1999, p. 195): "13 percent of French people attend service once a week, compared with 49 percent in the US according to a Gallup poll" (Corbett, 1994, p. 185). Numbers vary depending on the region. Places like Brittany, parts of the Massif Central, and rural areas across the country are still strongholds of Catholic faith and practices. (Your author remembers summers with her grandmother in rural Haute-Loire, where she attended church services every Sunday.) If Catholic practices are not followed as much as they used to (for example, the decline in marriages and higher rates of divorce), "most French people remain Catholic by tradition" (Davie, 1999, p. 201), and many aspects of everyday life are culturally Catholic, for example, vacations (Christmas, Easter, All Saints' Day, and so on) or the picturesque vista of church *clochers* (spires) across the country. Youth participate in Catholic rituals, such as communion and confirmation, inasmuch as their parents or grandparents still practice the religion.

The French Muslim community, the largest in western Europe (Davie, 1999), is changing the country's religious landscape, literally, with more than a thousand mosques built across the land. Muslim youth, much like their Catholic or Jewish peers, take part in (or don't take part in) religious rituals depending on the degree of membership experienced in the family. For example, many young Muslim women wear a veil (or foulard) in public places, and their clothing is purposefully nonprovocative. Ramadan is observed, as are daily praying times and attending the mosque with the rest of the family. The French Jewish community is the largest in Europe (Corbett, 1994). Such practices as Sabbath are observed, and in urban areas it is not uncommon to see young Jewish men wearing their prayer shawls and skullcaps strolling down the streets with their relatives. Again, these observations cannot be generalized to the entire Jewish, Muslim, or Catholic populations, as individuals choose whether to participate in the rituals of their religion.

Davie provides an interesting concluding reflection on the changing of nature of religious membership where faith and spirituality win over institutionalized practices and rituals: "Religion, whatever affiliation (or lack of affiliation) of the respondent, is becoming increasingly a matter of self-definition rather than a submission to institutional discipline. This is even more true of younger generations" (1999, p. 199).

CONCLUSION

French youth exist and evolve in similar sociocultural and economic contexts as their peers in other parts of the world. They live in economic democracies that teach conflicting values (of equality and fraternity) and yet, at the economic and political levels, show practices that suppress certain groups while favoring others. They also try to understand and come to terms with our post-9/11 world order and the consequences of governments' multiple actions since then (the war in Afghanistan and now in Iraq, the repressive measures taken against people of Muslim and/ or Arabic descent, and the growing anti-Semitism), and see where they fit in this globalization of terror and uncertain future. They are vocal about their concerns (through music, tags, and demonstrations; in classrooms; with their parents) and expect more and better responses than the ones found in history books. Through the Internet and the international connections they make every day, they have a heightened and more critical exposure to contemporary events and demand an education that will not insult their intellect, but rather aims at expanding it.

Young people also strong supporters of their families; like to spend time around a table where good food, wine, laughter, and arguments are shared on a weekly basis; and dutifully maintain the traditions, religious or cultural, of their elders. They know how to have fun, how to be with one another, as friends or as budding lovers, appreciating what is beautiful in life, such as the arts, nature, respect, and love. They enjoy what comes across the Atlantic: the fashion, the ideas, a faster pace of life and energy, and the English language. But they remain very French in certain traditions that will not easily die, such as hanging out at the local café, riding Vespas, and keeping a critical eye on everything and everyone.

Frenchness is a concept, an identity under reconstruction. The 1998 French soccer team showed the undeniable and inescapable diversity of French people, for example, Zinedine Zidane (Algerian), Christian Karembeu (New Caledonian), Lilian Thuram (Guadeloupean), or Bixente Lizarazu (Basque). Young people have long known this reality, through their daily experiences at school; through the friendships they build across racial, cultural, and religious lines; and through the common musical, political, and cultural grounds they exist in. They are all part of the postcolonial legacies, whether they come from the side of those who colonized or those who were colonized. They are learning together about the challenges of a heterogeneous society. Will they take them on and transform them into possibilities? The story continues ... and your author is reminded of the insightful words of the late poet Jacques Prévert, who, as he describes a young dunce, concludes,

Despite the teacher's threats,	Malgré les menaces du maître
under the disapproving	sous les huées des enfants
screams of the gifted ones,	prodiges
with chalks of all colours,	avec des craies de toutes les
	couleurs
on the blackboard of misery,	sur le tableau noir du malheur
he draws the visage of happiness,	il dessine le visage du bonheur
	(Jacques Prévert, "Paroles," 1949)

NOTES

1. A rock-and-roll radio program on Europe 1 in the 1960s that became a popular teen magazine in the 1960s and 1970s (when I was growing up) that described the lives and tribulations of popular French singers and actors.

2. This chapter cannot and does not represent the breadth and depth of experience of the entire French youth, which is too diversified and complex to fit within this summary. It is barely a snapshot of adolescent life through the eyes and experience of the author, a French/Italian native who grew up a small town

in the French Alps, with the support of contemporary sources on the subject. Generalizations would be inappropriate.

3. Only France Métropole and the DOM are considered part of the EEC. (See Commission of the European Communities, 1993.)

4. In the Provence region, the regional TV station airs every Saturday a program in Provençal about local events, economic issues, and so on. Provençal is offered in schools. So is Catalan in the southwestern part of France, where some primary schools are actually taught in both French and Catalan. Decentralization has also revived the voices of regional activists in places like Brittany, Corsica, or Le Pays Basque that have long sought independence from the mainland.

5. For example, Luc Ferry (the current education minister) is in his early 50s, a university professor and a famed intellectual and philosopher ("a philosopher in essence and a ministre by ambition" [L'Express Magazine, 24 October 2002]) whose philosophical inspiration lies in the works of Heidegger and Nietzsche: his books have been translated into 25 languages and he has won numerous esteemed literary awards, such as the Prix Médicis in 1992, and wrote a piece on "Philosopher at 18" that may give hints as to his vision for the French education system.

6. See the adventures of *Astérix le Gaulois*, the title character of which, with his small village and the help of a magical potion, fought the Roman Empire. A favorite cartoon from Morris and Gosciny, read by almost everyone, it portrays the Gauls as "boisterous, undaunted beer drinkers who love a fight and good food ... In reality, they were an ingenious and industrious people who invented soap and were skilled wheelwrights and barrel makers" (Corbett, 1994, p. 13).

7. For example, the regions where your author was born and grew up (Savoy and the French Riviera) are both closely knit to Italy, geographically (as bordering regions) and historically: Savoy was ceded to France by Duke Victor Emmanuel II in 1870 after years of being Italian. We feel this to this day, in our behaviors, our local traditions (cooking, local language, and so on), the architecture, and how we see ourselves as French/Italian people. Alsace-Lorraine, on the northeastern border of France, is the example of a German-influenced region. Annexed by Germany in 1871 after the Franco-Prussian War, it was returned to France through the Treaty of Versailles (1919). (See the *American Heritage Dictionary of the English Language*, 1996, 3rd ed., p. 54.)

8. Check the *Africana Encyclopedia* (Appiah& Gates, 1999), which contributes to a better understanding of colonization and decolonization times from an African perspective. Among other wonderful things, this encyclopedia provides useful geographical, sociocultural, economic, and historical information as well as philosophical reflections. A must-have.

9. "*Beur* is a slang derivation of *arabe* and refers to the children of North African immigrants brought up in France ... Not to be confused with the word *beurre* which means butter and is pronounced the same way. The term beur was coined by teenagers in the Parisian suburbs and has a deeper significance than people generally think. The second-generation immigrants do not feel entirely French but neither do they feel Arabic. 'I am beur means I am neither here nor

there. Unclassifiable. Have no desire to be [classified]'" (Corbett, 1994, p. 201, citing Begag & Chaouite, 1990, pp. 9–10 and 83).

10. "France is a Republic that neither recognizes nor supports financially any particular religion, but which guarantees to all its citizens freedom of conscience and freedom to practice their respective faiths. More specifically, it is a concept that denotes the *absence* of religion from public space and public affairs, the consequences of which are considerable in everyday life" (Davie, 1999, p. 201). See articles on the "Affaire du foulard," a national controversy in the late 1990s over Muslim girls wearing the *foulard* (the veil) in schools.

11. "No single race but between thirty and forty different ethnic groups— Ligurians, Iberians, Greeks, Teutons, and Romans, to mention but a few—have a valid claim to being the ancestors of the French" (Corbett, 1994, p. 20).

12. Again, it is hard to generalize depending on one's cultural or religious influences on the matter.

13. In light of increasing lethal car crashes among young people (usually due to alcohol and speed), the government imposes tight control and restrictions on young drivers. For example, they cannot drive over 90 kph until they have a year of driving experience, points are taken off their permit for each ticket they receive, and so on.

14. The government's objective is an 80 percent success rate for all forms of the *baccalauréat*.

RESOURCE GUIDE

Adamson Taylor, S. (1996). *Culture shock: France; A guide to customs and etiquette*. Singapore: Times Editions Pte Ltd.

Allègre, C. (2002, September). Oui, il faut réformer l'école. *L'Express Magazine*, 80.

Appiah, K. A., & Gates, H.L.J. (Eds.). (1999). *Africana: The encyclopedia of the African and African American experience*. New York: Basic Civitas Books/ Perseus Books Group.

Begag, A., & Chaouite, A. (1990). *Ecarts d'identité*. Paris: Editions du Seuil.

Caldwell, C. (2000). The crescent and the tricolor. *Atlantic Monthly*, 286, 20–34.

Cannon, S. (1997). Paname city rapping: B-boys in the banlieue and beyond. In Hargreaves, A., & McKinney, M. (Eds.), *Post-colonial cultures in France*. London: Routledge.

Chartier, C. (2001, April). Grandes Ecoles: Pour ou contre les quotas? *L'Express Magazine*, 101–106.

Commission of the European Communities. (1993). *Portrait of the regions: France, United Kingdom, and Ireland*. Volume 2. Brussels: Office for Official Publications of the European Communities.

Cook, M., & Davie, G. (1999) *Modern France: Society in transition*. London: Routledge.

Corbett, J. (1994). *Through French windows: An introduction to France in the nineties*. Ann Arbor: University of Michigan Press.

Davie, G. (1999). *Religion and laïcité*. In Cook, M., & Davie, G., Modern France: Society in transition. London: Routledge.

de Léotard, M.-L. (1998, March). *Lycée: Les jeunes avides de changement*. L'Express Magazine, 51–55.

Durand, C. (1999, September). *Lycées: Faut-il supprimer la mixité?* Marie-Claire, 236–240.

Haget, H., & Saubaber, D. (2003, October). *Les chantiers de l'éducation nationale: Le courage d'être prof*. L'Express Magazine.

Hargreaves, A.G. (1991). *Voices from the North African immigrant community in France: Immigration and identity in beur fiction*. Oxford: Berg.

Hughes, A., & Reader, K. (1998). *Encyclopedia of contemporary French culture*. London: Routledge.

INCA. (2002). *International Review of Curriculum and Assessment Frameworks archive*. http://www.inca.org.uk/.

INSEE. (2002). *Annuaire statistique de la France*. Paris: Institut National de la Statistique et des Etudes Economiques.

Jolly, P. (2003, February 23). *L'éducation nationale inquiète de la montée des tensions identitaires*. Le Monde.

Kidd, W., & Reynolds, S. (Eds.). (2000). *Contemporary French cultural studies*. London: Arnold.

Mucchielli, L. (1999). *Le rap, tentative d'expression politique et de mobilisation collective de jeunes des quartiers relégués*. Mouvements, Sociétés, politique et culture, La Découverte, 60–66.

Noveck, J. (1998, October 20). *French students follow example: Taking a tip from strike-happy adults, youths walk out to demand better schools*. Register Guard, Eugene, Oregon.

Rémond, R. (1987, January). *La fille ainée de l'église*. L'Histoire, 118–122.

Remy, C., Chartier, C., & Orgé, S. (2003). *Famille, je t'aime moi non plus: Parents-enfants, l'autorité plebiscitée*. L'Express Magazine. http://www.lexpress.fr.80/Express/Info/Societe/Dossier/parents/dossier.asp.

Rodgers, C. (1999). *Gender*. In Cook, M., & Davie, G., Modern France: Society in transition. London: Routledge.

Simonnet, D. (2002, October). *Les chiffres inquiétants de l'illettrisme*. Alain Bentolila: «Il existe en France une inégalité linguistique». L'Express Magazine.

Tarr, C. (1997). *French cinema and post-colonial minorities*. In Hargreaves, A., & McKinney, M. (Eds.), Post-colonial cultures in France. London: Routledge.

Warne, C. (1997). *The impact of world music in France*. In Hargreaves, A., & McKinney, M. (Eds.), Post-colonial cultures in France. London: Routledge.

Nonfiction

Popular Music in Contemporary France, by David L. Looseley (2003). Oxford & New York: Berg. While music lovers from all over the world have tried to re-create the ambience of French cafés by playing music from stars such as Piaf, Trénet, and Chevalier, intellectuals, sociologists, and policymakers in France have been embroiled in passionate debate about just what constitutes "real" French music. In the late 1950s and 1960s a wave of Anglo-American rock 'n' roll and pop hit Europe and disrupted French popular music forever. The cherished sounds of the chanson were sidelined, fragmented, or merged with pop styles and instrumentation. From this point on, French music and music culture have splintered into cultural divides—pop culture versus high culture; mass culture versus "authentic" popular culture; national culture versus Americanization. This book investigates the exciting and innovative segmentation of the French music scene and the debates it has spawned. From an analysis of the chanson as national myth to pop, rap, techno, and the state, this book is the first full-length study to make sense of the complexity behind the history of French popular music and its relation to "authentic" cultural identity.

Migration, Minorities, and Multiculturalism in European Youth Literature, by Heidi Magrit Muller (Ed.) (2001). Bern: Peter Lang Publishing.

Fiction

The Sorcerer's Apprentice, by François Augiéras (2001). London: Pushkin Press. Grasset. In the depths of the Sarladais, a land of ghosts, cool caves, and woods, a teenage boy is sent to live with a 35-year-old priest. The man becomes more than just his teacher.

£9.99: *A Novel*, by Frédéric Beigbeder (2004). London: Picador. These are the confessions of a disillusioned child of the millennium. Scathing, violent, tragic and hilarious, this exposé of advertising and universal consumerism by one of the most caustic authors of his generation makes £9.99 a truly unforgettable read.

Welcome to Paradise, by Mahi Binebine (2004). London: Granta. Tense, dramatic and bleakly compassionate, *Welcome to Paradise* is a striking portrait of human desperation, of countries allowing themselves to be bled dry of their people, and of media fantasies of Western life that can never live up to expectations.

Breathe, by Anne-Sophie Brasme (2001). London: Weidenfeld. The book tells the story of 19-year-old Charlene Boher, who recounts her past from her prison cell, beginning with her childhood memories and documenting a painful awkward adolescence.

The Round and Other Cold Hard Facts, by Jean-Marie Gustave Le Clézio (2002). Lincoln, NE: University of Nebraska Press. Set largely in locations near the French Riviera, these 11 short stories depict the harsh realities of life for the less privileged inhabitants of this very privileged region. Le Clézio lends his voice to the dispossessed and explores his familiar themes of alienation, immigration, poverty, violence, indifference, the loss of beauty, and the betrayal of innocence.

Desiderada, by Maryse Condé (1998). London: Distribooks Intl. A young woman from Martinique (La Desirade) is sent to France to an unknown mother and land, in the suburban environment of Savigny and Orge. She describes her struggles in this new cultural environment.

Tales from the Heart: True Stories from My Childhood, by Maryse Condé (2001). New York: Soho Press. A self-explanatory title.

All That Blue, by Gaston-Paul Effa (2001). New York: BlackAmber Books. As African village custom dictates, eldest child Douo, at the tender age of five, is handed over by his seemingly nonchalant father and grief-stricken mother to the missionary nuns who raise and educate him. At the age of 14 they send him to Paris, and the pain of thwarted familial love and dispossession decreed by tradition doom him to look for his mother in every woman he seduces and his father in every man he meets. Only his discovery of art and the French language, whose words and poems he so loves, allow him to keep alive his early childhood and fundamental happiness. From his unhappiness emerge many memories and sublime writing.

One Summer at Grandmother's House, by Poupa Montaufier (1985). Minneapolis: Carolrhoda Books. A reminiscence about a French girl and her family spending a typical summer with her grandmother in Alsace.

My Father's Glory and My Mother's Castle, by Marcel Pagnol (1986). Northpoint Press. Childhood memories of growing up in Provence, with a father as headmaster and a dutiful mother.

More Information

Historical Facts

Realms of Memory: The Construction of the French Past, by Pierre Nora (1998). New York: Columbia University Press. A wealth of cultural and historical topics and discussions that help explain contemporary France.

Economic Facts

Institut National de la Statistique et des Etudes Economiques (INSEE). Available at http://www.insee.fr/. The most accurate French database (since 1878) on economic facts and figures (population, employment, education).

Sports and Leisure

Facts about France. Available at http://www.discoverfrance.net/France/sports/.

French embassy Web site. Available at http://www.info-france.org/atoz/sports. asp/. General information on France. In the sports section, it offers a list of valuable links. The French embassy offers youth and sports grants to Americans age 18 to 25 with good French language skills who wish to participate in short-term cultural and linguistic programs in France. The programs usually include visits to the regions where the sessions are held. All expenses (accommodation and meals, activities, and so on) except for the airfare are paid for by the French embassy).

Ministry of Youth and Sports. Available at http://www.jeunesse-sports.gouv.fr/.

What You Need to Know about . . . France. Available at http://french.about.com/library/. A site filled with interesting information on the French language, pronunciation, grammar, and other interesting linguistic aspects.

French Diversity

Beur FM. Available at http://www.beurfm.net/. Rich information on *beur* life focusing on cultural events, for example, music, literature, and cinema. Also includes discussion forums on current events, such as the war against Iraq.

Islamic Beliefs among Youth of North African Origin in France, by A.G. Hargreaves and T.G. Stenhouse (1991). Modern and Contemporary France, 45, April, 27–35.

Education

Institut National de la Jeunesse et de l'Education Populaire (INJEP). Available at http://www.injep.fr/. Information on education, jobs, career strategies (how to interview, what to put in CV, and so on), cultural events, and numerous links.

Ministère de la Jeunesse, de l'éducation nationale et de la recherche [Ministry of Youth, National Education, and Research]. Available at http://www.education.gouv.fr/jeunesse/. A wealth of information about the ministry, its mission, its goals, its current activities, and links to sites of interest.

Phosphore.com: Le site des 15–25 ans. An online magazine that offers detailed articles on current issues, events, youth concerns (such as the preparation for June examinations, *bac*, or entrance exams for elite schools) in both French and English. For example, the March 2003 issue features an article on Ben Harper and his views on rock and roll and the United States, and a critical perspective on today's French demographics, about the "foreign origin" of French people (*Français certifiés double origine*).

Entertainment

FNAC. Available at http://www.fnac.fr/. One of France's largest store of music, books, photography, and other media services.

Lezarts Urbain. Available at http://www.lezarts-urbains.be/. A youth magazine of the *banlieues* that provides the latest hip-hop news as well as dossiers on topics related to hip-hop.

NRJ. Available at http://www.nrj.fr/. Discusses music, radio, appearances, and concerts, along with interviews with the stars.

Radio France. Available at http://www.radio-france.fr/.

Virgin Megastore. Available at http://www.virgin.fr/. All the services from the famous music store as well as the opportunity to listen to latest hits.

Media/Newspapers

Le Monde. Available at http://www.lemonde.fr/. French news, New York Times–style.

Le Monde Diplomatique. Available at http://www.ina.fr/CPMondeDiplo/monde-diplo.fr.html. Great archives for a variety of well-researched articles on France, a good number translated into English.

L'Express. Available at http://www.lexpress.fr/. An interesting weekly magazine on world events with a particular focus on France. Covers a variety of topics, from society, to culture, to politics, to arts, with critical written pieces from varied perspectives. Highly recommended are their dossiers that cover a particular issue in-depth each week.

Libération. Available at http://www.liberation.fr/. A more leftist paper with excellent free information.

Movies

La gifle, by Gilles Rappenau (1980). A look at the life and tribulations of a high school girl.

La gloire de mon père [My father's glory] and Le Chateau de ma Mère [My mother's castle], by Yves Robert (1992). Movies inspired by Marcel Pagnol's novels.

La Haine, by Mathieu Kassovitz (1995). The fracture of French society depicted not so much through ethnic difference as through social inequities, describing the bonding of a Jewish, black, and beur youth within a hybrid youth culture based on music, unemployment, police hatred, and exclusion.

Le Thé au Harem d'Archimède, by Mehdi Charef (1985), and Baton Rouge, by Rachic Bouchared (1985). Both movies address the troubled hybrid identity of second-generation members of minority ethnic groups stressing the new youth culture of the banlieue and its strong African American influences (Tarr, 1997).

Mohamed Bertrand-Duval, by Alex Metayer (1991). A bankrupt company director discovers life and love in a community of Arabs and gypsies camped near Marseilles (Tarr, 1997).

Ponette, by Jacques Doillon (1998). Coming to understand death, religious beliefs, and life lessons when you are barely six.

Souviens-toi de moi, by Ghorad-Volta (1996). A woman's perspective on strained relationships within the immigrant family (Tarr, 1997).

Pen Pal Information

http://www.opendiary.com/diarylist.asp?list=6&start=1&countrycode=FR&countryname=France

Chapter 4

GERMANY

Nicole Pfaff

INTRODUCTION

Germany at the beginning of the twenty-first century looks back on a long history, which is inseparable from the ups and downs of central and western Europe. During the eighteenth and nineteenth century Germany was known as a country with deep roots in science and culture. Some of the best-known philosophical theories of that time and some of the nineteenth century's most important innovations in the areas of science and engineering are of German origin. The first German Confederation was established in 1815 with 39 states and covered sections of the current territory of Austria, Switzerland, Poland, Luxembourg, Belgium, and the Netherlands. But the nineteenth century in Europe was a time of war, social conflicts, and unstable alliances, and only the Franco-German War, also called the Franco-Prussian War (July 19, 1870–May 10, 1871) marked the end of French hegemony in continental Europe and resulted in the creation of a unified Germany. The Germans' crushing victory over France in the war consolidated their faith in Prussian militarism, which would remain a dominant force in German society until 1945. Most important, Germany's annexation of Alsace-Lorraine aroused a deep longing for revenge in the French people. The years from 1871 to 1914 were marked by an extremely unstable peace between France and Germany. Their mutual animosity proved to be the driving force behind the prolonged slaughter on the western front in World War I.

In 1919, the year after the war's end, Germany adopted a democratic constitution. But assailed by serious domestic political instability, compounded by the Great Depression of the 1920s and 1930s—which hit Germany particularly severely—Germany with World War II and the Holocaust paved the way for one of the darkest chapters in world history: six years of global warfare and an estimated cost of 60 million lives. After Germany was defeated by the victorious powers of England, the United States, France, and the Soviet Union, in 1949 it was split, with the eastern sector under the control of the Soviet Union and the three western sectors under the control of the United States, France, and Britain. During the cold war, East Germany enjoyed the highest standard of living among the Warsaw Pact countries, though that prosperity was relative: West Germany forged ahead with the "economic miracle" spurred on by the Marshall Plan—massive economic support from the three Western allied powers, led by the United States. The Berlin Wall was built in 1963 between the two parts of the former capital and another between the two parts of Germany—a tragic symbol of the cold war for nearly 30 years. While the western Federal Republic of Germany took over the political system of most of its western-European neighbors, and soon became part of the western alliance and one of the leading economic powers in the world, the eastern German Democratic Republic was not as democratic as its title asserted. Political power in the GDR was vested solely in the hands of the Socialist Unity Party, which constituted a totalitarian regime. But in 1985 the dramatic process of German reunification began with the accession of Gorbachev in Moscow and steadily gathered momentum until its climax at the end of 1989 with the fall of the Berlin Wall and the collapse of the Soviet bloc in eastern Europe. Less than two years later, the two Germanys were reunited—with the agreement of the former wartime Allies.

The present constitution of the reunified Germany dates from May 1949, the Federal Republic of Germany being formally established four months later. Germany is a parliamentary democracy with a bicameral legislature (the Bundesrat and Bundestag). Executive authority lies with the federal government, led by the federal chancellor. The federal president is the constitutional head of state. Each of the federal states has its own legislature with power to pass laws on all matters not expressly reserved for the federal government. The former German Democratic Republic has been absorbed into this system, adding five states to the total. Since 1991, Germany—with a surface area of about 350,000 square kilometers—is the fourth-largest country within the European Union, behind France, Spain, and Sweden. Now 16 states belong to the Federal Republic of Germany. In the north it borders Sweden and Denmark; in the east Poland; in the south the Czech Republic, Austria, and Switzerland; and in the west France, Luxembourg, Belgium, and the Netherlands.

Berlin is the capital and also largest city of Germany (3.4 million inhabitants); other famous cities are Hamburg (1.7 million), Munich (1.2 million), Cologne, and Frankfurt. All in all, there are 80 German cities with over 100,000 inhabitants, where over 30 percent of the population lives.

The German economy is the world's third-largest and accounts for about one-third of Europe's GDP (gross domestic product). Two-thirds of the yearly national GDP is composed of services and one-third of industries; agriculture only makes up one percent.[1] Germany belongs to the world's largest and most technologically advanced producers of iron, coal, cement, chemicals, machinery, vehicles, machine tools, and electronics, and it is the United States' second-largest European trading partner and fifth-largest global partner.[2] More than half of Germany's volume of trade passes within the European Union.

But Germany's affluent and technologically powerful economy turned in a relatively weak performance throughout much of the 1990s. The modernization and integration of the eastern German economy continues to be a costly long-term problem, and unemployment has become a chronic problem—especially in the east. Germany still practices a "social market" economy that largely follows free-market principles but with a considerable degree of government regulation and generous social welfare protections, which are in serious trouble due to a stagnating economy and current demographic trends. Germany has about 83 million inhabitants and is therefore the most populous nation in Europe. In line with most European countries, Germany has a greater number of deaths than births, as well as the problem of significant aging of the population during the last few decades. Without population gains attributed to migration, the number of people in Germany, as well as in Greece, Italy, and Sweden, would be declining.[3] At the end of 1999, 7.3 million immigrants lived in Germany, accounting for about nine percent of the total population.[4] This figure falls in the upper range for a European country.

One in four foreigners in Germany is from a member state of the European Union. The largest groups among the foreign resident population are the Turks (28 percent), nationals of the Federal Republic of Yugoslavia (Serbia and Montenegro; 10 percent), Italians (8.4 percent); Greeks (5 percent), Poles (4 percent), Croatians (2.9 percent), Austrians (2.5 percent), and Bosnians (2.3 percent).

Although Germany has to rely on immigration, during the 1990s xenophobia and nationalism rose up here as well as in many other European countries. In eastern Europe there was a revival of nationalism, and in western Europe a continuous electoral success of right-wing and populist parties.[5] In Germany, xenophobia and right-wing extremism are seen as problem of young people, because the flare-up of neo-Nazi violence in Germany during the 1990s mainly traces back to right-wing extremist youth cultural styles and groups. On the other hand, xenophobia is highly concentrated in east Germany, although the total representation of immigrants is lower than in the west. Also, unemployment in the east is higher and social prestige is lower than in the west. However, xenophobia and nationalism in Germany are, thanks to German history, kept under careful surveillance by social research and by a long list of governmental and nongovernmental antiracism organizations.

While right-wing populists and conservative parties in western Europe have succeeded during the last two decades in France, Austria, Belgium, Italy, and other countries, Germany since 1998 has had a left-wing government, consisting of Social Democrats and the socially and ecologically oriented Green Party. The main focus of the Social Democrats lies in the field of domestic politics on rising social problems, such as high unemployment and rising costs for the social security and pension system as well as questions of ecological protection. The public support for environmental issues in Germany and abroad is strong among the Germans.

In the field of foreign politics, the unification of Europe is the main topic. Germany is founding member of the European Union and, particularly because of its history and geographical position, acts as a bridge between eastern and western Europe, with its leading role in the process of EU enlargement to eastern European countries. Additionally, Germany belongs to the group of eight most industrialized countries (G8). It was admitted as a full member of the UN in 1973 and has been active in the past years in promoting many international projects, such as the International Criminal Court and questions of global environment policy. With regard to international military mandates, Germany participated in Operation Enduring Freedom, under the auspices of the UN mission in Afghanistan, and the International Security Assistance Force (ISAF), raising a joint contingent in conjunction with the Netherlands and Denmark; German soldiers also contributed to SFOR (Stabilization Force) in Bosnia-Herzegovina, KFOR in Kosovo, and Fox in Macedonia. Humanitarian aid is another main focus of German foreign policy. Germany funds aid projects around the world; the overall focus of German financial and technical development assistance is on direct aid to the poor.

Compared with other countries, Germany is still a relatively peaceful place. Not social conflicts but their own beliefs lead German people to the streets; only wage negotiations and impending wars have led to significant demonstrations since 2002. But times get harder, and the critical situation of the social security system and rising unemployment are harbingers of different times to come. For the first time in postwar German history, a significant number of young people are suffering from these problems.

TYPICAL DAY

Media and institutions mainly influence the daily routines of teens in Germany. From that point of view, the daily life of young Germans is the same as those from other industrialized countries. Children and adolescents spend much time in institutions and associations, taught or supervised by adults, and in the meantime entertained by mass media and games—all made by adults. The former is typical for the daily timetable of most German teens, who far more often spent time in youth centers, sports clubs, and other associations than their European neighbors.

There are lots of different influences on individual daily routines, such as residence, family situation, religious beliefs, and schooling, but also individual habits, a demand for sleep, time to get ready in the morning, personal interests, and favorite dishes.

Most German teens go to school or serve an apprenticeship (88 percent of 15- to 19-year-old teenagers do one or the other),[6] so for them, Monday to Friday is spent either in school or at work. This, in most cases, means getting up between 6 and 8 in the morning, preparing, and leaving the house for school, which usually starts between 7:30 and 8 all over Germany. In provincial regions, but also in big cities, getting to school by way by public transportation or a school bus might take up to an hour.

On the one hand, school time is an opportunity to acquire skills for private life, a job, or travel. On the other hand—and more important for most students—school is a place for meeting friends. The breaks between classes, especially, give an opportunity for chatting with people of the same age. Many German schools by some means or another either provide lunch for their students or give them the possibility to buy sandwiches, snacks, sweets, and drinks.

At present, most schools in Germany practice half-time schooling; only upper grades have afternoon classes. Additionally, most schools offer afternoon activities such as optional sports, theater, music, tutorials, or language classes. But for most German students, school is over in the early afternoon, and only homework has to be done later in the afternoon. Consequently, afternoon and evening time is spare time. However, teenagers who are serving apprenticeships or visiting vocational schools have full-time jobs with their companies and therefore have less time for leisure activities.

German teenagers' spare-time activities include meeting friends, watching TV, doing sports, surfing on the Internet, and reading.[7] The younger the teens, the more time they spent either in afternoon homes for schoolchildren (up to age 14), at home, or with relatives. Older teens spent more time unattended with friends or in institutionalized youth groups. Eight of 10 German teenagers have more than two fixed dates per week, and half of German children up to age 12 already help their parents at home.[8] Half of 14-year-old German teenagers work at least sporadically in part-time jobs;[9] this provides money for extra shopping and expensive leisure activities.[10] Even if German teenagers seem to be very busy, there is still enough time for friends. Most 15- to 19-year-old Germans belong to a set of young people they get together with nearly daily. They meet at home, in youth centers, or at public places—usually in shopping areas, around stations or in pubs. Adolescents from the age of 16 in Germany have limited access to pubs, bars, and discotheques. Low-percentage alcohol (beer, wine, mix drinks) and tobacco are also allowed.

There is also a wide range of organizations working on youth issues in Germany; therefore public youth centers and analogous institutions are very popular with the German youth. All in all, the daily life of most German teenagers follows clear routines—but not for all. Social research on socially underprivileged children and teenagers again and again shows that the most obstructive factor to social integration is the absence of daily routines. Massive welfare efforts are made for homeless and unemployed adolescents or truants, which official estimates place at between 20,000 and 700,000 young people in Germany. Not much public attention has been spent on these children and adolescents, but in the last few years their numbers have been rising dramatically.[11]

FAMILY LIFE

German family life has changed during the last century. Three-generation households, where children live with their parents and grandparents in the same house, are a rarity. Thirty percent of the children are short distances to the nearest relatives, as they live in the same neighborhood. Most teens grow up with both parents, but a significant percentage live with only one parent, usually the mother. But the more fundamental change for families is the number of children growing up in one family, which declined drastically during the last 50 years. One out of every five German homes has only one child. More and more children stay, at least temporarily, in their parents' home until their late 20s, or until the end of their vocational qualifications. Another change that has been observed during the last century concerns the age of marriage and starting a new family. Only one of three 25- to 29-year-old Germans are married.[12] Slowly but surely, people become parents at an older age. The higher the social status of a woman (indicated by school and vocational qualification), the more seldom and the later she will have children. So most German children grow up today with older parents and fewer brothers and sisters than 50 years ago.

Not only family structure but also family life has experienced profound changes in the last century. This affects family roles, which are not as rigidly gender-specific anymore, but cast more pragmatically in each family. In Germany, half of married women work in at least a part-time job (and in the eastern part of Germany even more).[13] Consequently, men have to share family duties such as bringing up children, doing housework, and so on. But within German families, the mother is still the first person of reference for her children.[14] The relationship between children and parents has changed. That is to say, parents and children no longer have hierarchical relationships, but are living in a more equal relationship. The age of consent in Germany is 18, where citizens are permitted to participate in elections, drive cars, marry, and so on.

There are massive differences between upper- and lower-class families in Germany, which affect all matters of family life (relationships, housing, and so on) as well as schooling and chances for adolescents' individual futures. On the one hand, lower-class kids' learning conditions are nothing compared to those of middle- and upper-class children.[15] This concerns support at home, at school, and at vocational training, and access to information and education. On the other hand, there is more violence and more fear of the future in lower-class children's life.[16]

FOOD

Thinking of German cuisine as of a mix of beer, sauerkraut, and bratwurst would be an unforgivable simplification. Thanks to immigration and European unification, Germany is a country with many influences on its food market. To give one example, the most popular street food in Germany is *döner kebab*, a Turkish sandwich of lamb or chicken and salad, with falafel and Italian pizza running a close second and third. In most German cities snacks like this are available in so-called *imbiss* (fast-food restaurants) all around the clock. Also there are Italian, American, Mexican, and Asian restaurants, and famous foreign cuisine has also reached German food preparation at home. Most teens like pasta, pizza, and french fries and hamburgers more than traditional German dishes.

Traditional German food is characterized by its forcefulness and caloric content. Most traditional dishes contain meat, above all pork, but also poultry, beef, lamb, or fish and vegetables according to season and region. In most homes there is one warm common meal a day, where women typically prepare the dishes. Germany has a special tradition in the bakery; there are bakery shops in every supermarket, and also many single shops in every town. Bakeries especially feature bread, but cakes are also made in many different styles with different cereals, vegetables, and fruits. Bread is served for breakfast and dinner and is prepared in the morning, often then given as a snack for school and work.

Food in Germany is sold in supermarkets; however, both in the country and in big cities there are markets where local farmers sell their fresh products. In times of epidemics among animals in European piggeries, cattle farms, and fowl farms and the genetic manipulation of plants, Germany and other European countries support biological farming, which augurs more healthy but more expensive food.

Breakfast in the early morning in Germany is not a substantial meal. The traditional morning food is bread, cheese, or marmalade with tea, coffee, juice, or milk. Traditionally, in German families lunch was the most important meal of the day; it was eaten together at home, prepared by housewives. But nowadays this culture has changed, and lunch is eaten at school or work. So for most families, at least during the week, dinner has become the only shared meal.

SCHOOLING

English students on average spend 15,000 hours in school in their lives,[17] and that's nearly the same in Germany. German students mostly have more than 10 courses, and one class takes 45 minutes. In Germany, after every class there is a small break (5 minutes) and after two classes there is a big break (15 or 20 minutes). Depending on age group, students have between five and eight classes a day, five days a week. German classes are normally between 15 and 30 students, depending on the type of school. The class sizes are fixed and usually don't vary between grades and classes. Every class has its own room, and in the case of special subjects like chemistry, music, sports, or art, the teachers switch rooms. Students are allowed to wear what they want in German schools; school uniforms are very unusual. In terms of vacation, students generally have six weeks of summer vacation, one week of autumn vacation, two weeks of Christmas/winter vacation, two weeks of Easter/spring vacation, and one or two weeks of June vacation, depending on the federal state. To a foreign observer, the German school system is like a jungle. To describe this system is nearly impossible, because the 16 German federal states have 16 different school systems.

In Germany school is compulsory from the age of 6 to 18. On average, children start school at the age of six. Junior school then lasts until the fourth or fifth grade. After this, parents and children decide on what type of high school they want to continue the education: secondary modern school, secondary school, grammar school, or comprehensive school, where subjects at all levels can be studied. The distribution of the frequency of different school types varies in different states. In high school, the 5th or 6th to 10th grades form is called the "secondary level one" or middle level. The term between grades 11 and 13 is called "secondary level two" or advanced level. This advanced level culminates with the completion of the "A" level (*abitur*). Universities can only be attended with A-level qualifications. If adolescents go into an apprenticeship at a company, they have to attend vocational school while working in the company ("dual system"). For handicapped people or adolescents with special needs, there are different kinds of special schools in Germany where all kinds of qualifications can be reached.

German public schools and universities depend on public spending; school attendance is usually free of charge. However, fees for college are under discussion, which has caused many students all over Germany to enter protests. The exception to the rule in this whole system is private schools and universities. Some of them are raising school fees, which have to be paid by parents. There are currently about 2,900 private schools in Germany, many of them boarding schools. There are also international schools where the classes are taught in English and also schools with bilingual education. Knowledge of foreign languages is taken very seriously in German education. German students have classes of at least one foreign language over three years.

In 1999, the percentage of those leaving school with a secondary general school certificate was 30 percent, 40 percent left school with an intermediate school certificate, and another 30 percent left with a university entrance qualification. One out of every 10 adolescents left school without even the lowest qualification, which is the secondary general school certificate. Since 1995, German girls are reaching higher school qualifications more frequently than boys.

Education in Germany still is a matter of social prestige and the economic status of one's family—this was revealed recently by the results of an OECD-sponsored survey of reading, math, and science skills among 15-year-olds, the Program for International Student Assessment (PISA). Proud of their heritage of *dichter und denker*(poets and thinkers), Germans were shocked to learn that their students finished 25th out of 32 countries for literacy. A national follow-up, the PISA-e, confirmed the bad news. Additionally, it has been found that children with lower-class backgrounds or immigrants showed serious shortcomings.

SOCIAL LIFE, RECREATION, AND ENTERTAINMENT

Socializing of teenagers in Germany, as well as everywhere else, takes place in different manners. Teens meet other teens at school or at work, within associations and institutions, at public places, at youth centers, or in private. There is only a little separation between girls and boys; most things in their daily lives they do together. Separated girls' or boys' schools are rare in Germany. Only sports clubs and some religious, cultural, and community associations care about the gender of their members. More important for young Germans' social lives is their social status and the neighborhood or environment they grew up in. This determines school, memberships in clubs and associations, and at least one's own acquaintances.

On the other hand, youth cultural preferences of teenagers, such as music, style, and cultural or spare-time activities, and also their individual values and theories, are very significant for social relations. In Germany, as well as in most industrialized countries around the world, there are a confusingly large number of different styles and scenes, fashion, music, values, and behaviors.

Music styles include hip-hop and hip-hop clothing, which have especially extended among youngsters, and also techno and rock styles, all specified in many subcultural and crossover styles. The clothing of young people is usually a bit more colorful, eccentric, and provocative than other people's clothes—especially when they are together with their peers. Teenagers clothe themselves according to pop and movie stars as much as to models and other celebrities. Their most important values for clothing are that they be cool and sexy.[18] Body decorations, such as tattoos and piercing, are also very popular among older adolescents.

More uncommon and exotic styles, such as punk, heavy metal, skinhead, and gothic, also inspire subgroups of young people's fashion and living style. Some only use the fashion trends, and some get deeply involved in scenes and networks. Military fashion is widespread, much more so among boys than girls. A special German example of youth cultural styles is called *müslis* (from cereals for breakfast). Dressed in colorful or natural T-shirts and trousers or coats, with comfortable shoes and long hair, they are also often critical of governmental policy and interested in ecological and peace actions. In many ways they are similar to styles in other countries, such as American hippies.

Teens in Germany usually can make their own decisions, and from a certain age parents are more seen as partners or consultants than as decision makers. This, in most cases, is also true concerning love affairs between adolescents. Sexual liberty is an important attitude practiced by many youth in Germany. Sex before marriage is usual and accepted, and different kinds of contraceptive methods are encouraged and easily available for teens. Schools, associations, doctors, and parents are concerned with telling teenagers the facts of life. But usually most of the young people in Germany get to know the facts of life on their own. Generally accepted, especially among the young, is homosexuality. German teens want to experience social life, relationships, and love affairs in their early years, but constancy in romantic relationships and the unity of family are the most important values, as youth surveys show again and again.[19]

Sports is one of the big businesses in most European countries, especially in Germany. There is sports TV, sports radio, sports magazines, and sports reporting on the Internet, and sports events take place every weekend, with thousands in the audience. The favorite sport in Germany is soccer, where professional players from all over the world earn massive amounts of money and are adored by the public. This is true with other kinds of sports too, such as Formula One, tennis, and skiing.

One out of every three adolescents does sports after school and on the weekend. Also, sports classes are the favorite subject in school. Therefore public sports clubs are the most attractive spare-time institutions for kids and teens, as well as for older generations. Generally, sports clubs in Germany have the most members and most volunteers.[20] There are leagues and competitions in Germany for nearly all sports. There are huge numbers of youngsters practicing their sports every day, having competitions and games every weekend, in hopes of becoming a sports star one day. Girls and boys can play soccer, handball, volleyball, basketball, tennis, and table tennis, or like to trek through the German forest, the famous German *wandern*. Water and winter sports are also very popular, depending on the region. There are also various options for the physically disabled, senior citizens, and mothers with small children to exercise their bodies in Germany. Physical health and exercise are important values for most Germans.

After school, teenagers in Germany love to dance in clubs, at parties, or at parades, and they jog and go to fitness centers. Volleyball and hand-ball, gym, and dance sports are more practiced by girls; boys more often play soccer, bicycle, or do martial arts or body building. Fun sports, such as climbing, horseback riding, golf, snowboarding, and sailing are very popular among upper-class youngsters. Doing such sports as skating or basketball also depends on youth cultural affiliation.

Nevertheless, the rise in the number of teenagers having only little physical exercise in their daily life is worrying the medical profession. More and more indoor activities, such as watching TV, surfing the Internet, and playing videogames, capture teens' spare time. Also, in Germany, the number of teens who spend a lot of time in front of the computer playing games, chatting, or surfing the Internet is increas-ing. On average, 6 of 10 German teenagers at home have access to the Internet, but 8 of 10 in the upper class and only 4 of 10 in the lower class.[21]

"Music makes the world go round"—for German teens as much as for those anywhere There is music everywhere in the lives of the young. Music is played not only in clubs and pubs, but several TV and radio stations bring music to teens' homes, their cars, the streets, and even their mobile phones. Many types of music are popular among German adolescents: all-ahead pop and dancesounds, techno, house, hip-hop, and R&B. But there are also many rock and heavy metal fans as well as gothic, punk, and reggae fans. Only a few teens like German folk music, jazz, or classical music.

One out of 10 kids make their own music by singing or playing an instrument. There are many unknown teen bands playing in their par-ents' cellar or garage, in back rooms of youth centers, or in the afternoon at school. Record companies, TV or radio stations, and local companies organize music competitions, where some have a chance of getting a contract.

During the last decade Germany has developed a range of youth festi-vals and youth parades, such as the Love Parade, where millions of young techno fans dance through the streets of Berlin every year on a Saturday in June. In everyday life youngsters meet at public places, youth centers, pubs, and on weekend in clubs or discotheques to listen to their music and have fun together.

Most drugs are forbidden by law except alcohol and tobacco. However, hashish and marijuana are allowed in small amounts in some federal states. One out of three Germans in between the ages of 12 and 25 has had experience with illegal drugs,[22] almost always hashish or marijuana.

But four percent of this age group has taken chemical drugs, such as Ecstasy. In big cities there is also a problem with youngsters addicted to heroin or speed. Social workers care for those in different organizations, and antidrug campaigns are made by public associations in schools and youth centers to guard others against drug abuse.

RELIGIOUS PRACTICES AND CULTURAL CEREMONIES

In general, people in Germany have left the Christian churches (both Catholic and Protestant) by the millions. Since the Second World War, Germans have stopped going to church. This especially happened in big cities and in East Germany, where in the GDR the government didn't accept any religious beliefs and rituals. Even though 66 percent of children and adolescents are Christian, 6 percent Muslim, and 3 percent other religions, 25 percent of the young are without religion, only 20 percent go to church, and only 27 percent claim to pray regularly.[23] This number increases on Christian holidays such as Christmas and Easter, which have become more and more consumption-based rather than religious festivities.

Contrarily, there are several religious youth organizations and scenes, and a rising number of teenagers participate in them. They belong to the worldwide phenomenon of new Christianity, and should be understood as an example of the independence of cultural expressions of the young. Religious youth organizations and scenes are places for socializing, talks and discussions, youth festivals, and parades with pop music and Christian slogans. Young people in Germany have their own calendar of cultural events and festivities. Fans of different scenes and styles celebrate at different times and at different places. Techno fans go to the Love Parade in Berlin, dark-music fans go to the Pfingsttreffen in Leipzig, and heavy metal fans go to the Full-Force-Festival in the southeast of Germany. Additionally, there are many other festivities for members of different scenes. Last but not least, the political action of the young, which has increased continuously in the past two decades, is a third type of youth culture; for example, the relatively small right-wing extremist scene, with skinhead groups and fascist organizations, frighten the public with demonstrations in military style in the streets of German cities. But there are many young people from all styles and scenes who work together against racism and xenophobia. They organize concerts and festivals, cultural exchanges, and intercultural meetings. Others are engaged in environmentalism or in the peace movement, as on the day of the beginning of the Iraq war in 2003, when most German students did not come to school and demonstrated in the streets against the war.

There are two national holidays and some religious holidays in Germany. May 1 is the day of workers in Germany and October 3 is the day of reunification, which was first celebrated in 1991. Religious holidays depend on the region. Additionally, in some regions, especially in the Rhine area around Cologne, there is a whole holiday season at the beginning of February. This is called Karneval, and includes several days of clownish parades and parties, where masked people dance on the streets of their cities and make jokes in public speeches about current developments in policy and society. There are similar festivities with different names at the same time all over Germany.

CONCLUSION

Youth in Germany need time to learn and have their own experiences in all battlefields of life. Compared to teenagers in other countries of the world, young people in Germany live a relatively safe, luxurious, and independent life. They enjoy social peace and freedom, sexual liberation, and enormous educational efforts. Chances for education and learning are distributed relatively equally between boys and girls and also, although less successfully, among lower- and upper-class kids.

Youth is the time for important decisions: what qualifications to reach and where to go and what to do in the future. Most teenagers in Germany nowadays, compared to older generations, have many possibilities and excellent support.

In contrast to their parents' generation, German youth will live a more autonomous life, with less social security and unsteadiness in social relationships. Current trends in policy turn away step by step from state responsibility for the stability and social security of German citizens.

NOTES

1. Data from Statistisches Bundesamt, Datenreport 2002. Zahlen und Fakten über die Bundesrepublik Deutschland, Bonn, 2002, p. 246.

2. Taken from U.S. Department of State, FY 2001 Country Commercial Guide: Germany (prepared by U.S. embassy, Berlin, and released by the Bureau of Economic and Business in July 2000 for fiscal year 2001). U.S. & Foreign Commercial Service and the U.S. Department of State, 2000. http://www.state.gov/www/about_state/business/com_guides/2001/europe/ germany_ccg2001.pdf (last time visited: 11 March 2003).

3. Information from Eurostat yearbook 2002.http://www.eu-datashop.de/veroeffe/EN/thema1/jahrb_02.htm (last time visited: 15 March 2003).

4. Data taken from Federal Government's Commissioner for Foreigners' Issues: Facts and Figures on the Situation of Foreigners in the Federal Republic of Germany. 19th edition. Berlin, October 2000. http://www.integrationsbeauftragte.de/publikationen/facts00.rtf (last time visited: 20 March 2003).

5. See, for instance, Othon Anastasakis, Extreme Right in Europe: A Comparative Study of Recent Trends. Hellenic Observatory, European Institute. London School of Economics & Political Science, London, November 2000. http://www.lse.ac.uk/collections/hellenicObservatory/pdf/AnastasakisDiscussionPaper3.pdf (last time visited: 10 March 2003).

6. Data taken from Bundesministerium für Bildung und Forschung (ed.), Grund- und Strukturdatenreport 1999/2000. Magdeburg, 2000.

7. Deutsche Shell (ed.), Jugend 2002: Zwischen pragmatischem Idealismus und robustem Materialismus. Fischer Taschenbuch Verlag, Frankfurt am Main, 2002, p. 78.

8. Institut für Jugendforschung München, 2002. http://www.institut-fuer-jugendforschung.de/German/ index_blickpunkt.htm (last time visited: 13 March 2003).

9. Bundesministerium für Familie, Senioren, Frauen und Jugend (ed.), Elfter Kinder- und Jugendbericht 2002, p. 146.http://www.bmfsfj.de/Anlage18653/Text.pdf (last time visited: 28 March 2003).

10. Ibid.

11. Ibid., p. 154.

12. Ibid., p. 124.

13. Statistisches Bundesamt, Datenreport 2002. Zahlen und Fakten über die Bundesrepublik Deutschland, Bonn, 2002, p. 88.

14. As traced by J. Zinnecker et al., Die erste Jugendgeneration des neuen Jahrhunderts. Leske & Budrich, Opladen, 2002, p. 25.

15. Bundesministerium für Familie, Senioren, Frauen und Jugend (ed.), Elfter Kinder- und Jugendbericht, p. 109.http://www.bmfsfj.de/Anlage18653/Text.pdf (last time visited: 28 March 2003).

16. Ibid., p. 232.

17. M. Rutter et al., 15000 Hours: Secondary Schools and Their Effects on Children. Open Books, London, 1979.

18. As traced by J. Zinnecker et al., Die erste Jugendgeneration des neuen Jahrhunderts. Leske & Budrich, Opladen, 2002, p. 158.

19. Deutsche Shell (ed.), Jugend 2002: Zwischen pragmatischem Idealismus und robustem Materialismus. Fischer Taschenbuch Verlag, Frankfurt am Main, 2002, p. 143.

20. As found by Bundesministerium für Familie, Senioren, Frauen und Jugend (ed.), Freiwilliges Engagement in Deutschland. Band 1 Gesamtbericht, Stuttgart (Kohlhammer), 2001, p. 45.

21. Data taken from Deutsche Shell (ed.), Jugend 2002: Zwischen pragmatischem Idealismus und robustem Materialismus, Fischer Taschenbuch Verlag, Frankfurt am Main, 2002, p. 83.

22. Data taken from Bundesministerium für Familie, Senioren, Frauen und Jugend (ed.), Freiwilliges Engagement in Deutschland. Band 1 Gesamtbericht, Stuttgart (Kohlhammer), 2001, p. 221.

23. Taken from Deutsche Shell (ed.), Jugend 2000. Leske & Budrich, Opladen, 2000, p. 157.

RESOURCE GUIDE
Nonfiction

Heneghan, Tom. Unchained Eagle: Germany after the Wall. Pearson Education, London, 2000.
Kershaw, Ian (ed.). The Nazi-Dictatorship: Perspectives of Interpretation. London: Penguin, 1993.

Fiction

Becker, Jurek. The Boxer. Arcade, New York, 2002.
Kaminer, Wladimir. Russian Disco: Tales of Everyday Lunacy on the Streets of Berlin. Ebury Press, Random House, London, 2002.
Rhue, Morton. The Wave. Penguin Books, London, 1988.

Web Sites

http://www.about-germany.org/literature/literature2.asp (information about some famous German authors and their work)

http://www.deutsche-kultur-international.de/ (information about international exchange programs with Germany)

http://www.deutschland.de/en/ ("deutschland.de is the official and independent portal of the Federal Republic of Germany. It offers a representative list of links to important German information sites under the headings of Education, Health, Culture, Media, Sports, State, Tourism, Economy and Science")

http://www.germany-info.org/ (the portal of the German embassy in Washington, D.C., providing news about life, politics, and economy in Germany, as well as everything about traveling and working in Germany)

http://www.germany-tourism.de/ (the National Tourist Board, with information about different regions, sights, and travel tips for Germany) http://www.goethe.de/enindex.htm (the site of Goethe Institutes, who present German culture in 76 other countries; Information on culture and society, study materials, and links and news from Germany are provided)

http://www.government.de/ (the official site of the German government, with actual statistics, links to state organizations, and policy news)

http://www.jugendseiten.de/ (a portal for German-speaking teenagers, with information on adolescents' special interests, such as music, spare time, parties, and so on)

http://net-thinkers.scram.de/index1.php (another youth site in German, an e-magazine made by young people for young people)

http://www.spiegel.de/ (the site of one of the most famous German weeklies)

More Information

German Embassy
4645 Reservoir Road NW
Washington, DC, 20007-1998
Tel: 202-298-4000
German Information Centre
871 United Nations Plaza
13th & 14th floors
New York, NY 10017
Tel: 212-610-9800
Fax: 212-610-9802
E-mail: gic1@germany-info.org

Pen Pal Information

http://interpals.net/index.php
http://penpalsnow.com/
http://www.opendiary.com/diarylist.asp?list=6&start=1&countrycode=DE&countryname=Germany
http://www.studentsoftheworld.info/

Chapter 5

IRELAND

Claire Lambe

INTRODUCTION

Ireland is a relatively small island situated on the western edge of Europe. One could drive the length of it in a day and the width of it in an afternoon and still have time to stop, take in some sights, and have a few cups of tea. The Irish name for Ireland is Erin, and the country is divided into 32 counties comprising four provinces: Munster in the south, Leinster in the east, Connaught in the west, and Ulster in the north. The six counties of Ulster are under the jurisdiction of the British government and are known as Northern Ireland; the remaining 26 counties make up the Republic of Ireland, with a population of 3.9 million people. The majority of people in the Republic of Ireland are Catholic, while the majority in Northern Ireland are Protestant, which has resulted in centuries of turmoil, struggle, and fatalities—as some of the ensuing paragraphs will explain.

Ireland has been through many changes in its history, and in the last 20 years has gone from being an "extra" on the edge of the European stage to one of Europe's fastest-growing economies. Traditionally, Ireland has been a country largely dependent on agriculture. In the second half of the twentieth century, tourism became a major industry. Ireland has a great deal to offer the visitor, since in a short distance one can experience many different landscapes, although not necessarily a suntan: Ireland can be quite rainy, which accounts for its reputation for being so green. More recently, a wide range of industries have found a home in Ireland, and have become an important source of revenue and employment, with urban areas growing to accommodate this. Better known for exporting people than importing them, Ireland has seen this process reversed in the past six years. An increase in the population of over 290,000 has brought the overall population to figures not recorded in Ireland since 1871, although still 1 million short of the figures for 1841, before the famine, a decisive event in later Irish history, decimated the population and forced a great wave of emigration. Over one-third of the population currently live in the capital city, Dublin, and surrounding areas. Ireland has a large youth population: children from birth to age 14 make up 24 percent of the population according to the 2002 figures, while all those under age 21 account for approximately one-third of the population.

Ireland is a democratic republic with an elected government. There is a president, but the role is more honorary and diplomatic than political. The primary political figure in the country is the *taoiseach* (pronounced *tea-shock*). The voting age is 18, and most teenagers can't wait for their first time at the polling booths. Ireland has a very high rate of voting in all elections, local and national. Failure to vote is considered a dereliction of duty, as not voting is still a vote and possibly one that might favor the wrong party, depending on one's politics. Ireland favors a system whereby votes are cast differently from the voting procedure practiced in the United States. In Ireland, each voting slip has all the names of the candidates on it, and a number is placed next to the ones favored in order of preference. If one's first choice is knocked out of the race, the vote goes to the second choice, and so on. Obviously, one doesn't put a number next to a candidate not wanted, in case all the preferences get knocked out and this candidate eventually picks up a vote. The Irish consider this a fairer way of voting, and it gives the individual more power, if not to get their first-preference candidate into government, then at least someone of whom they approve. It also helps smaller parties to get representatives into governmental positions.

To understand a people and have an idea of what makes them tick, one must know something about where they came from and how they got where they are—one must know something of their history, and since no country exists in a vacuum, it is good to learn some surprising things about one's own history.

Like most European countries, Ireland was subjected to many successful invasions, although it is one of the few places in Europe that repelled the armies of the Roman Empire. Ireland's history of human occupation dates back to approximately 5000 B.C. Little is known of these first inhabitants of the island except for what they left behind: fantastic cairns, or graves, to house their dead. These graves were built with miraculous skill and rival the great stone circle of Stonehenge in Britain and even the

Egyptian pyramids in their builders' understanding of astronomy. The Celts came to Ireland in about 500 B.C. and brought new skills, particularly in the area of metalwork. They also brought the Gaelic (Irish) language and became the dominant force in the country. Nobody knows exactly where the Celts originated, although on the basis of artifacts that have survived, various scholars think that they may have come from as far south as North Africa or perhaps even the Middle East. They made their way up the western edge of Europe, leaving pockets of settlers all along the way: the Basques in Spain, the Bretons in France, and the Cornish, Welsh, and Scottish in Britain.

Around 450 A.D., a young boy was captured on the coast of England by marauding Irish pirates and taken to Ireland as a slave. He eventually escaped, but returned later to convert his former captors to a new religion that was spreading through Europe: Christianity. This boy's name was Patrick, and he became the patron saint of Ireland, his feast day on March 17 being celebrated by Irish people and their descendants all over the world. From 500 to 900 A.D., after the fall of the Roman Empire left the rest of Europe vulnerable to successive waves of pagan invasion by the Vikings, Goths, Saxons, and Vandals, Ireland lived through a time of peace. The arrival of Christianity in Ireland had heralded a new beginning on the island and resulted in the building of churches and monasteries, the creation of wonderful art, and scholarship. Eventually the Vikings invaded Ireland too, but the end result was not that the Irish became Viking but that the Vikings became Irish. This phenomenon was to be repeated when the Normans invaded in the twelfth century.

By the time peace reigned again in Europe, the continent was devastated from centuries of war. The year 1000 was fast approaching, and many believed that the world would end. When this didn't happen, there was great relief, and people looked with renewed faith toward Christianity. Charlemagne, a convert to Christianity and emperor of the Holy Roman Empire, turned to Irish monks and scholars to help educate people and bring back the new learning to Europe. At this time, Ireland was known as the Land of Saints and Scholars. However, this moment was short-lived, and soon Ireland was plunged into successive invasions, first by the Anglo-Normans in 1169, and then by the English.

Unlike the Vikings, who were primarily adventurers and traders, or the Normans, who became totally integrated into the fabric of Irish society, the English were imperialists whose true home was elsewhere. They remained strangers in the country. The conquest of Ireland was merely a rehearsal for the creation of what was to become the British Empire. The colonization of Ireland took the form of land being forcibly settled by the English aristocracy or, in some cases, estates given by way of reward for services to the Crown or to the occasional discarded mistress of a king. Ireland remained an unhappy and rebellious colony for the next 700 years. The Irish people by and large found themselves reduced to being tenant farmers on the lands of their new overlords, often with as little as a quarter of an acre or less to grow their food on. This was not enough land to sustain the grain crops that had traditionally been the staple food in Ireland. However, a new and nutritious food source, the potato, was discovered in the new world of America and imported to Ireland as an alternative to grain. Potatoes were particularly useful, as they produced a far better yield than grain from very little land, and so they were ideally suited to the smallholdings of the Irish peasantry.

This was to backfire horribly when the crop failed as a result of potato blight in 1840, resulting in hunger for the peasantry. Things went from bad to worse as blight followed blight over the next 10 years, the worst of which were in the years 1845–47. During the last five years of the famine, over 1 million people died of starvation, while others emigrated in droves. Huge numbers of Irish came to America at this time, many "encouraged" to leave by landlords who wanted to modernize their holdings and saw these smallholders as being in the way of progress, and because the alternative was to provide famine relief, which cost more money than the fare abroad. Already sick when they boarded the ships, many people died en route from seasickness and the terrible conditions. The ships they traveled on had recently been retired from their work in the African slave trade.

Famine suggests that there is no food at all to be had. In Ireland at that time, while people died of hunger on the roadsides, plenty of food was being exported out of the country—only the potato suffered a blight, after all. In Ireland, the famine is referred to as the Great Hunger. People didn't die for lack of food in the country but because of the British government's policy of achieving modernization in farming and their unwillingness to face the costs of famine relief. A faction in England actually regarded the failure of the potato crops and subsequent suffering as God's will: he was culling an overpopulated island. In Ireland, the Great Hunger is looked upon by many as a form of genocide, a crime against humanity.

When the tragedy finally became public knowledge around the world, public opinion (including many Britons) forced the British government to set up soup kitchens. By then, the worst was almost over. Many of these soup kitchens were run by evangelical Protestants who doled out soup on the condition that their almost exclusively Catholic clients embrace Protestantism in return. Most refused. Other groups, including the Quaker and Jewish communities in Ireland, also ran soup kitchens, thankfully without any conditions. Aid also came from other countries, including America, and none more touchingly than from the Choctaw Nation in Oklahoma, a people who themselves had suffered greatly on the Trail of Tears, when they were marched from their homes in Virginia to Oklahoma, only 15 years earlier.

Finally in 1921, Eamon de Valera and his illegal ragtag army, the IRA (Irish Republican Army), fought a successful war of independence against the British, eventually resulting in the formation of the Irish Free State. By then, as resources on both sides showed signs of thinning, de Valera sent a delegation under his general, Michael Collins, to broker a treaty with Winston Churchill in London. Unfortunately, the agreement that was reached excluded the six largely Protestant counties of Ulster (Northern Ireland), which were to remain part of Britain. The treaty included the demand that the government of Ireland would retain the oath of allegiance to the British Crown. In Britain, this development was greeted with some trepidation. There were those who believed that to allow an independent Ireland to exist was the slippery slope that would lead to the demise of the British Empire, and indeed this proved to be true. Within the next 40 years, many British colonies sued for the right to independence and self-determination, including India, which was considered to be "the Jewel in the Empire's Crown." In Ireland, the treaty received mixed reactions. Some felt that it was the best that could be reached under the circumstances, while others felt it was a betrayal of everything that they had fought for; the latter included Eamon de Valera and IRA officers and soldiers loyal to him. Before long, Michael Collins was assassinated and Ireland plunged into civil war. The war didn't result in any changes to the treaty, although successive governments in the ensuing years attempted to negotiate new Anglo-Irish treaties to effect the unification of Ireland. In 1937, with de Valera in the office of *taoiseach* (prime minister) of Ireland, the Irish Free State declared itself a republic, ratified the Irish constitution, scrapped the oath of allegiance to the British Crown, and formalized its claim on Northern Ireland. By this time, the antitreaty IRA was outlawed. Today, the two main political parties have their origin in the two sides who fought each other in the civil war, although now they have other rival parties to contend with, including the Green Party.

Meanwhile in Northern Ireland, the Catholic community (also known as nationalists), who favored the unification of all Ireland, suffered great discrimination under a system of apartheid comparable to the apartheid practiced in South Africa before the collapse of the white regime. They lived in the poorest areas with the worst housing and schools, unemployment was high, and entry into many government agencies such as the police force, the RUC (Royal Ulster Constabulary), was discouraged. In addition, only those who owned property could vote, and since few in the nationalist communities owned their own houses, they had very few votes and so were severely underrepresented in government. A democratic voting system wasn't implemented in Northern Ireland until as late as the mid-1970s.

In 1969, a group of Catholic students, inspired by the success of the civil rights movement in the United States under the leadership of Reverend Dr. Martin Luther King Jr., organized marches and protests in the province. These marches met with a heavy-handed reaction from the police; protesters were arrested, beaten, and shot at with rubber bullets. These events galvanized the communities, and the divisions between Catholic nationalists and Protestant loyalists (loyal to Britain) became even more entrenched than before. In the cities of Derry and Belfast, nationalists erected barricades to prevent the police and loyalists from entering their communities. Soon the British government sent over army divisions to help keep the peace.

The Irish civil rights movement gained momentum, and peaceful marches continued. The soldiers, who were supposedly there to keep the peace, reacted with even more heavy-handedness to the marchers than did the police. In one infamous incident, 14 civilians were killed. Militant members of the nationalist community formed breakaway groups from the IRA to promote violent response—these have included the Provisional Irish Republican Army and, more recently, the "Real IRA." In turn, militants in the loyalist community created their own paramilitary groups, the most notable being the Ulster Volunteer Force, who targeted Catholics and declared war on the IRA. None of the paramilitary groups have any legal status, and although they consider themselves to be legitimate armies with legitimate causes, they are deemed to be terrorists by both the British and Irish governments. The "Troubles," as the conflict is called in Ireland, continued throughout the next 30 years with varying degrees of intensity, resulting in 3,000 dead and 38,000 injured. It occasionally spilled over into mainland Britain and to a lesser extent the Republic of Ireland, in the south of the island.

In 1999, with the help of the American administration under President Clinton, with Senator Jim Mitchell acting as intermediary and conciliator between the factions, a cease-fire was brokered and a power-sharing Northern Ireland Assembly convened to administer the province. The terms of the treaty involved a great deal of compromise on both sides, and as such it is an uneasy truce, but after over 30 years of civil war, the people of Northern Ireland are hungry for peace and the right to live their lives without the fear of violence. Parents have had enough of seeing their children walk to school through a gauntlet of soldiers wearing battle fatigues and carrying machine guns to protect them from stone-throwing adults from the other side. Teenagers want to go out and meet their friends without being stopped and asked threatening questions by strange men wearing masks, whether they are Catholic or Protestant.

TYPICAL DAY

As Ireland is so small, it will be obvious to the reader that nobody living in the Republic of Ireland is very far away from the troubled northern province of Ulster and the specter of terrorist gunmen and bombs. The capital city of the republic, Dublin, is less than a two-hour drive from the border that divides the north from the south, so you would be forgiven for thinking that Irish teenagers live in fear for their lives and never set foot outside their homes unless they absolutely have to. Yet even in Northern Ireland, teenagers have insisted on being teenagers, and many of them, regardless of their proximity to the areas most affected by the conflict, have managed to have friends from "the other side." There are also a number of organizations who have worked to bring together teenagers from both sides to discuss their situations and get to know each other, and to learn that they are not so different from each other and share the same concerns and fears. Unfortunately, it is hard for many to overcome feelings of hate, especially for young people who have lost a parent, sibling, or friend to violence. This is the tragedy of war and the challenge of peace.

Whereas teenagers in Northern Ireland live with the threat of daily violence, a visitor to the republic, in the south, might be hard-put to find any evidence of anxiety at all among teenagers. It is strange given how close everything is, but to someone south of the border, the events in the north seem to be happening in another world. They are always there in the background, however, as is the possibility that the problems in the north could engulf the whole country, despite the cease-fire and the apparent progress that is being made in the Northern Ireland Assembly. Irish people of all ages have lived through and rejoiced at news of cease-fires, only to find that they were short-lived, so if one asked any young person in Ireland whether they are glad the war is over, there might be a funny look or an answer that isn't entirely optimistic. Yet we do live in hope that this peace will be the one that lasts.

Times are changing rapidly, and more and more young people feel that the aims and goals of the two opposing parties in Northern Ireland, separatism for the loyalists and unification for the nationalists, are being made obsolete by recent history. For some years now, Europe as a whole has been moving toward the formation of a political and economic union. In 2002 there is an even greater sense that borders are dissolving, with most countries agreeing to share a single European currency, the euro, and make passports or visas no longer a requirement to travel, work, or study from one country to another. Up until 15 or 20 years ago, Ireland seemed cut off from continental Europe, and provincial by comparison to many countries. The present generation of teenagers feel as much European as they feel Irish. Increased wealth and travel opportunities have been a factor in this, as well as the increase and diversity of people who have chosen to emigrate to Ireland to live. Of course, most Irish people, like most people in other European countries, are still very protective of their cultural identity and traditions, so there is a limit to how integrated or "Europeanized" any of the countries' people want to be. If there is a particular reservation to the European Union that is common to all its member states, it is this.

As everywhere, the lifestyle, expectations, and demands made on young people differ according to whether they live in a big city, a small town, or a rural area. The son or daughter of a farming family would almost certainly be expected to do some chores before breakfast, like milking cows or feeding animals. In other respects, the school day would be similar in towns as in the country. Most schools start their day at nine o'clock, so students should be ready to catch the school bus in time unless they live close enough to walk or cycle. The school day ends at between 3 and 4 P.M., depending on the school and the grade. Students have a short break in the middle of the morning and lunch at between 12:30 and 1:30. They take their lunch with them or buy it in the school cafeteria. At the end of the school day, how much time a student has to stay and chat with classmates depends again on the distance to home (if they are taking the bus, not so much time). During the school week, most students will go home directly, while those who live close to a town center may go to a café or hang out in the town square or shopping center before going home to get some homework done before dinner. In both urban and rural areas, dinner would most likely be served between 5:30 and 7 P.M. Teenagers would be expected to help prepare the meal in most families and/or help out with younger siblings—exceptions or reductions in chores may be made for boys and girls studying for one of the state exams. After dinner, there is more homework and maybe some MTV or a chance to check e-mail or play a computer game before bedtime. It is now not uncommon for a teenager to have a TV in their bedroom, unlike a few years ago. A separate phone would be more unusual, and whether a teenager would have his or her own computer would depend first not only on the wealth of the family but its size. It would still be unusual to have more than one computer per household.

Most Fridays after school, teenagers will congregate in whatever place, café, or shopping center is popular at the moment. If you live in Dublin and favor a hippieish or grunge look, the broad steps of the Bank of Ireland on Dame Street in the center of the city might be the meeting point. Some kids will head for home at dinnertime and choose to get their weekend homework out of the way, while others may put it off until Sunday evening. Many teenagers aged 16 and over will have weekend jobs, in stores or supermarkets, restaurants, or bars. Few 16- or 17-year-olds will be permitted to serve alcohol behind the bar, especially in urban areas, but they can get jobs as busboys or girls. The legal age for drinking alcohol in bars is 18.

FAMILY LIFE

Farmers' children will tend to help out at home, since a farm is a family business. Now that the age when it is legal to work has been raised to 16, there aren't a lot of opportunities for younger teens. Paper routes are virtually nonexistent, but cutting grass for neighbors and washing cars are still options. On the weekend, most teenagers will find time to catch a film at the cinema or, if older, go clubbing.

How much freedom an individual teenager has depends on how strict their parents are, and also on where the teenager lives. Although people can legally drive at the age of 17 (not alone, unless they have a full driver's license), very few high school students will own a car, and not many will get the keys to their parents' car either, regardless of the family's income. Parents in rural areas are more likely to be relaxed in this regard than urban parents. As in other parts of the world, a country boy or girl has probably been driving farm vehicles since the age of 14 or earlier, off the road at least, as soon as they can reach the pedals and see over the steering wheel. And country teenagers need to travel greater distances to get places. For older college age teens, the good old thumb—hitchhiking—is still a popular way of getting from A to B, and on Friday evenings the main roads outside college towns and cities will be lined with young people holding up destination signs for passing motorists who might give them a ride home for the weekend.

Of course, in Ireland just as much as elsewhere, hitchhiking can be a risky business, best done in pairs. But many Irish motorists—including this author—remember being needy students themselves and are amenable to stopping if they are going in the right direction and have room in the car. Also it is a national characteristic of the Irish that they love meeting new people and chatting, and what better way to while away a boring car journey than to give a student a ride and see them safely deposited in their hometown?

In the past, most married women didn't work outside the home. The exceptions to this were women who worked in family businesses, and the so-called professions, medicine and education. There were few opportunities for the average woman. Some jobs literally disappeared when a woman got married. Banks didn't employ married women, so female bank clerks had to "retire" when they married. This persisted up until the mid-1970s. Thankfully those days are gone, and like the United States and elsewhere, there are gender-discrimination laws in place in Ireland now. Many women work outside the home today, and even farmers' wives, who traditionally worked the farms beside their husbands, are likely to have careers that they are no more prepared to give up than are their city counterparts. Since farmers' daughters are less likely to inherit the farm, they tend to be more widely educated than their brothers, who will often go to an agricultural college. Even there, the boys are finding more and more that they are sharing their classes with girls. Consequently, many teenagers, both in rural and urban areas, come home from school to empty houses. So far Ireland has not had a woman *taoiseach*, but the last two presidents of Ireland have been women, including the present one, Mary MacAlease.

FOOD

People in Ireland used to eat their main meal or dinner in the middle of the day. In the evening they would have tea, which was a light meal more like lunch. Schools allowed time for children to go home for dinner, as did companies and businesses, so that workingmen could join their families for the midday meal. For the same reason, bars used to close for an hour from 2 to 3 P.M., and this was euphemistically called "the Holy Hour." Where once it was considered rather pretentious to eat dinner in the evening, today most people do so. Schools no longer allow a full hour or more for lunch, and as so many women have careers, they are not available to spend half the morning cooking big meals. Most families would like to eat dinner together, but the pressures of modern-day living often make this impossible. In the past, food preparation was usually the domain of women and girls. Now, as in the United States, men and boys are now expected to do their fair share in the kitchen.

In former times, people ate mainly whatever fruit and vegetables were in season locally, and for this reason dishes varied throughout the year. Imported food was not only more expensive but also harder to find, unless you lived in one of the three main cities of Dublin, Cork, or Limerick. Porridge was a common breakfast food, along with homemade bread, usually traditional Irish soda bread. Dishes for the main meal tended to be fairly simple: potatoes, meat, and a vegetable or two, or an Irish stew. Nowadays, one would be more likely to be served up a dish of pasta than an Irish stew, even in the heart of the countryside. At one time, if one wanted a Chinese, Indian, or authentic Italian meal, or even McDonald's, one would have to go to one of the cities. The Italians were the first to bring different food to the small towns of Ireland—alas, not wonderful pasta dishes or even pizza, but the new American-style fast food: hamburgers and fries, or chips, as they are called in Ireland and England. Teenage tastes led the fast-food revolution, and now every town will have a range of restaurants and takeout places, including the ubiquitous McDonald's and Burger King, while Chinese or pizza restaurants are everywhere.

SCHOOLING

For a time during the 1800s the British forbade Irish Catholics to go to school, on the grounds that an educated person is potentially more dangerous and harder to control than an uneducated person. This did not sit well with the Irish, who had a centuries-old interest in learning. The Irish language, which was banned as a school subject until independence, is the oldest written language in Europe. To counteract this law banning Catholics from formal education, underground schools called "hedge schools" were founded by teachers, many of whom were priests. Despite the name, outdoor schools would not have been a very practical solution in a climate as wet as Ireland's, and in fact most hedge schooling took place in "safe" houses, often the home of one of the students. The school would be in a different place every week to avoid detection by the authorities. Even the poorest people managed to find the few pennies to pay the teacher for the classes, which not only included the basics of reading, writing, and math, but also the classics—Latin was still the international language at that time, and nobody could claim to be educated without a knowledge of Latin.

After independence, in the early 1920s, there was very little money to set up schools, and the job of educating the young was taken up by religious orders: nuns for the girls and Christian Brothers or priests for the boys. (The Christian Brothers take vows of celibacy, as priests do, but are not ordained to say mass or perform the duties of a priest.) Coeducation was common only up to first grade, except in small rural schools, and these only taught up to sixth grade. Most poor and working-class children didn't go on to secondary school but went to the world of work or apprenticeships at age 12. Over the decades since then, the minimum school-leaving age gradually rose to the present age of 16. Today, over 80 percent of teenagers are still at school at age 18 and earn the Irish equivalent of the high school diploma, and close to 50 percent continue on to do at least one year of higher education. About 10 percent more girls than boys complete high school and go on to college.

Religious orders still play a large part in the education system, although the numbers of nuns and Christian Brothers has declined, so that a student going to a convent school may find that the majority of their teachers are nonreligious or lay teachers. Some things haven't changed: Catholic schools are rarely coeducational even today. But there are now many interdenominational schools (catering to all religious beliefs) founded by the state, and these tend to be coeducational. Also, a number of Protestant schools that were coeducational have become interdenominational in recent years.

In the past, the republic's minority population of non-Catholic students went to schools founded by their own churches or temples, and it was rare to find a Protestant or a Jewish child in a Catholic school. Today this is less true, and it is very common to find children and teenagers from Catholic backgrounds in the schools of other denominations. Some parents who were educated in Catholic schools themselves want alternatives for their own children, including coeducation. In the 1990s the Muslim community built a huge, lavishly equipped school in Dublin to accommodate the growing numbers of Muslim children in the city.

The education offered in the republic is similar to the French *baccalauréat*, whose purpose is to provide as broad an education as possible through high school, so that students will be well placed to make career choices appropriate to them and be educated to a high enough standard to prepare them for their chosen specialization in or out of college. Schooling in Ireland is divided into three levels: the primary level, from kindergarten through 6th grade; the second level, also called secondary school, from first year through sixth year (equivalent to 7th through 12th grades); and the third level, which refers to degree or diploma courses at universities or vocational and technical colleges and other similar institutions. The primary and secondary levels follow a national curriculum—a standardized curriculum set down by the state's Department of Education, and which is the same in both state schools and private or independent schools. There are countrywide state examinations in all subjects in third year (9th grade) and sixth year (12th grade). The third-year exam is called the junior certificate, and the sixth-year exam is called the leaving certificate. The latter is the equivalent of the high school diploma in the United States. These exams are supervised by external examiners and sent away to be graded by outside assessors. The core subjects are English and Irish language and math. All other subjects are optional. Students must pass a minimum of five subjects to qualify for the leaving certificate, but most students take a minimum of six subjects to allow for a failing grade in one, particularly a compulsory core subject in which they may not be particularly strong. Ambitious students take up to 9 or even 10 subjects. Each grade in each subject is worth a certain number of points; the total determines whether a student will qualify for his or her first choice of university or college, and in particular for the college course they are applying for. Medicine, veterinary studies, engineering, and law usually demand very high points. The theater-studies course at Trinity College in Dublin also demands high points, as it is popular but only takes a small number of students each year, so competition for a place is great.

Whether in Northern Ireland or the Republic of Ireland, students would be expected to budget about three or four hours every evening for homework, especially in the exam years, if they want to get good grades and the points necessary to qualify for their dream courses at college. In the republic, if they fail to get adequate points, they do have the option of repeating their leaving certificate exam the following year, but that is more difficult than it sounds. Apart from having to do an extra year at school and, in this case, pay for it, some subjects change from year to year. The novels and plays on the Irish and English language core courses are different every year.

While most schools have sports teams, sports is not an exam subject and there are no such things as sports scholarships to colleges, although occasionally talented Irish athletes are offered scholarships to colleges in the United States. In Ireland, once a student is accepted to a course or discipline at university, they then concentrate on their area of interest: for example, if you wanted to study law, you do not have to do a primary degree first, but would go directly from high school to studying first-year law at college. There are other types of colleges and schools open to students who do not wish to go to a university where a variety of courses are offered, including secretarial, catering, technical and technological, marketing, and design studies. There is even a "rock" school in Dublin for students who hope to carve out a career in the music business.

Ireland, unfortunately, does not have the variety of high schools available in a large country like the United States. There are no specialized high schools for the arts, and the national curriculum doesn't allow much room for alternative schooling. The good thing about the national curriculum, however, is that an A from the poorest school in the most disadvantaged area is worth exactly the same as an A from the wealthiest school.

And some variety of high schooling is there for the taking. There are Irish-language schools all over the country where all subjects are taught in Irish, and these are becoming more numerous as their popularity grows. There are also a number of foreign schools, especially in Dublin, where students can have a taste of another culture. These tend to be independent schools and consequently are fee-paying. If a student is not very academically minded, there are technical and vocational schools where he or she can go after a junior certificate and get a more practical education. While "gifted" schools and programs are not part of the system, most state schools, including those run by religious orders, have different streams to accommodate different abilities, and gifted students will usually find plenty to keep them going in the higher-level classes. There are also special advanced courses run by the universities that offer the exceptional students added academic challenge. At the other end of the scale, most schools will include remedial or special classes for those students who need extra help.

A certain percentage of parents opt for private, fee-paying schools for much the same reasons that people who can afford it make the same decision in the United States: smaller class sizes, higher teacher/student ratios, and perhaps more choice of optional subjects and extracurricular activities. Private or independent schools in Ireland are far less expensive than in the United States, as the state decrees that every child regardless of parental income is entitled to a free education. Therefore the Department of Education allows every school, including the private ones, a certain amount of money per student, including the cost of one teacher for every 30 students. Schools that decide to have two or more teachers for every 30 students must fund the extra staff themselves through school fees and/or fund-raising.

The quality of state schools and teachers is generally good, although there are some schools in certain city areas that have a hard time keeping teachers on the staff. These are in the most disadvantaged areas, where poverty and crime are high and interest in school is often low. As in other countries, the state school system is constantly trying to accommodate too many students, and the average class size often exceeds the desired maximum of 30.

State-funded schooling also extends to higher education, so state universities and colleges are free. This wasn't always the case, and is a recent and welcome development, especially since the vast majority of young people attend state schools and colleges. In fact, the only reason to attend a private university or college is if you are unlucky enough not to gain entry into the state system but lucky enough to have the money to afford the fees in the private system.

In Northern Ireland, schools follow the British system of education, with two state-mandated exams during secondary schooling, in 10th and in 12th grade. In the latter, known as A level, students specialize more narrowly than in the Irish system, and usually take no more than three subjects (more ambitious students might take four or even five), preparing for the even greater specialization at college level, as in the republic. Many parents in Northern Ireland and mainland Britain are questioning this kind of specialization at the high school level, and are calling for a broader, more *baccalauréat* style of education.

Many British students take a "gap" year after high school to work or travel, prior to entering college, and in Ireland this is more common in the north, where high school graduates can apply for college and then defer starting for a year without losing their place. Taking a gap year is considered to be a good idea, as it gives young people a chance to mature before taking on the rigors of college and, for some, provides a chance to save some money—since even though they will not have fees to pay, full-time education always costs money. Many students use the gap year to travel and work abroad, and some go to third-world countries through organizations that place them in areas that need teachers, or simply manpower. Although sometimes these students get paid a small stipend for this service, many try to get sponsorship from companies and businesses to supplement the costs.

SOCIAL LIFE, RECREATION, AND ENTERTAINMENT

Teenagers will always find places to get together, meet new friends, and hang out. Even in the most unpromising of towns, some café will become a haven for them to sit over the same cup of coffee or soda for hours at a time chatting to friends. Most Irish towns do try and accommodate young people in some way and provide venues for them to get together, like youth clubs, tennis clubs, and other sports clubs. Churches, schools, and sports clubs run discos and dances, and these are always a good place to meet up with friends and kids from other schools, particularly important for teens who go to single-sex schools. These discos will usually be supervised by adults, including parent volunteers, although supervision at the sports-club dances is often pretty limited, thus making them the most popular.

A highlight of many teenagers' lives is going to the Gaeltacht in the summer. The Gaeltacht (pronounced *gail-tackt*) is a bit like a summer camp and takes place mostly in the rural, Irish-speaking areas of the western side of the country. The Irish language suffered greatly under English rule and almost disappeared in many parts of the country, so although it is the official first language of Ireland, it is only spoken as a first language in a minority of households. But it did survive as a first language in much of the west coast. The reason for this is because the poorest farming land is on the west coast and was of less interest to the colonists. Nonetheless, most of the Gaeltacht villages are in scenically beautiful areas, and those that aren't next to the ocean always seem to have lakes or great swimming

An Irish teenager "hanging out" in Dublin. Courtesy of David Hewitt.

holes nearby. Enormous numbers of young people are sent to the Gaeltacht areas by their parents for a month at least once during their teenage years, to bone up on their Irish, and they stay with local families while they are there. Whole villages give themselves over to these visitors, and homes have extra rooms especially to accommodate their summer visitors. While the mornings are taken up with Irish-language classes, the afternoons are free for swimming and the evenings for dancing, mostly *ceilis* where the dancing is traditional Irish dancing.

Strictly speaking, the teenagers are supposed to speak only Irish while they are there, but how much this rule is adhered to depends on how strict a particular Gaeltacht is. For the most part, the teenaged visitors are left to their own devices, and supervision is in short supply—yet one rarely hears horror stories about the goings-on at the Gaeltachts except for the occasional student who is sent home for the crime of talking too much English. Since all children learn Irish in school from kindergarten, most will have a pretty good knowledge of it by age 12, but only the keenest students or those who come from Irish-speaking homes will be fluent. The Gaeltachts are great places to meet other young people from all over the country, and often great friendships are made there. The other good thing about the Gaeltachts is that it doesn't cost a lot to go, as they are subsidized by the government to give young people an opportunity to spend time in places where their language is spoken on a daily basis. Until about 20 years ago, girls went one month and boys the next, which was great for the village boys and girls, who were inundated with dates for at least one month every summer. Now all the Gaeltachts are coed, making them even more popular than ever (though no doubt less popular with the village teenagers).

Older teenagers usually meet up in whichever local pub is popular with their age group at the moment—always changing from generation to generation. Although the legal age to go to bars is 18, many Irish teenagers celebrate their 18th birthday in a bar where they have been regulars for months, to the annoyance of the duped bartenders.

In small towns and villages, it is common for teenagers from different economic backgrounds to mix and be friends, but in the cities this is less frequent. City demographics tend to be more sharply divided along economic lines. Teenagers, especially younger ones, tend to hang out close to home and go to school locally, and often don't come across others from vastly different backgrounds. There are exceptions: some secondary schools straddle both working-class and middle-class neighborhoods, where teenagers from different backgrounds will share classes and have opportunities to get to know each other and often become friends. Young people who attend private schools are less likely to have opportunities to meet people from working-class backgrounds except through friends outside of school.

Sports are very popular among young people in Ireland, especially among boys. The most popular is soccer, and most schools will have teams. In the more middle- and upper-class schools, rugby is played more, while in rural and small-town schools, traditional games like Gaelic football and hurley hold their own. Hurley is an ancient Irish game played with a specially shaped stick and a small hard ball, and is a very fast, furious, and sometimes dangerous game. These days many hurley players wear small helmets to avoid injury. Girls are more likely to play basketball and hockey in school. The really committed will belong to sports clubs outside school and play against clubs from other parts of the country. Ireland has its own national soccer team, and when the team qualifies for the various stages of the World Cup, the whole country is glued to their televisions.

Most teenagers engage in premarital sex in Ireland at some point, despite the discouragement of parents, teachers, and the church. Sex among younger teens is not so common, and the legal age is 15—so if a girl is discovered to be having sex before that age, her boyfriend would be in deep trouble. The younger generation of parents are more permissive and open-minded than their parents were about sex, and are more likely to be confided in and to ensure that their children know about contraception. In the not-so-distant past, it would be a huge disgrace if a girl became pregnant out of wedlock. Often she would be sent to a home for unmarried mothers, usually a convent, and the baby given up for adoption in the hope that the whole thing could be kept a secret. Some of these homes still exist, but these days people have a different attitude toward such things: not that anyone would think a school-age teenager becoming pregnant was anything but a tragedy, but more for the girl and her future than for the whole family or even the whole community. Unfortunately, many teens do make mistakes and find themselves to be parents too soon. Terminations are not legal in Ireland, but many Irish girls and women travel to England if they become pregnant. It is an expensive route, and difficult for young people who do not have a lot of money. The country is greatly divided on this issue, with strong pro-life organizations constantly campaigning not to change the constitutional articles on the rights of the unborn, and equally vocal organizations campaigning for a woman's right to choose.

RELIGIOUS PRACTICES AND CULTURAL CEREMONIES

Ireland is essentially a Catholic country, and in the past the division between church and state was fuzzy, to say the least. Even today most schools will have religious education, including state schools, but in recent decades the Catholic Church has lost a lot of ground in Ireland, particularly in the big towns and cities. Less than 30 years ago, every Sunday service from 7 A.M. to 12:30 P.M. would have been packed, and even in big churches the tardy would have trouble finding a seat. Each age group in a given town would have a service or mass that they favored. Afterward they would meet up with their friends, so going to church was as much a social event as a religious one. This no longer holds true. Church pews are emptying, and some of the larger buildings are being sold to other faiths, while many of the smaller ones are finding their way into private ownership.

The separation of church and state is becoming more palpable with every generation, as more and more young people feel that the Catholic Church is out of step with the times and resent its dictates, particularly with regard to family planning and other things that people today consider basic human rights. In the early 1990s, Ireland moved ahead of England in decriminalizing homosexuality. To underscore this change in the law, the then president of Ireland, Mary Robinson, invited a delegation from the gay rights movement to the Presidential Residence, sending a clear message not only to the country in general but also to the church that the state would no longer support discrimination against gay men and lesbians.

The second-largest church in Ireland is the Protestant Church of Ireland, and the country has long-standing Jewish and Quaker communities. Other faiths are becoming more common too, as the diversity of people in the country becomes greater with every passing year.

Politics is not often high on the agenda in the average teenager's mind, and this is as true of Irish teenagers as anywhere else. Nevertheless, probably because of Ireland's turbulent history and the conflict in Northern Ireland, the average Irish person is something of a political animal, and most teenagers have a rudimentary idea of what's going on in the world. All the political parties have a junior section that allows young people to become actively involved in the workings of the party. Membership in Amnesty International and other such organizations is not uncommon. There have been times in recent history where teenagers in Ireland came to the fore on important issues. Famine, wherever it happens in the world, is always taken very seriously in Ireland, and the young people of Ireland have played a significant role in raising funds for famine relief. In the 1980s, not only was the enormously successful Live Aid fund-raiser for Ethiopia organized by the Irish musician Bob Geldof, but there was more money donated per capita in Ireland than anywhere else in the

world. It is also common on city and town streets to see teenagers collecting money for good causes. One of the most memorable moments in
Irish teenage history also happened in the 1980s, the last decade of apartheid in South Africa and Nelson Mandela's imprisonment. The young
employees of one of Ireland's largest chain stores, most of whom were
under 21, asked their employer not to stock South African goods in the
stores. This request was refused, and the employees voted to strike. The
strike, which was countrywide, lasted for close to a year, during which
time the strikers gained huge support from the public, who refused to
cross the picket lines, and resulted in the shutting down of all the stores.
With the company on the brink of bankruptcy, it had to be bailed out
by the government. When the stores reopened their doors to the public,
they no longer carried South African goods. This strike was a great hardship for the workers, most of whom were working class, and although the
public made contributions to augment their limited strike pay, the strikers
took huge losses in salary during that year. These young people, many of
whom had left school at 16 with a limited high school education, made
a huge impact on every person in Ireland and helped make many of their
"better educated" peers aware of the injustices practiced in a faraway
country. They were well rewarded, however, as Mr. Mandela put Ireland
on his agenda as one of the first places to visit after he was released from
prison and elected president of South Africa.

CONCLUSION

Have Irish teenagers become Americanized? Certainly American culture has had an effect: films and television programs have brought at
least a Hollywood version of American life into Irish living rooms, and
McDonald's and Burger King have taken care of the fast food, almost kill-
ing off the fish-and-chip shop. And if Americanization is also synonymous
with modernization or globalization, then Irish teenagers are certainly
Americanized. An American teen and an Irish teen would certainly be able
to chat about their favorite episodes of whatever American soap or sitcom
is currently popular with that age group. Also, the Irish teen is likely to be
well up on the latest American music, including hip-hop and rap. When
it comes to sports heroes, however, they might find they have little to say
to each other. The average Irish teen won't have a clue about American
football or baseball. And a word of warning to fans of the Irish rock group
U2: if you do meet an Irish teenager, don't call Bono "Bone-o," or you
might find yourselves the butt of huge laughter—the first o in Bono's name
is short and rhymes with Ron.

Today's Irish teenagers face many of the same challenges as their American counterparts, struggling to fit into a world made both larger and smaller by globalization and dealing with serious environmental issues, school exams, boyfriends and girlfriends, and the difficult question of whether it is baby-snatching to go out with someone from the grade below yours—and, of course, the ever-present question of what to be when you grow up. Possibly the greatest challenge they and the Irish generations to come after them face is the new diversity at home. In the last half-dozen years, Ireland has gone from being a very monocultural society to the beginnings of real multiculturalism for the first time. There has been a great influx of refugees and immigrants from eastern Europe and also from Rwanda and other parts of Africa. Many of these families will return home when they can, and many will stay and their children will be Irish. Let us hope the present generation of Irish teenagers remembers their own history of oppression and emigration and the example of past generations of teenagers, including the strikers of the 1980s, and welcome these new Irish into their hearts, their communities, and their world.

As an Irish saying puts it: Do not walk behind me, I might not lead. Do not walk ahead of me, I might not follow. Walk next to me and be my friend.

RESOURCE GUIDE
Nonfiction

Cunningham, Bernadette (editor). *Women and Work in Ireland, 1500–1950*. Four Courts Press, Dublin, 2000.

Lyons, F.S.L. *Ireland since the Famine*. London: Weiderfeld and Nicolsa, 1971. (The best reference on modern Irish history for 11th and 12th grades.)

O'Connor, Frank. *The Big Fellow: A Biography of Michael Collins*. London: Picador, 1934.

Fiction

DeValera, Sinead. *Irish Fairy Tales and More Irish Fairy Tales*. London: Piccolo, 1979.

Jacobs, Joseph. *Celtic Fairy Tales*. New York: Dover Publications, Inc., 1968.

Lenihan, Edward. *Strange Irish Tales for Children*. Cork: Mercier Press, 1987.

Lynch, Patricia. *Tales of Irish Enchantment*. Cork: Mercier Press, 1998.

O'Connor, Ulick. *Irish Tales & Sagas*. Dragon Books, London: Granada Publishing LTD, 1985.

Tunney, Paddy. *Ulster Folk Tales for Children*. Cork: Mercier Press, 1990.

Novels by Irish Authors Set in Ireland

* Suitable for young teenagers aged 12–13.
** Suitable for teenagers aged 16 and over.

Brown, Christy. *My Left Foot*. London: Mandarin Publishing, 1989

Doyle, Roddy. *The Commitments*. UK: King Farouk Press, 1987.**

Hickey, Tony. *Where Is Joe?* Baldoyle, Ireland: Poolbeg Press, 1990.*

Lingard, Joan. *Across the Barricades*. London: Puffin, 1995.*

Lingard, Joan. *The File on Fraulein Berg*. London: Beaver Books, 1980.*

Lingard, Joan. *The Gooseberry*. London: Beaver Books, 1978.*

Lingard, Joan. *Hostages to Fortune*. London: Puffin, 1976.

Lingard, Joan. *Into Exile*. London: Puffin, 1973.

Lingard, Joan. *A Proper Place*. London: Puffin, 1975.*

Lingard, Joan. *The Twelfth Day of July*. London: Puffin (also Beaver Books), 1970.
    (First in a series about two young people from different backgrounds trying
    to have a relationship in conflict-torn Ulster.)*

Macken, Walter. *Flight of the Doves*. London: Silver Burdett Gin, 1992.

Macken, Walter. *The Scorching Wind*. London: Britain Books, 1966.

Macken, Walter. *Seek the Fairland*. Omagh, Northern Ireland: Irish Book Center,
    1962.

Macken, Walter. *The Silent People*. London: Pan Books Ltd., 1965.

McCourt, Frank. *Angela's Ashes*. New York: Touchstone Books, 1996.**

O'Brien, Edna. *The Country Girls*. London: Penguin, 1960.**

O'Brien, Flann. *The Poor Mouth*. Normal, IL: Dalkey Archive Press, 1996.

O'Brien, Flann. *The Third Policeman*. Normal, IL: Dalkey Archive Press, 1999.

O'Connor, Frank. *Collected Stories*, edited by Richard Ellman. New York:
    Picador, 1981.

O'Connor, Frank. *Guests of the Nation*. New York: Picador, 1931.

Web Sites

http://www.cso.ie/ (the Central Statistics Office, Ireland)
http://www.ireland.com/ (information on current events in Ireland and Europe)
http://www.irlgov.ie/ (information on the Irish state)
http://www.local.ie/ (historical, social, and religious information on Ireland)

Pen Pal Information

http://www.irishpenpals.com/ (adult pen pals)
http://www.ipf.net.au/ (International Penfriends; all ages, including school class
    applications)
http://www.opendiary.com/diarylist.asp?list=6&start=1&countrycode=IE
    &countryname=Ireland

Chapter 6

ITALY

Antonio Petrone

INTRODUCTION

Italy is one of the most beautiful countries in Europe and among the richest in history. It is certainly not an easy task to summarize its essential characteristics in a short chapter.

Italy has a surface area of about 300,000 square kilometers but is spread along a good 1,400 kilometers in an elongated shape that resembles a boot. The resident population is approximately 58 million, in addition to which there are about 1 million resident foreigners. There are a few large cities, such as Rome (the capital), Milan (where the stock exchange and the major businesses are based), Naples, Turin, Palermo, Genoa, Bologna, and Florence. Most of the rest of the population lives in the approximately 8,000 towns scattered all over the country, which vary in size from 800 to 200,000 inhabitants. This is something that is peculiar to Italy, the legacy of the *periodo comunale*, that is, the time before the various states within Italy were unified and became one country. From this also comes a weak sense of unity with the state and a strong localized and individual drive.[1]

From the point of view of the population, in line with many other European countries but in a more pronounced way, two phenomena stand out. On the one hand there is the greater number of deaths than births, which, thanks to immigration, has not caused a decrease in the population. On the other hand, there is the marked aging of the population; indeed, the average life expectancy is very high (76 for men and 82 for women), with a large increase in the number of older people and a sharp fall in the number of births, which has caused a reduction in the number of children and young people. These phenomena are worrying the government and social forces, who are evaluating a reform of the pension system and the welfare system in general.

Italy does not possess any important natural resources (in strictly economic terms—oil, gas, precious minerals, and so on) and depends largely on imports, especially of crude oil, which supplies fuel for the thermoelectric power stations that produce most of the country's energy. Agriculture, which during the period following the Second World War was the principal occupation, was greatly reduced after the economic boom of the 1960s and today occupies only six percent of the active population. However, it has developed a high rate of mechanization and above all has transformed itself from subsistence agriculture (principally the production of cereals and pulses essential for the survival of the population) into quality production. Italian wines are well known throughout the world, but so too are Italian olive oil and cheeses, ingredients that form the basis of the so-called Mediterranean diet (of which pizza is only the most famous example).

Central to the Italian economy is the role of the manufacturing industry, which has seen radical changes in the course of the last few decades. In fact, it has gone from the predominance of heavy industry during the 1960s (production of steel and cars), established by large firms that were often the property of the state, to the manufacturing of consumer goods with a significant technological element, as with the fashion industry and "made in Italy" in general (for example, clothing, spectacles, furniture, jewelry, items for the home, stationary, publishing, and so on), for the most part carried out by small, sometimes family-run companies.

Finally, what always characterizes the Italian production material now is the marked expansion of the service industry, which employs nearly two-thirds of the workforce and in the last few years has seen an explosion of new sectors within industry, such as tourism, communications, cultural production (that is, culture-related media products), and scientific production (both research and manufacturing).

To summarize, we can say that in 1945, just after the Second World War, Italy had just started the process of industrialization, and at the end of the century it is recognized as the fourth- or fifth-most-important industrial power in the world. This series of progress and modernization of the Italian economy is the result of profound modifications that have benefited the country's economic structure and its position internationally. In the background serious structural problems still remain unresolved, including the fact that the south is still lagging behind, the decline of big industry, industry's lack of technological autonomy, and the inadequacy of many social services.[2]

Among these problems, perhaps the most strongly felt is that of unemployment, which at 9.5 percent in Italy is rather high; unfortunately, this figure is the result of the pronounced territorial inequality between the north and south of the country and also of marked gender differences. In fact, women persistently find it difficult to get into the world of work, particularly in areas where there is significant unemployment. In recent years, with the introduction of forms of work referred to as atypical (part-time work), the problem of unemployment, which toward the end of the 1980s and into the mid-1990s had reached dramatic levels (in some areas of the country one family in four generally relied on the income of only one person, often working in precarious and badly paid conditions), is being reduced consistently and significantly even though situations remain that urgently need to be addressed. Italy retains the unpleasant lead in youth unemployment in Europe. One young person in four between the ages of 15 and 29 (more than 21 percent) is unemployed, but this depends on many factors linked to the way in which the workforce is made up, the Italian education system, and the differences in the availability of work according to geographical area.

Italy is one of the seven most industrialized countries in the world and attends the many contested/challenged meetings of the G8, one of which, up to now the most tragic, was held in August 2001 in Genoa and saw Italy as the hosting nation. It is above all one of the founding nations of the European Union, with the *trattato di Roma* (treaty of Rome) of 1957, which came from and then rendered more concrete the idea of a transnational community in the "old continent": it certainly plays a leading role, particularly because, given its geographical position, history, and culture, it acts as a bridge between continental Europe and North Africa and above all as a point of reference for the Mediterranean countries.[3]

Italy is a parliamentary republic (with two chambers, one for the members of the Senate and one for the members of Parliament, with the same functions) with a president of the republic who guarantees respect for the constitution and a prime minister, elected by Parliament, who holds executive power. Although the electoral system was changed in 1990 from a proportional to a majority system,[4] the role of the parties remains central. Their number has not dropped by very much, and neither has the possibility that one party can tip the scales with very few votes and therefore few seats in Parliament and thus determine the success or failure of a government. However in order to better understand recent events in Italian politics and the current institutional structure, it is necessary to remember that in 1992, following an inquiry by a magistrate in Milan, a judicial storm blew up that was referred to as "Tangentopoli" (or "Kickback City"), which would lead to the political standing being revoked and the disbanding of the two most important political parties, who held the majority and were governing the country at that time, namely the Democrazia Cristiana (a Catholic party) and the Partito Socialista Italiano of Bettino Craxi (who would later take refuge in Libya, where he would later die).[5] To fill the space in the political arena created by Tangentopoli,[6] in 1994 Silvio Berlusconi came on the scene, an entrepreneur from Milan and owner of three private television networks, who founded a new party (called Forza Italia) and won the elections, thus becoming the prime minister. His government was, however, held to ransom by the Lega Lombarda of Umberto Bossi, a secessionist and slightly xenophobic party established in three regions of northern Italy, which after about a year spelled the end of the government: in the following elections the center-left won, and would run the country for five years. However Silvio Berlusconi won the latest election and is once again the prime minister.[7]

Like the majority of European countries, Italy has also seen in its recent past periods of great social disputes, from 1968 until the end of the 1970s. Considering, however, the period from 1981 to 2000, a reduction can be seen in the working hours lost through absence due to social conflicts. This period of relative social peace, which has also seen the advent of great social reforms (including, for example, pension reforms) is about to end. In fact, the mobilization of workers and of the most disadvantaged social classes has increased significantly in the past year because of a series of reforms announced by the government, particularly in the areas of flexibility in work and the reduction of health and social spending in general. Nevertheless, it is in the unfolding of these various turbulent sequences of events that the positive and innovative potential for solutions that expand the social relationship become established. A tight network is bringing together more and more individuals, as demonstrated by the more than 221,000 nonprofit institutions operating in Italy (almost 40 for every 10,000 inhabitants). Of these, more than 55 percent were set up during the course of the last decade and are mobilizing, among workers, volunteers, and conscientious objectors, more than 3.8 million people, managing resources of the value of nearly 40 billion euros.[8]

It is well known that the state of Vatican City, over which the pope reigns, is situated in the city of Rome, which is also the capital of Italy. It is also well known that Italy is historically a Catholic country, even if that has been changing over the last few years. In fact, until 1984 the Catholic faith was by law the national religion and was an obligatory subject taught in school (owing to agreements dating back to 1929 between the Italian state and the Holy See). This obligation has since become less, and the presence of the Catholic Church within Italian society has become much less imposing.[9] The phenomena of the secularization of society and the separation of church and state that occur in all European countries have also made their presence felt in Italy. From a political point of view, the political unity of the Catholics became less in 1992, when only one political party (La Democrazia Cristiana) represented the interests of all Catholics and the clergy in Italy; from the social point of view, faith in the church and the clergy has been less and less, and religious practice has fallen greatly. Contraception, premarital relations, cohabitation of unmarried couples, homosexuality, and to some extent even abortion are accepted practices by the general public even if they are against the principles of the official church. In spite of this, 80 percent of the Italian population consider themselves Catholic,[10] and even though religious practice is somewhat low (only 42 percent go to mass at least once a month), neither can we ignore the fact that a return to religious commitment through voluntary work involves large chunks of the population. To conclude, thanks to the process of globalization and significant immigration in recent years, the religious offerings[11] are rather structured, and now diverse non-Catholic communities can be counted, from the historical Jewish, Muslim, and Hindu faiths to the cults and minor churches.

Italy is one of the countries defeated in the Second World War and freed from Nazi and Fascist occupation by the allied American and British forces. For this reason it was immediately influenced by America and became a strategically fundamental country in NATO as a direct contact with countries such as the dictator Tito's Yugoslavia under the influence of the Soviet Union. Now that the cold war is over, Italy remains one of the United States' most important allies and has been involved and has sent soldiers to various peacekeeping operations in various parts of the world. Currently the most critical situations that have seen Italian soldiers in active service have been in Afghanistan and the Balkans (Kosovo and Bosnia). Italian citizens support their soldiers but often express strong doubts about the usefulness of war to achieve peace.

Before moving on to describe, as far as is possible, the life of young Italians, it is necessary to ask questions of methodology that involve the Italian territorial structure. In fact it is impossible to talk, from an economic, social, or political point of view, about one single Italy: it is necessary to take certain points into consideration. In the first place is the north-south divide, which has existed for many years, characterizes all social and economic studies undertaken about the country, and still causes us to talk about Italy in two parts. Second is the lack of homogeneity, within the distinction between north and south, of the country and therefore the subdivision into zones of major and minor development. On this point it has been said that there are three Italies,[12] but some experts have multiplied that, in extreme cases, to as many as eight.[13] Finally, we must mention the distinction between rural and urban areas, which in the Italy of the new millennium is still shown to be very pronounced in socioeconomic analyses of the population. For all these reasons, in the following pages a concise and much simplified "typical/ideal" image is conjured up of youth and adolescence in Italy. It is not possible to explain here the reasons that prevent even a partial reconstruction of the complex experiences of the young Italian, which span an age range from the end of compulsory education (around 14–15 years old) up to, if we are to believe the latest piece of research on the topic, the beginning of adulthood at 30 years old. If the international stereotypes linked to the image of Italy are to be avoided, it is necessary to read these pages with a critical attitude, using the information contained within them as a point for reflection and an opportunity for further investigation into the topics considered, but without being deceived into thinking that it's possible, by walking the streets of Rome, Cuneo, or Isernia, to meet the "typical" boy or young man whom we are going to describe, because he exists only in these pages.

TYPICAL DAY

It would seem natural when thinking about the typical day of a teenager to talk about his schoolwork, homework, and free time: all of this is right, but in Italy around a quarter of boys between the ages of 15 and 19 don't go to school.[14] They work on more or less temporary terms or they leave school and begin the often unfruitful search, particularly in the south, for a job.

For the majority of young Italians, during the week (from Monday to Saturday), the typical day begins with getting ready for school: washing, breakfast, a little TV, and then leaving the house to go to school. These are treated as repetitive daily actions that don't have any particular symbolic value and can therefore be defined with difficulty as ritual actions in an anthropological sense.

The routes and methods for getting to school are very different according to the size of the town where a person lives. In large cities the route is almost always of an urban nature, and young people can expect to spend a good hour in traffic if their parents take them by car or if they use public transportation. However, what happens more often is that they go by scooter, facing all the dangers that go with negotiating rush-hour traffic. In smaller cities students often make their way to school on foot or by bicycle, and even the traffic is less of a problem. In rural villages public transportation is used, such as the school bus, which collects children from various villages and drops them near the school of the nearest town; in such cases youngsters can often lose several hours traveling and are therefore often tired, reducing their capacity to study.[15]

Only 23.5 percent of children at junior high school have lunch at school, while in public senior high schools there is no canteen and therefore students go home for lunch, or perhaps to a fast-food restaurant or sandwich shop in the big cities; in small towns where (and this is rare) there is a senior high school, they go home or to relatives' homes for lunch, often to their grandparents'.

Usually students are at school all morning until one or two o'clock, according to the type of school attended. Approximately 90 percent of children have homework to do in the afternoon and therefore spend about an hour and a half studying, usually alone but sometimes helped by their mother, or very rarely by their father.[16] Also, thanks to a school reform approved in the last term of office but blocked by the current government, which intends to "reform" it, more and more schools are popping up that offer afternoon activities. These activities are extremely varied: students can do their homework, helped by the teachers, particularly those who need to improve low grades, and there are courses in theater, music, art, sports, and so on. However, by five or at the latest six o'clock in the afternoon adolescents are free from educational obligations; usually Italian youngsters are not involved in any domestic chores (with the exception of keeping their own things tidy and setting the table for meals),[17] and can therefore spend a good deal of their free time however they want.

A day in the life of a youngster who works is completely different. In fact, we can't ignore the fact that 10 percent of young people between 15 and 19 have more or less steady jobs. Unfortunately, they are young people who do menial work because of their lack of educational qualifications, for the most part employed in industry in the north and in the building trade in the south. A proportion of these young people, about whom there is no precise data, work without a contract and in hazardous situations, if not in conditions of out-and-out hardship. It is often from among these youngsters that the mafia and criminal organizations recruit their members. For working teenagers the day is principally marked by the pace of work, and recreation and entertainment are confined to the weekend.

Free time is usually taken up by sports, clubs (such as the Scouts), or voluntary work, but also in more trivial pursuits like shopping (especially in large stores, which have become common meeting places), going around town with their friends (either on foot or on their mopeds), going to amusement arcades, bowling, and so on. The rise in the number of teenagers who spend their free time at home alone playing on their PlayStation, at the computer, or in front of the TV is worrying, while the number of adolescents who fill their free time reading nonschool books or going to the cinema or theater is minimal.

In Italy the weekend is short; it begins on Saturday afternoon and ends on Sunday evening. During this time young people have a rest from their study or work obligations. There are no specific weekend activities; young people who live in big cities often go away to the country with their parents or friends or sometimes with organized groups or clubs (Scouts, local church groups, sports clubs, and so on), in winter to the mountains skiing (especially those who are well off), or in summer to the sea. Saturday evening, older teenagers in particular go to discotheques and dance until dawn, and only get up the following day for lunch.

FAMILY LIFE

The structure of the Italian family has experienced profound changes in the last 50 years. Until the whole of the second postwar period (up to the end of the 1950s), Italy, with rare exception, was a largely agricultural land, underdeveloped and poor, and the family practically throughout the country took the form of the extended patriarchal family. In the houses scattered around the countryside or in little castle villages on the inland hills would live a male head of the (often very large) family: in an economy based on traditional and underdeveloped agriculture, the sons represented an indispensable workforce for field labor.[18]

The situation today has completely changed. With a birthrate among the lowest in the world, the number of people in the average Italian family is around 2.7.[19] It is very difficult to give a single family model because this changes in different areas of the country and varies based on social class. Speaking very generally, it can be said that usually the Italian family is formed from the marriage of two young people (although not too young) between the ages of 25 and 35. The man in vast majority of cases works away from home and plays a very minor domestic role compared to that of the woman. The woman with a family still has some difficulty getting into work, even though in recent years there has been a constant increase in the number of working women and a reduction in the number of full-time housewives. We should also not discount the number of households made up of only one person (21.7 percent), usually single people or lone elderly people, or those composed of one parent and one child.

Firm family roles no longer exist as they did in the past in the traditional family,[20] but jobs are divided up in a much more pragmatic way. In any case there remain activities carried out mostly by the woman, such as the preparation of meals and helping the children with their homework. Usually the father spends his free time with the children (something that men have more of compared with women), or perhaps will go shopping, at times accompanied by the children.

The way in which the day is organized is quite standardized and dictated by hours of work and those of school for children, although a tendency toward greater flexibility in working hours is developing, also due to people traveling more, principally because of one of the parents' jobs.

The legal age for driving a car is 18, although the majority of teenagers own a scooter or moped that they can legally ride from the age of 14. There are few young people who when they turn 18 own a car, and only in well-off families are cars given as 18th birthday presents.[21]

One of the differences in family life for rich and poor young people is the presence of a housekeeper or domestic help, in richer families, who take care of the housework and cooking and therefore allows the mother to dedicate the majority of her attention to the lives of her children.

What has remained of the traditional idea of family? Even though the Italian family has completely mutated in its structure, it remains central to Italian society. Educating and training the younger generation is still very much the family's job, as is the protection and assistance that has distinguished the Italian family in the past: sociologists talk about the "long family,"[22] in which young people don't manage to fly the nest and start their own family until they are in their 30s. The causes of this phenomenon, which in Italy is taking on alarming proportions, are multiple and are linked to the education system, the system of work, and the social system in general.

FOOD

It is not easy to talk about any one traditional dish or dishes, because Italian cuisine is among the most important, delicious, and varied in the world. Well known around the world, pasta and pizza are not the only symbols of the famous Mediterranean diet: to give examples, we could talk about the hundreds of ways to serve the various different types of pasta, according to the recipes. However, when talking about Italian cuisine we cannot stop at pizza and pasta. Also renowned are Italian cheeses and cold meats, among which *parmigiano reggiano* (reggiano parmesan, which takes its name from the city of Reggio in Emilia where it is produced) and Parma ham (which also takes the name of the city of Parma, where it is produced) are the market leaders. To these we should also add olive oil and wine, which in the last few years have become leading products throughout the world, overtaking other countries that used to be the leading exporters, such as France (for wine) and Greece (for olive oil). In Italy eating "traditional" food, that is, food that is not imported or typical of other countries, is the norm and is still widespread, especially in smaller towns and cities, and people generally prepare food at home, often buying their products from markets with local suppliers.

Obviously the situation is very different in large cities, where people buy their food for the most part in supermarkets and sometimes consume ready-prepared or easy-to-prepare products. The main meal is still lunch,[23] which is prepared at home by the mother of the family. However, other ways of eating are appearing: in large cities, where daily movements take up a lot of time, the lunch break is not long enough to go home and consume a complete meal, so people prefer to go to a public eating establishment where they can eat something quite quickly. Hence, in the last few years sandwich shops, self-service restaurants, and McDonald's have been flourishing.

In Italy the Americanization of eating habits has not established itself as it has in many other consumer areas. McDonald's and other such chains are not very widespread, and even teenagers with a tendency to eat hamburgers or hot dogs are not numerous and frequent such establishments rather sporadically, and in any case not on a daily basis.[24]

The Mediterranean diet is based on a healthy and balanced food intake, as is recognized by dieticians and nutritionists throughout the word. Problems of obesity and associated illnesses are for the most part the result of food and alcohol abuse. In reality there is an increase in attention to obesity among younger teenagers due, in particular, to the use of industrial snacks and all the other ready-made products.

SCHOOLING

In Italy there are approximately 9 million students (besides those attending university), of whom 1.2 million attend private schools (14 percent).[25] School is currently compulsory up to the age of 15, irrespective of whether students attain their *scuola media inferiore* (also known as *scuola media*), or junior high school certificates, which are generally taken around the age of 14. Therefore all children are obliged by law to go to school until they are 15. Junior high school is completely free of charge, and students are entitled to be reimbursed for 50 percent for the cost of books; nevertheless, families spend a lot of money on buying books, stationery, and transportation: this is one of the things that generates in Italy the phenomenon, although now much reduced, of children leaving school early. In fact, about 2 percent of children who finish primary school (from the age of 6 to 11) don't enroll in lower middle school (between the ages of 11 and 14) or leave before the end (2.2 percent)[26] of the course; 14- to 19-year-olds then attend *scuola media superiore* (referred to in slang as *superiore*), or senior high school, for five years. Senior high schools are divided into three types:

- Professional institutes (for business, industry, or crafts), which mainly teach students a trade
- Technical institutes (for business, tourism, or surveying), whose objective is training that leads to a technical profession such as surveying, accounting, and office management in medium to large companies
- *Licei*, senior high schools specializing in traditional academic studies, which are of four types: *liceo classico* (specializing in classical studies—ancient Greek, Latin, philosophy and so on), *scientifico* (specializing in sciences), *linguistico* (specializing in languages), and *artistico* (specializing in the arts); in these schools students receive a general cultural education that prepares them for college

The choice of senior high school, at the end of junior high school, is completely free and is often a joint effort between the teachers, family, and the student him/herself. Access to college is also completely free. Obviously youngsters who receive high grades at the end of junior high school are strongly advised to enroll in a *liceo*, while those with lower grades are advised to go to the technical or vocational schools.

Whether in public or private school, the classes are mixed: boys and girls coexist, meeting and facing one another every day. The typical school day in senior high depends on the type of school attended: as a rough guide, it begins at eight or nine o'clock in the morning and finishes between one and two o'clock in the afternoon. Rarely do students have lunch at school, and only a few students return to school for the afternoon activities that happen a couple of times a week and are optional.

Special schools do not exist; students with a disability, be it physical or psychological, attend mainstream classes, although followed by an assistant teacher who supports them. Public schools are predominant and are also attended by youngsters from well-off and wealthy families. Prestigious private schools do exist, however, which expect rather high enrollment fees, where children from rich families study. The difference between these institutions and "normal" ones is almost nonexistent for junior high school, slight for senior high school, and more noticeable at the university level.

Teachers are of both sexes but with a higher number of female teachers (70 percent in junior high schools and 60 percent in senior highs) and are on average on the older side (average age 47);[27] they are for the most part graduates, but their social background is white-collar and middle class. Today the teaching profession is in serious crisis, and it is more and more difficult to find young, motivated, and capable teachers (this is also due to inadequate pay, which is among the lowest in Europe). Public schooling is completely financed by the state, although the cost of textbooks and materials is almost entirely carried by students' families.

For the overwhelming majority of parents, school is seen as the solution to all teenagers' problems. Parents and society in general place a lot of faith in the educational and training capacity of schools, even though in reality the education system is in profound crisis. Resulting from this crisis is the general school reform that was passed by the last government but has not yet been put into action because of the block put on it by the present government: when this reform is put into operation, the system outlined above will be completely turned around, with schools subdivided into cycles, the abolition of the vocational and technical school, and the creation of training courses leading exclusively to immediate work placement.

SOCIAL LIFE, RECREATION, AND ENTERTAINMENT

There is no standard way in which young people meet and spend time together: the ways of meeting up in a large metropolitan city are different compared with a small provincial town and different again compared with a mountain village. Even within a city it changes between central districts and those in the suburbs.[28] In big cities, partly because of a certain distrust on the part of families, the socializing of teenagers is entrusted to associations and institutions: in the first place in school with afternoon activities, then in sports groups and clubs, and finally in educational and recreational religious associations. There is also the spontaneous meeting of friends and acquaintances near their own homes, especially in districts on the outskirts of town, as was represented a short time ago in the TV series titled *I ragazzi del muretto* (*The Little Wall Kids*).

In smaller cities, besides the usual organized afternoon activities, friends and companions usually meet each-other at the *struscio*, that is, they go for a walk along the main streets closed to traffic or in pedestrian areas where youngsters of various ages hang out. In smaller towns, the bar or *circolo* (club, usually some kind of hostelry) represents the only meeting place. Rarely do Italian teenagers go with their families to meet relatives or friends of the family, and often this practice, where it does occur, is considered tiresome by the majority of teenagers.[29]

Meetings can be random, sometimes organized by teenagers themselves, often using mobile phones or e-mail, or otherwise more simply they meet up, going to the places frequented by their friends.

The vast majority of young people go to discotheques or places where they can dance with the intention of meeting new people or at least socializing and being among people of the same age. There are more expensive places frequented by rich youngsters, and it is with difficulty that rich young people mix with poor ones and vice versa, with the exception of special occasions such as concerts and events open to everybody. Schools, regardless of activity or location, are open to both sexes, and young people choose their sexual and emotional partners freely, including, often around the age of 30, the man or woman they choose to marry.

Clothes and day-to-day behavior, from the type of language used to relational attitudes, are mediums for communicating social status and differences in class, whether between youngsters or adults. For rich youngsters, designer clothes, expensive watches, and luxury items are ways of affirming their own social background and recognizing one another at a glance Obviously youngsters from modest backgrounds and those who come from the middle classes also have ways, in their possessions and behaviors, of identifying themselves and enabling themselves to be recognized.[30] Parents don't manage or perhaps don't want to control their own children, who are therefore left with a lot of freedom to decide what to wear and who to hang out with. It is not easy, in Italy, to say what young people wear; the ways people dress vary a lot depending on social status, age, where they live, and political leaning. It is possible to find, in large cities, young people dressed in punk, dark, and heavy-metal styles, but there are also those who wear designer suits, known as *pariolini* (from the name of a rich residential district in Rome), or you can see youngsters dressed in army shirts with berets in the style of the revolutionary Che Guevara, a clear symbol of left-wing political orientation. In big cities small gangs of Nazi skinheads roam the streets with the classic dress of leather jackets, jeans, army combat boots, and closely shaved heads.

The current fashion, especially among younger teenagers, imposes American dress, with very wide, low-waisted jeans worn almost falling down, sports shoes, and enormous sweatshirts with dangling sleeves (sometimes with chains hanging down—useful for not losing keys or wallets). The differences between males and females for what concerns fashion and lifestyle are very limited.

The sexual behaviors are also very similar between sexes; both have sex before marriage and use contraceptive methods. Italy is still a Catholic country, but sexual liberty, achieved during the 1960s and 1970s, is becoming a fundamental value of the young; it is now completely normal for girls and boys to have their first sex near the majority age. Homosexuality isn't still considered a perversion or illness, and people, the young in particular, accept gays. Two-thirds of Italian young men and women know at least three contraceptive methods, but the most widespread is the condom, because it is very important to prevent HIV.[31] The increase of sexual freedom corresponds, on the other side, to the rise of the importance of a couple's fidelity and the unity of family, which is considered the most important value, as chosen by people in every survey.

Over 1.8 percent of Italian youngsters dedicate themselves to sporting activities.[32] Many sports are practiced in Italy, by far the most popular being soccer. Sports are practiced in school either in the morning or afternoon but have not been completely integrated into young people's education. In reality, in the majority of cases, school time dedicated to sports is limited (a couple of hours a week), often carried out with totally inadequate structure, practiced in very large groups (classes are usually made up of about 30 students), and directed by elderly teachers with outdated training who are not familiar with new or less well-known sports. Adolescents and young people are therefore forced to join private sports clubs, and even they are often short of equipment and resources.

Sporting activities are mostly practiced in the north of Italy, where the sports structures are better and the local authorities invest more public money in this sector. The sports most practiced by teenagers from 13 to 19 are soccer, swimming, gymnastics, dance, volleyball, tennis, and skiing. There are very few youngsters who follow the lesser-known sports: horse riding, polo, climbing, sailing, canoeing, fencing, rugby, and so on.

All sports can be practiced by both sexes, although there emerges a marked gender characterization of sporting activities. Exercise, gymnastics, and dance are more popular among the girls (42.8 percent compared to 10.7 percent of boys), as are swimming, water polo, diving (28 percent compared to 17.2 percent of boys), and volleyball (11.1 percent of girls to 3.8 percent of boys). Excluding these sports, the proportion of boys to girls practicing all other activities is higher. In particular, some sports have developed as typically masculine: among these are soccer (practiced by 41.4 percent of boys compared with 1.7 percent of girls), but also cycling (9.6 percent compared with 2.8 percent of girls), tennis (9.8 percent compared with 4.5 percent of girls), and hunting and fishing, which surveys show as not being practiced by women at all.[33] The majority of youngsters practice their sport noncompetitively two or three times a week. Those teenagers and young people who join teams and take part in national championships or leagues in various sports train every day for several hours and on the weekend take part in competitions and tournaments, whether they be at the national or European level.

Hikers at the peak of Labbro Mountain, Italy.
Courtesy of Marco Cecchini.

The national sports heroes are the highly paid, extremely famous soccer players: among the Italian ones we can include Roberto Baggio, Alessandro Del Piero, and Francesco Totti among the forwards, and Fabio Cannavoraro, Alessandro Nesta, and Paolo Maldini among the defenders.

Bodybuilding and other gym activities such as spinning (fitness classes in which participants follow a program on an exercise bike), aerobics, step, and martial arts are on the increase, but mostly involve adults. Besides sports, teenagers also entertain themselves with pastimes like bowling, rollerblading, ice skating, pool, and playing video games.

In Italian schools very little space is given over to the study of music and even less to listening to music. In Italy all types of music are listened to: rock, pop, and Italian singers, but also heavy metal, rap, and hip-hop. In the discotheques people listen and dance to techno, dance, and alternative music. Themed establishments exist in large cities, where it's possible to listen and dance to many different types of music, from reggae and jazz to Irish folk music.

There are also youngsters who, as well as listening to music, play in small bands (which sometimes even become famous), in local (brass) bands, or even in the large national symphony orchestras such as the La Scala theater orchestra in Milan or the RAI symphony orchestra. (RAI is the national public television broadcasting company, Italy's equivalent to Britain's BBC.)

The consumption of alcohol is forbidden to minors under the age of 14; nevertheless, pubs are often frequented by teenagers, especially the older ones.

The phenomenon of drug taking in young Italians is complex, widespread, and difficult to describe, because it is clandestine and little-known. In Italy taking drugs is against the law, and it is a criminal offense to sell, traffic, or consume in company any substance that alters a person's psychophysical capacities: this includes those classed as hard drugs, like cocaine, heroin, and opium, but also those classed as soft drugs, like hash and marijuana, as well as the so-called synthetic drugs, such as hallucinogens (LSD, amphetamines) and the modern ones like Ecstasy. Despite the fact that is against the law, the use of prohibited substances among the youth is quite widespread: the official data from the Ministero per le Politiche Sociali (Department for Social Policy) on the official number of drug-dependent people undergoing treatment in rehabilitation centers talks about a few thousand people, of whom young people between 13 and 19 represent a further minority. Many people under medical care by state institutions have taken heavy drugs like heroin or cocaine.[34]

The sociological studies show that the phenomenon is underground and very large. In fact, a research study on 35,000 18-year-olds has pointed out that one teen in five uses drugs, or has used at least them at least one time (mainly hashish or marijuana). The teens usually use drugs during the weekend when they are in groups, often in the discos. In Italy, like in most European countries, the consumption of drugs is a phenomenon with steady growth: in fact, the consumption of heavy drugs has had a partial reduction in our time, but at the same time, the consumption of hallucinogenic drugs is increasing among young people.

The rapid increase in the amount of free time teenagers spend alone at home is worrying: almost all youngsters between 11 and 19 watch television every day, and the majority spend several hours in front of the TV; another very popular pastime, especially among the younger ones, is video games (Nintendo, PlayStation, Xbox, and so on), so much so that they avoid leaving the house to be with their friends or to play sports because of a real obsession with their favorite game.

Finally, but recently on the increase, is time spent in front of the computer playing games or surfing the Internet; 60 percent of teenagers have a computer[35] at home and a connection to the Internet: the Net is used to chat, play, and collect information. In the age of the telecommunications society, young Italians are not behind their European contemporaries, and spend the majority of their free time, especially during the week, in a virtual world, which seems very real but is not.

RELIGIOUS PRACTICES AND CULTURAL CEREMONIES

As we said in the introduction, Italy is still a strongly Catholic country, even though sudden changes in recent years have brought the traditional model of religious practice into crisis. Italian youngsters are still linked to the Catholic Church by a double cord, and in any case in their early youth are strongly socialized within the religion of the same family: 33 percent of youngsters between 14 and 19 go to religious functions at least once a week, while the percentage rises considerably if we consider participation in religious occasions like Christmas and Easter.

One should not underestimate the phenomenon of religious youth groups, which despite a marked decline compared with past years still involve one youngster in five: at the top of the list we find Catholic scouting and the Franciscan "speakers." Also voluntary work, which principally involves older youngsters, often has religious connotations (mostly Catholic).

In Italy the festivities over the Christmas period are very important. Besides the religious importance, which sees even the slightly "distracted" Catholics joining in, is the fact that Christmas represents, especially for teenagers, who have about two weeks of school holidays, a time for enjoyment and getting together. During this time of year a lot of time is dedicated to shopping, gifts, and the often excessive consumption of goods of all kinds. Teenagers are not exempt from this phenomenon; they take advantage of this period when they can receive gifts such as items of designer clothing, more and more powerful computers, or the latest cell phone, if not a scooter or car.

There are also the more minor religious festivals like the Immaculate Conception of the Virgin Mary, Mother of God (December 8), the Ascension of Mary (August 15), All Saints' Day and the Festival of the Dead (November 1), and the festivals of the patron saints, which are celebrated on different days by each city.

There are three civil festivals: celebrations of liberation from the occupation of the Nazi-Fascists (April 25), the workers (May 1), and the foundation of the republic (June 2). These festivals are not strongly felt by the population in general, and even less by teenagers. The lack of civic feeling among the younger generations and the stronger and stronger tendency to forget Italy's recent history are phenomena worryingly on the increase, and are undermining at the source the national and civic identity on which our country is based.

CONCLUSION

It is impossible to talk about Italian adolescence in general, or to define once and for all what an Italian teenager is and does. There is no sense in talking about "youngsters" as a homogenous category. There are many youthful conditions, many routes to adult life, many ways to live through this phase of life's journey. And yet there are also some elements that teenagers and young people share, not only in Italy but all over Europe and perhaps even in the entire part of the world to which Europe belongs.

Teenagers are simply those who are just starting to get a taste of life, for good and bad, and still have everything to discover. In the condition of youth the dimension of time and in particular the image of the future takes on great importance. Here there is a great deal of uncertainty. There are those who relish uncertainty as an opportunity and those who view it with fear and suspicion. For both categories, in any case, the future is unpredictable. The dimension of uncertainty is the one that best defines being a young Italian today.

Childhood and adolescence are by definition the most carefree periods of a person's life, in which the greatest anxiety is about growing up; for the majority of Italian youngsters, it is exactly like that. The family thinks about and satisfies all their needs, from those of sustenance to those that are unnecessary, sometimes to an unrestrained an excessive extent. This characteristic is also a limit: parents are more and more becoming friends with their children and are losing the function of guidance that is essential to a young person's upbringing.

The problems and anxieties of adolescence are resolved by unrestrained consumption and the escape into virtual worlds such as the Internet and TV. School and society are becoming less and less interested in young people and their education, but are looking at all costs to teach them something that is immediately usable in the job market, leaving social, civil, and cultural education to other centers and institutions, which, if studied carefully, are either absent or much reduced.

The future is, however, one of the greatest Italian contradictions: a short life of rituals and standardized, globalized styles contrasted with the solidity of the younger generations' values. The family, fidelity, and true feelings such as love, friendship, solidarity, and attachment to freedom are the values most shared and promoted among Italian young people and teenagers, who represent the future of our Italy.

NOTES

1. Martinelli, Chiesi, 2002.

2. Taken freely from Graziani, 2001.

3. On the role of Italy in Europe, see Di Palma, Fabbrini, Freddi, 2000.

4. On the little difference between the two electoral systems in the Italian version, see the contribution of Sartori, 1995.

5. For a reconstruction of the institutional and political setup from 1988 to the present day, see Di Palma, Fabbrini, Freddi, 2000.

6. See Altan, Cartocci, 1997.

7. A cautious analyses of voting in the last political elections can be found in Itanes, 2001.

8. Data taken from CENSIS, 2002.

9. The sociological and political reconstruction of this phenomenon can be found in Martinelli, Chiesi, 2002.

10. Data taken from Cesareo, 1995; Gubert, 2000.

11. The concept of religious offerings and religious space was introduced by the sociologist Peter Berger in 1969.

12. Bagnasco, 1977.

13. Statera, 1987; Di Franco, 1996; Golini, Mussino, Ravioli, 2001.

14. Thirty percent of Italian youngsters between 14 and 19 do not define themselves as students, as reported by OECD, 2000, and confirmed in the last Iard survey (Buzzi, Cavalli, De Lillo, 2002).

15. This is information is based, as far as possible, on data taken from ISTAT, 1998b.

16. Taken from ISTAT, La vita quotidiana di bambini e ragazzi, 1998b.

17. Calculations performed on ISTAT data, 1998b.

18. Taken from Martinelli, Chiesi, 2002, pp. 53–57.

19. In this case it is ridiculous to talk about the "average"; in fact, it is logically incorrect to apply an average to "natural" or invisible units such as human beings. It is more correct to say that the nuclear families made up of two or three components are those that are most widespread: in the first case this refers mainly to elderly people, given the high number of the country's elderly people, and in the other case to couples with only one child, which represents the typical Italian family at present.

20. Barbagli, Saraceno, 1997.

21. From ISTAT (Italian Governmental Data) data it can be seen that only 1.7 percent of youngsters between 18 and 19 drive themselves to work or to their place of study, of whom even fewer actually own a car.

22. See Buzzi, Cavalli, De Lillo, 2002.

23. It is not easy to find available data on the eating habits of Italians, if we exclude the newspapers' surveys and pseudo-investigations (whose scientific value is rather low); in this case reference is made to data reported by D'Egidio, Da Fermo, 2002, pp. 223–35.

24. About seven percent of youngsters between the ages of 14 and 17 frequent fast-food restaurants once a week (ISTAT, 1998b).

25. Data taken from the Ministero dell'Istruzione (Department of Education), 2001.

26. Taken from Gasperoni, 1997, page. 26.

27. This data is taken from Cavalli, 2000.

28. ISTAT, 2001, confirms that 67 percent of youngsters between the ages of 11 and 19 meet their friends every day, and almost all of them at least once a week.

29. These statements are based on the observations of ISTAT, 1998b.

30. A study that has recently described these phenomena in Italy is Bovone, 1997.

31. These statements are based on Buzzi, 1998.

32. Data from ISTAT, 2001.

33. Taken from ISTAT, 2002a.

34. Data taken from Ministero delle Politiche Sociali (Department of Social Policy), 2001.

35. Data taken from ISTAT, 2002b.

RESOURCE GUIDE

Nonfiction

Altan, T.C., Cartocci, R., *La coscienza civile degli italiani. Valori e disvalori. L'Italia di tangentopoli e la crisi del sistema partitico* (The civil conscience of the Italians: Values and disvalori in the national history), Udine: Gaspari, 1997.

Bagnasco, A., *Tre italie* (Three Italies), Bologna: Mulino, 1977.

Barbagli, M., Saraceno, C. (eds.) , *Lo stato delle famiglie in Italia* (The state of the family in Italy), Bologna: Mulino, 1997.

Berger, P., *The sacred canopy: Elements of social theory of religion*, New York: Doubleday, 1969.

Bovone, L., *La moda della metropoli* (The fashion of the metropoli. Where the young people from Milan meet themselves), Milano: Angeli, 1997.

Buzzi, C., *Giovanni, affettività, sessualità* (Love, tenderness, and intimacy), Bologna: Mulino, 1998.

Buzzi, C., Cavalli, A., De Lillo, A., *Giovani del nuovo secolo* (Young people of the new century), Bologna: Mulino, 2002.

Cavalli, A., *Gli insegnanti nella scuola che cambia* (Teaching in the school that it changes), Bologna: Mulino, 2000.

CENSIS, *35° Rapporto annuale sulla situazione sociale del Paese La società italiana al 2001* (Census: Annual Report of the Social Situation in the Italian Society), Roma: 2002.

Cesareo, V. (ed.), *La religiosità in Italia* (Religion in Italy), Milano: Mondadori, 1995.

D'Egidio, P., Da Fermo, M., *I giovani in Abruzzo* (Giovanni in Abruzzo), Milano: Angeli, 2002.

Di Franco, G., "Le otto italie della Camera e del Senato," (The eight italians in the room and senate), *Sociologia e ricerca sociale*, 50, 22–49, 1996.

Gasperoni, G., *Il rendimento scolastico* (Scholastic reading and social status), Bologna: Mulino, 1997.

Golini, A., Mussino, A., Ravioli, M., *Il malessere demografico in Italia* (The demographic malaise in Italy), Bologna: Mulino, 2000.

Graziani, A., *Lo sviluppo dell'economia italiana. Dalla ricostruzione alla moneta europea* (The development of the Italian economy: From the reconstruction to the European currency), Torino: Bollati Boringhieri, 2001.

Gubert, R. (ed.), *La via italiana alla post-modernità* (Italian life after postmodernism), Milan: Angeli, 2000.

ISTAT, *I cittadini e l'ambiente* (The citizens and the atmosphere), 1998a.

ISTAT, *Cultura, socialità e tempo libero* (Culture, society and free time), 2001.

ISTAT, *Cittadini e la pratica sportiva* (Practice for sports for all), 2002a.

ISTAT, *I cittadini e le tecnologie della comunicazione* (Technology and communication for all), 2002b.

Martinelli, A., Chiesi, A. M., *La società italiana*, Laterza, 2002.

Ministero delle Politiche Sociali (Department of Social Policy), "Relazione annuale al Parlamento sullo stato delle tossicodipendenze in Italia" (The annual report of Parliament on the state of drug dependency in Italy), 2001

OECD, *Education at a Glance: OECD indicators*, 2000 edition, Paris, OEDC, 2000.

Price, J., Ramella, A., Vattimo, G., *Italia America, America Italy*, Gribaudo, 2002.

Sartori, G., *Come sbagliare le riforme* (Like mistaking the reforms), Bologna: Mulino, 1995.

Statera, G. (ed.), *Le basi sociali dei poli elettorali* (The social basis of the electoral poles), Milano: Angeli, 1987.

Web Sites

http://www.agesci.it/

This is the site of the Italian Catholic Scouting Association.

http://www.censis.it/

This is a research site on society and customs in Italy.

http://www.enit.it/

This is the National Tourist Board site, where the innumerable tourist opportunities are outlined.

http://www.gamberorosso.it/

This is the most important guide to eating well in Italy, with places to eat, foods, wines, recipes, and lots of other gastronomic information.

http://www.ilsole24ore.it/

This is one of the major Italian newspapers; this site is a true portal, where you can find a bit of everything.

http://www.istat.it/

This is the Istituto Nazionale di Statistica (National Statistics Institute) site of official statistics in Italy, where is possible to find all official Italian statistical data.

http://www.ministeroistruzione.it/

This is the site of the Education Department, with information about schooling and the education reforms.

http://www.moda.it/

This is the site of a well-known fashion magazine.

http://www.musicaitaliana.it/

This is a site where you can listen to Italian music; all the major Italian radio stations are listed.

http://www.ragazzinet.it/

This is a site entirely dedicated to teenagers.

http://www.rai.it/

This is the site of the Italian state TV broadcasting company, with lots of opportunities to see and hear Italy.

Pen Pal Information

http://www.opendiary.com/diarylist.asp?list=6&start=1&countrycode=IT& counryname=Italy

Chapter 7

MALTA

Anthony E. Azzopardi and Marilyn Clark

INTRODUCTION

The Maltese Islands consist of Malta, Gozo, and Comino. The total surface area is 315 square kilometers, of which Malta covers 246, while Gozo and Comino together cover 69. The resident population in Malta is around 376,000, giving a population density of 1,193 persons per square kilometer.

Situated at the center of the Mediterranean Sea, Malta is approximately 90 kilometers south of European Sicily and 290 kilometers to the north of Tunisia and to the east of Libya. It is almost equidistant from the Straits of Gibraltar and Alexandria in Egypt.

Malta's small size and population density have had an impact on the character of the nation. The structure of Maltese society is influenced by its micro-status, resulting in insularity. However, Europe and its value systems have also determined some of its social characteristics. An important consequence of its small size is the high degree of social visibility and absence of anonymity. This may be experienced as comforting but also as claustrophobic at times. The hot climate means that people are drawn outdoors, leading to a strong sense of community manifested, for example, by the eager participation of people of all ages at the village *festa*.

In Malta, it is hard to distinguish between urban and rural areas. The term *urbanization* cannot be applied as it has been in other countries, probably due to the absence of an intense period of industrialization. In Malta urbanization has taken a different form. There has occurred an amalgamation of different urban districts with towns and other localities merging into one another. But in spite of this, Maltese society still has features of urban growth, such as high population density, changes in family structures, and a decline in agricultural land. A characteristic of Maltese urban localities is a merging of the old and the new.

The fact that Maltese society has always been, and still is, at the crossroads of development is reflected in a number of apparently contrasting issues. Both politically and economically, Malta can be considered a developed country, with an array of statutory democratic institutions and a thriving economic system. People's rights and obligations are safeguarded by a constitution, and elections to the House of Representatives are normally conducted in a free and democratic manner. The economy, mainly based on the free-market principle, is relatively stable and in the main supported by the tourist and services industries.

There are, however, other issues that may be considered as indigenous as they are controversial and that often lead to protracted polemics. For example, while the Maltese are known to be proud homeowners, the state of the environment in a number of locations leaves much to be desired. People's houses and apartments are generally very well kept, and one can find in them all the amenities that go with a comfortable lifestyle. Yet there seems to be a general lack of interest in keeping public places, like the countryside, beaches, historical buildings, and building sites, in a good state of maintenance. Efforts by the government, NGOs, and public-conscious individuals to improve the situation are often thwarted by careless and indifferent persons.

The small size of the country also contributes to a number of distinguishing features. Notwithstanding the short distances involved in going from one place to another, driving along Malta's roads can become a daunting experience. The number of cars on the road and the state of some of the roads are two alarming factors. A 7-minute walk can easily become a 20-minute drive if one decides to use one's car instead.

As already pointed out, Malta can boast of a number of architectural gems dating from a very early age. With the fast development of the construction industry in terms of housing, tourism, entertainment, and industrial estates, Malta's skyline and land surface have become a mosaic of contrasting shapes and colors. The Millennium Tower at St. Julian's overlooks one of the most pleasant and popular fishing villages; a block of concrete high-rise apartments may be found sitting next to a row of traditional Maltese stone houses; and a spacious bungalow, with swimming pool and maybe tennis court, is not an uncommon sight right in the middle of a wide, flat area of the countryside. In short, one ends up feeling sorry for the Malta Environment and Planning Authority and its enforcement officers in their effort to preserve Malta's geographical features.

Yet the number of foreign visitors who throng the Maltese islands throughout the year, and particularly during spring and summer, is also in itself a phenomenon. The latest figures published in 2002 by the National Statistics Office indicate that an average of 1 million tourists visit Malta annually. This is a figure equivalent to almost three times the resident population, and it is a figure that sometimes worries entrepreneurs because of periodic downward trends. Tourists from all over the world travel to Malta because they find in it an island of culture, hospitality, a warm climate, and a safe environment. The vast majority of Maltese, who pride themselves on their language, can also communicate in English. Italian, French, and German are also spoken fairly widely.

The history of Malta goes back to the Stone Age. Neolithic and megalithic remains, many of which symbolize fertility and life, testify to the inhabitation of the islands since the third millennium B.C. The first known colonizers were the Phoenicians, who, around 800 B.C., had already introduced their alphabet and taught the people how to build and repair ships. They were followed by the Carthaginians in about 500 B.C. Around 200 years later, Malta became a *municipium* of the Roman Empire. For over a thousand years (218 B.C. to 870 A.D.), the Romans ruled over Malta. During this epoch the Maltese were introduced to Christianity, and they still make reference to the account of St. Paul's shipwreck on the island in the year 60 A.D., as illustrated in the Acts of the Apostles. They also lived through their first experience of having to identify closely with the ruling power's culture.

The end of the Roman era was followed by 200 years of Arab occupation (870 A.D. to 1090 A.D.). Consequently, the island of Malta was introduced to a new way of life, a new religion, and a new language. Notwithstanding the relatively short period of Arab rule when compared to the Roman times, the basic elements of the Maltese language today are still significantly rooted in Arabic.

In 1090, the king of Sicily, Count Roger of Normandy, freed the islands from Arab domination. The islands were also freed from the Islamic culture, and Christianity flourished again. A new turn in the cultural orientation of Malta also took place at this time. The link with the North African region was almost completely severed, and links with Europe started to grow roots. The unification of Malta with Sicily, through the successive passage from one feudal lord to another, came to an end in 1530. The island was then ceded to the Knights of St. John by Emperor Charles V of Spain.

When the Knights arrived in Malta, they were received with mixed feelings. The common people looked upon them as protectors against corsair attacks, while the notables felt betrayed by the cession of the island as engineered by the viceroy of Sicily. The Knights, however, settled down to what was later defined as the most glorious period of Maltese history. Their popularity reached its climax following the triumph registered at the expense of the invading Turks in their 1565 siege of Malta. The "Great Siege" led to an era of prosperity as the Knights lavished extravagant attention on the island by building a new capital city and other architectural gems in the form of *auberges*. This was later to become the downfall of both the Maltese and the Knights themselves. The finances of the order were reduced to a precarious position, unemployment became rife, poverty was widespread—and, in the meantime, the Knights were engaging in activities far removed from their monastic vows. Concurrent with this decline, Napoléon had been gradually confiscating the property of the Knights that lay in France. His plans to capture Malta were subsequently realized in 1798.

The French soon imposed their own form of government. Although they immediately set about introducing a primary education program and an adult education program, the university was suppressed, the church was divested of almost all of its treasures, and the *auberges* and other buildings were stripped of everything of value. This behavior subsequently sowed a climate of rebellion among the people. It also sowed a new sense of identity and patriotism. Unable to get rid of their oppressors, the Maltese sought the help of Admiral Nelson and the British fleet for protection.

The British effectively took over in 1800, ending a short two-year period of French rule. With the Treaty of Paris, Malta became a British colony in 1819. The return to a fortress status was soon established when the British Mediterranean fleet made Malta its official headquarters in 1827. With the opening of the Suez Canal in 1869, Malta also became a major landmark on the way to Asia. This event turned Malta's location into a shipping, trading, and military base.

The Maltese and the British forged a relationship that lasted for over 160 years and still figures prominently in Malta's present society. The two countries lived together through the experiences of the two world wars (1914–18 and 1940–45). The British colonial administration was alternately considered, on the one hand, a blessing to the development of the Maltese economy and its political structure, and on the other, a domineering and arrogant colonizer. Throughout most of the nineteenth and early twentieth centuries, the social condition of the population was very poor and politically degrading. However, significant progress was registered in the development of democratic processes and in the field of education. These were also interspersed with periodical breakdowns of good relations because of the opposing aspirations that emanate from the status of the colonized and the colonizing agent, respectively. Because of their lasting and still pervasive effects in Maltese social and political life, some events deserve mention: the fluctuation between support and opposition shown reciprocally between the British government and the Catholic Church in Malta; the suppressive behavior of the British military during the *Sette Giugno* (seventh of June) 1919 riots; the undisputed effect of the British language and way of life on the Maltese in terms of the island's immersion in a Western-inspired culture; and, finally, the political and economic battles fought, both diplomatically and less so at times, in 1964 in connection with Malta's independence within the British Commonwealth, and in 1979 in connection with the departure of British forces from the island.

Throughout the 38 years of independence, Maltese society carried forward most of the characteristics that were identified by its historical development. A number of battles were fought between 1972 and 1987. For example, the Maltese were witnesses to "the battle of the economy," which began to depend heavily on government; "the battle of social welfare," which was institutionalized; the closure of the British military base; and "the battle of the church schools" through the discontinuation of capitation grants (1978) and the freezing of school fees (1981).

The late 1980s and the 1990s were marked by a drastic change in the political and economic life of the Maltese. The last event of major significance for the people occurred in 1990, namely the adoption of a market-oriented economy linked with Malta's application to join the European Union.

At the turn of the century, Malta finds itself engaged in an ongoing, often partisan debate on its accession process to European Union membership. Malta's application was frozen in 1996 with a change in government and then reactivated in 1998. At the moment, the focus of Malta's political future lies with the people's choice at a referendum in connection with the EU issue and at the next general election.

TYPICAL DAY

As in most countries, teenage life in Malta is regulated by a variety of factors, among which one can mention the age factor, the seasonal factor, and the socialization factor. Early teen life (13 to 16) is characterized mainly by the parameters of the education system. Education in Malta is compulsory up to the age of 16 unless a special exemption is granted by the Education Division. During the scholastic year, which runs between September and June, teenagers in Malta start their day by preparing to go to school. School transportation, starting as early as seven in the morning, is available to most schools, and although distances are very short on the island, most students make use of this service, which is provided for free in state schools. Students attending church schools are expected to give a donation, and those attending private schools pay both school and transportation fees. As a general rule, the day at school ends in the early afternoon at around half past two. Although the number of working parents or guardians is on the increase, on returning home the majority of schoolchildren find one of their parents at home with a meal on the table. After a short break, young teenagers would probably do one of many things, such as homework, going to private lessons in one or more subjects, or attending extracurricular activities, such as ballet, music, drama, or sports. Later in the day, they may watch TV, pass some time playing computer games, or even go to the local youth center, where available. However, there are also some young people whose life appears to be less idyllic because they are required to work in order to contribute to the family or required to care for a sick or elderly member of the family. These kids often miss out on the carefree period of early adolescence.

The picture, in most cases, changes completely during the weekend. A considerable number of young teens are known to spend a good number of hours during the end of the week in outdoor activities. These would include sports activities, going to the cinema, participating in youth organizations, hiking, going to the library, or congregating at particular spots with their friends. It must be pointed out, however, that there are also young boys and girls who have to attend to their family's needs by, for example, helping in the home or business, whether this is a sales outlet or, as happens in some villages, in the agricultural sector.

Toward the end of the scholastic year (around May and June), most young teenagers are occupied with the necessary preparations for the end-of-year examinations. Now the pattern changes to a significant degree. Most of the days are taken up by studies, but, since the weather at this time of the year changes to longer hours of sunlight and the temperatures soar to the higher 20s in degrees Celsius, study periods may be interspersed with visits to the seaside or to late evenings and nights out. As summer holidays take over, these last two activities become very popular, and outdoor life takes over until the end of August. There are, however, a number of schoolchildren who for reasons both social and economic cannot enjoy outdoor life as much as others. There exists a distinction in the pattern of a typical day's routine between urban and rural life. And there are also some teenagers who do not follow any pattern at all and spend a considerable number of hours "doing nothing."

In the case of the late teens (17 to 19), some changes in the typical day described above do occur. At this age, most of the young people are engaged in further studies at higher secondary schools or college, or in part-time or full-time employment. In this category, one can easily distinguish between those who opt to enrich their academic record and those who prefer to start earning a living. While those who are still in school tend to carry forward the routine they had followed earlier, with the difference that timetables are now more flexible, employed young people are known to spend their nonwork time either attending evening adult classes or engaging in a variety of activities, such as playing sports; going to band clubs, political groups, social clubs, or fitness centers; or spending evenings out. Their spending capacity encourages a different lifestyle. They then move away from adult-supervised entertainment and leisure to a more consumer-oriented leisure pattern, centering around bars, clubs, and nightspots.

The problem of unemployed youth is on the increase. This category of young people very often finds itself totally dependent on the hope that this period is cut short. A considerable number, though, take the opportunity to attend work-related training programs organized by the Employment and Training Corporation.

FAMILY LIFE

The family has a central place in Maltese society. The sociological literature gives compelling evidence of the strength and stability of the Maltese family. Church-related pastoral studies, however, express concern over the family's rapid transformation under the influence of foreign and local social change. This transformation naturally impacts on the life world of young people in Malta as well as that of other generations. The traditional values of the Maltese nuclear family have been affected by the many socioeconomic changes that have marked Maltese society since the war. Some clear examples of this are the shrinking size of the Maltese family, a change in traditional gender roles, and the democratization of parent-child relationships.

Despite this, the unity of the family is a value strongly upheld in Maltese society. Relationships with extended family members remain strong, even though with the increasing pressures of modern life, family members are required to spend more time away from home. Most Maltese families are very close-knit, and this serves as an important social-control function, especially with regard to adolescent behavior. The family in Malta remains a major social institution with an impact on young people's lives and an important form of social control. With regard to adolescent behavior, this means that young people in Malta remain very concerned about their families and what they think of them long after they have come of age. Many Maltese people continue to meet with their family members on a daily basis, even though they are no longer living in the same house. Parents and siblings continue to play a major role in the life of the young person after that person has formed his or her family. Many young adults continue to live with their family of origin long after they have come of age. The family tops the list of priorities for what people in Malta find important in life, followed by work, religion, leisure, friends, and politics.

In Malta, both men and women attach great importance to the family. In recent years the nature of work and the way it is distributed between the genders has changed dramatically across many European countries, including Malta, although to a somewhat lesser extent. While women have started to gain employment outside the home, they still lag consistently behind men both in terms of numbers and status of employment. This is once again related to the great importance attached to family life and the traditional role of women as caretakers. An analysis of census data in the mid-1990s reports that 26 percent of all working-age women, in contrast to 74 percent of working-age men, have full-time employment. This difference is considerably less among the younger generation. In fact, the largest percentage of women working outside the home are the under-20s. Full-time employment falls sharply for women in their mid-20s and continues to fall thereafter, probably because once women have children they no longer retain full-time employment. Directly related to different participation rates in the labor market is the fact that women are underrepresented in almost all major occupations.

Traditionally, expectations for the genders have been different. Young women were expected to work until they had children. Once they had children, it was felt that the children should come first, and most women abandoned their jobs. With such short career prospects, investment in terms of preparing for a career was much less likely for girls than for boys. Boys, on the other hand, were expected to make long-term decisions about education and training for a career. However, this trend would appear to be changing with the increasing numbers of young women entering higher education. While in 1997, 50.8 percent of the student population at the University of Malta was female; in 2002, this percentage rose to 56.2 (University of Malta, 2002). With increased investment in their education, young women may, in the near future, find it less attractive to relinquish their working role and their investments in career in order to take on the role of homemaker. Thus the Maltese family is becoming less patriarchal and more democratic, with young people at the forefront of such social change. Social class is another source of difference among young people in Malta. Traditional gender roles are more predominant in the lower than in the middle classes as the level of educational investment increases.

In a national youth-values study, respondents were asked about their priorities in life. Most young people gave great importance to the family, their boyfriend or girlfriend, leisure, and work. The overriding importance young people attach to their partner and the family suggests that the traditional patterns of marriage and a family-centered life are still alive with the younger generation. Marriage thus remains one of the primary goals of young people in Malta, but with the breakdown of more traditional gender roles the family is becoming more democratic and less patriarchal. Recent changes in family law have also contributed to this development.

FOOD

The food consumed in any one country is often a reflection of the cultural identity of the people of that country. Malta is no exception. The blending of the old and the new, the traditional and nontraditional, is common in all aspects of Maltese life, and food is certainly no exception.

Maltese gastronomy is a fascinating blend of influences that reflects Malta's location and history. Primarily Italian in character, Maltese cuisine also borrows extensively from the kitchens of North Africa and the eastern Mediterranean. Over the centuries, all of these distinct components have been integrated into a uniquely wholesome and flavorful mélange.

Naturally there is bound to be a difference in the food-consumption patterns of the different generations. Maltese cuisine is the offspring of a long relationship between the indigenous people of the island and the foreign domination over the centuries. Although Malta is now an independent republic, the influences from other countries, especially the industrialized West, are very strong. Thus young people in Malta are as likely as other Europeans to be eating in fast-food restaurants like McDonald's, Burger King, and KFC, several branches of which have, in the last six years, sprung up all over the island. The fast pace of many young people's life makes fast food an attractive option to them. In Malta, in this respect, once again one finds an interesting mélange of the old and the new. One may find a McDonald's outlet next door to a traditional *pastizzi* outlet, and both may be equally popular with local youth. *Pastizzi*, probably Turkish in origin, are small boat-shaped delicacies of ricotta cheese and egg wrapped with thin crisp pastry, something between phyllo and puff. *Pastizzi* may also be filled with peas or anchovies. They are sold on street corners and village bars. It is rather common that after a night of clubbing, young people will, in the early hours of morning, join the farmers and fishermen having their *pastizzi* before they go off for their day's work. However, one is as likely to find them in all-night cafés and fast-food outlets like McDonald's and Burger King, which remain open until early morning. Thus, while young people are out and about they are likely to be eating junk food. However, since family ties are strong and Maltese housewives pride themselves on feeding their family well, Maltese youth are likely to be eating traditional food also.

Pastry of all kinds is used to encase vegetables, cheese, fish, meat, pasta, and rice. *Timpana*, an everyday concoction of pasta in a meat sauce topped with a layer of pastry, is very popular, as is *lampuki* pie, which is filleted dorado mixed with spinach and cauliflower in a short crust pastry.

An ice cream van in Malta. Courtesy of Giuseppe Costanza.

Spinach and anchovy pies are also very popular. Stewed and stuffed dishes are also an important feature of Maltese cuisine—for example, stuffed cuttlefish in spicy tomato sauce, stewed rabbit cooked in wine and herbs, and *bragioli*, that is, parcels of mince, eggs, and breadcrumbs wrapped in thin sheets of beef. There are many restaurants that specialize in Maltese food, and these are popular with young adults rather than teens. A very popular night out is a *fenkata*, where young people meet in special restaurants and eat rabbit.

Seasonal salads and vegetables are an important feature of the Maltese kitchen. The best-loved and most healthy dish is probably *minestra*, a thick vegetable soup combining numerous fresh and dried vegetables, served with fresh or grated *gbejniet*—sheep or goat cheese. With the advent of summer, the variety of locally caught fish increases. Swordfish is very popular and is often used for barbeques.

During the summer, when each village commemorates the feast of its patron saint with a pyrotechnic display, elaborate gilded stalls sell unusual sweets such as deep-fried date-filled pastries (*imqaret*), treacle rings, and nougat made with sugar and nuts. These are popular with young and old alike.

The process of globalization has also reached Maltese shores, and one may indulge in a variety of exotic foods from all over the world. Particular favorites are Chinese restaurants, which abound, and American diners. However, one may also find Indian, Malaysian, Thai, and Mexican restaurants. Alternative eating habits are also gaining more ground. For example, vegetarianism is becoming more popular among young people on the Maltese islands.

SCHOOLING

Education in Malta is compulsory up to the age of 16. There are a variety of schools available: playschools (age 1–3), kindergarten schools (3–5), primary schools (6–11), secondary schools (11–16), postsecondary schools (16–18/19), college, adult evening courses, and the University of the Third Age (over 60s).

Primary schools are found in every town and village, while secondary schools are spread out in a number of catchment areas. There are four sixth form colleges (postsecondary), one state and three church/private ones, and one university.

Early teens who attend secondary schools can find themselves in modern buildings with spacious classrooms, fully equipped science laboratories, a library, a drama center, a school hall, and large playgrounds.

Others may be working in a less pleasant environment, since some of the schools they attend had been built a number of years ago and the refurbishing process may not have been yet completed. All schools are equipped with computer rooms at the rate of one computer for every five or six students.

State schools are open to all and are free of charge. There are, however, common entry requirements for all secondary schools, state, church, and private. The latest development within the education system of Malta is the introduction of the National Minimum Curriculum, which has as its motto "Creating the Future Together."

Although there are different approaches to schooling, the educational vision of Malta's schools is one that, according to the Ministry of Education, "promotes fundamental values," "facilitates [students'] holistic development," and "motivates them and prepares them to be lifelong learners" (1999). However, the economic situation of the family is known to influence the placement of a child within the educational system. The integration of children with special needs into the mainstream has also become a common practice, although severely disabled children do attend special schools.

With the exception of primary schools and two private secondary schools, schools in Malta are single-sex. Most of them require the wearing of a uniform, and discipline is generally well kept. Coeducation and the wearing of casual dress is permitted in postsecondary schools. Another distinction that can be made at this stage is that there are formal classes for early teens, while there are lectures and tutorials for those above the age of 16.

A school day is normally divided between formal classes and extracurricular activities, with emphasis being given to the former. As students move up to higher classes, then one may notice a decrease in extracurricular activities because of the pending matriculation examinations. In this respect, it must be stated that certification is still a predominant issue within Maltese society, and so one finds that homework is given much importance and that private lessons, after school hours, also take center stage within a competitive ethos. End-of-year examinations together with continuous assessment is one of the means used to grade students before the end of their secondary school period. At the end of this period, then, one finds that higher education institutions require a stipulated number of passes in matriculation ordinary-level and/or or advanced-level examinations, depending on the individual's choice of course of study.

Between the age of 13 and 16, Maltese young people attend secondary schools. After that period, the majority move on to postsecondary schools and then to universities or to the newly established vocational college, if they are successful at the matriculation examination. There are a number of alternatives for those who fail to make it at the first attempt, and consequently one finds that young people in Malta make extensive use of extended educational programs.

Teachers in most schools are trained at the University of Malta. There are also those who have entered the teaching profession as instructors or facilitators after having followed special part-time courses organized by the Education Division in conjunction with the university. All teachers require a warrant, which is awarded after successful completion of a full-time training course or after completing a number of years of teaching at the end of a part-time course. At the end of each scholastic year, all teachers are required to attend an in-service training course.

Formal education in Malta is also complemented by the professional training of youth and community workers at the Programme of Youth Studies at the University of Malta. Informal and nonformal education is considered an essential feature of the education system, and, progressively, one can witness the introduction of this type of education in a number of institutions, both governmental and nongovernmental, which provide for the personal, social, and political education of young people.

SOCIAL LIFE, RECREATION, AND ENTERTAINMENT

Over the past few years there has been a significant increase in the importance of leisure. In relation to young people, leisure has most often come to signify entertainment based on consumption. This holds for youth in Malta in the new millennium. The traditional festive culture in Malta has been given a new dimension by the emergent materialistic and consumerist lifestyles and the diffusion of a tourist way of life. Naturally, because leisure is often based on consumption, there are inevitable differences in leisure patterns, resulting from structural inequalities inherent in Maltese society. Perhaps these inequalities are most evident in terms of gender and class, with leisure opportunities more available for males and those of a higher socioeconomic status.

In Malta one may find diverse entertainment venues catering mainly to the young. Maltese young people are generally very hip, that is, up to date on the latest fashions, music and dance styles, and other trends. Many clubs boast "Ibiza-style" open-air dance floors with parties continuing through the early hours of the morning. Although in recent years there has been much media panic about the effect of such parties on young people, with particular emphasis on drug abuse at such venues, the party scene is still as strong as ever, especially during the summer months, when parties hosting internationally acclaimed DJs abound. The dance scene is not the only scene with strong following for young people in Malta. One may also find rock clubs, jazz clubs, and (rather popular in the last three years) Latino clubs. Higher spending power, greater mobility, and a considerable increase in privately owned cars coupled with a need for a good time and relaxation of the formerly more restrictive religious morality have all had an impact on the new leisure patterns and lifestyles in Malta. Many young people in Malta exhibit a willingness to pay for their entertainment (even though there are differences in the capacity to do so). However, one must not assume that young people in Malta only engage in consumerist social-life experiences. According to a survey by Abela in the 1990s, young people go out very often for their leisure. However, many are members of an association, group, or social organization. Most popular, in descending order of importance, is membership in sports, religious, social, cultural, ecological, and, least of all, political organizations. Abela also highlights that most young people belong to mixed groups and meet their friends on a regular basis.

In recent years the most popular entertainment venue is Paceville, an area that has grown as an extension of St. Julian's, a seaside village. This area is a hub of activity—discotheques, bars, restaurants, cinema complexes, and open-air venues are built almost side by side. Although young people are prohibited by law from purchasing alcohol or tobacco before the age of 16, many of these places of entertainment are, in the early evening, frequented by younger teens, and therefore one finds that these substances are in fact consumed by these young people. In fact, recent results from the European School Survey Project on Alcohol and Other Drugs (ESPAD) (Bezzina, Borg, & Clark, 1995) indicate that the consumption of alcohol is predominant among teenagers in Malta. It is easily available both at home and in public places. Alcohol is not primarily viewed as a drug but rather as a social lubricant. In Maltese society alcohol is used extensively on social occasions and is often served at the family table during meals. An updated report of 1998, in fact, concludes that Maltese young people are being socialized into a culture in which alcohol plays an intrinsic role.

In the past the Maltese had a very strong religious morality, but the process of secularization is resulting in the declining significance of religious institutions, especially among the younger generation. The youth of Malta thus have a more liberal morality than did their forefathers, especially with regard to sexuality. Over the last decade the Maltese have become more accepting of different sexual orientations and behavior, but compared to their European counterparts, their sexual standards may still be considered strict. Abela concludes that young people in Malta "are more inclined to hold liberal views on issues related to their immediate needs and practices like contraception, pre-marital sex and life-long fidelity in marriage, but tend to be more restrictive on issues that seem removed from their present concerns." In fact, it is in the arena of sexual attitudes that there is greatest divergence between the generations. Young people seem to agree with their parents with regard to political views, religious attitudes, and moral standards, but are more liberal with regard to sexual matters.

A number of studies carried out in Malta and its sister island, Gozo, indicate that young people attach importance to leisure time as distinct from free time. Free time is considered to be that time when they can do whatever they like, be it following a hobby, just relaxing, or being free from school or work duties. Leisure time is seen as being congruous with entertainment through activities such as being with friends, listening to music, or practicing a particular sport. It is not easy, however, to distinguish between the two, since both free time and leisure time are means of recreation, that is, a time during which one usually takes a break from the normal routine. As stated earlier, the age of the young person, his or her status (whether still at school or in employment), and the time of the week and year play an important role in the choice of activity one engages in.

Malta can boast of a number of locations where sports activities can be pursued. There are three to four large sports complexes of international standard, and Malta has, on more than one occasion, hosted the Small Nations Games and the FISEC games for schoolchildren with huge success. Football (soccer), track, basketball, volleyball, and "leisure center" activities are very popular with both boys and girls. In summer, competitive water polo and going to the beach are taken up in earnest by many youngsters. One must also mention that indoor activities like badminton, bowling, gymnastics, dancing, martial arts, and chess are played throughout the year. Other activities of a more selective nature, because of the expensive equipment required and the high membership fees charged, include horse riding, archery, and polo. One sport, which has been the subject of controversy among sportsmen, environmentalists, and even politicians, is bird hunting and trapping. This activity is very popular with Maltese of all ages, and there seems to be a family tradition where teenage boys are almost encouraged to take up their father's hobby. Girls do not, as yet, seem to entertain such a hobby. The controversy rages about the duration of the shooting season and which species of birds should or should not be targeted.

Without much doubt the two most popular sports among kids are football and track in winter and water polo is summer. Large crowds, including many young boys and girls, attend league games, and their support for their favorite team is very energetic and vociferous.

However, not all teenagers in Malta participate in sports activities. One can distinguish between those who consider recreation time to be a time when one could be a physically active participant and those who prefer to be either less active or even passive, in activities such as going to the cinema, reading, watching television, using PlayStations, or even attending game rooms in popular entertainment centers. What is certain is that there is no significant form of discrimination or separation between boys and girls in any one of the activities mentioned above, apart from particular games such as netball, which is predominantly a girls' game. What some time ago used to be considered male-dominated sports have practically disappeared from the Maltese scenario. Just to stress the point, both boys and girls engage in sports such as judo, wrestling, boxing and kickboxing, hockey, and rugby.

Perhaps it is to the credit of Malta's education system that recreation time is given so much importance. Almost all schools have their own teams, and various games and competitions are held throughout the scholastic year. The Education Division, through the Department of Youth and Sport, also organizes weekend activities for all young people free of charge. "Skolasport" is one such activity that incorporates all kinds of sport, from swimming to gymnastics to aerobics to track, for all ages and with the participation of parents and guardians, who prefer to be active while their offspring are in action. Another organized activity gaining popularity with young people is that of cultural tours throughout the islands of Malta and Gozo during the winter weekends.

But recreation time means different things to different people. As young teens grow in age, one can notice that changes occur in terms of interests and attitudes. While the majority of young teens often prefer organized activities, as they grow older they opt for more casual forms of recreation. In this respect, one therefore notices that the older Maltese teenagers, while many of them still practice some form of sport, tend to change their idea of free time more to one of socializing than competing. That is, more time may now be devoted to other forms of activity that one would describe as entertainment rather than recreation. This is not to make a clear distinction, but more to point out that there is another world of recreational activity than sports. Going out with friends, dancing, dining, hiking, and hanging out become the more popular forms of entertainment. Attendance at youth centers diminishes, boys' and girls' outings become mixed-sex activities, and campaigns for or against a particular social issue are organized by mixed groups of young people from all forms of socioeconomic background.

Teenagers' interest in recreational and entertainment activities has, throughout the years, contributed to the development of a social and economic domain of some importance. The state, church, and business community have all become aware of the importance of making provision for young people's need to let off steam. While the state looks at the social aspect of the issue and the business community sees the opportunity for investing its financial capital wisely, the church tries to strike a balance between the educational and moral side of the situation. All three—the state, church, and business communities—speak of the importance of safe and healthy lifestyles, and all three attempt to make adequate provisions. In terms of glamour, attraction, and convenience, the business community comes out as the winner, while in terms of popular support it is the state that makes the most of the prevalent interests. The church cannot compete financially, and one reason why youth centers are becoming less and less popular is that they are mainly run by the church. The time limits imposed and the voluntary nature of the management process are its two biggest enemies. This means that young people's choice of recreation and entertainment, outside their home and school, is circumscribed by a number of divergent options. The lack of alternative leisure activities, the danger of misuse of substances, dress codes, time limits, excessive costs, and the occasional misdemeanors of young adults are some of the issues that create reactions of concern among adults and that surround young people's recreation and entertainment scenarios in Malta.

RELIGIOUS PRACTICES AND CULTURAL CEREMONIES

Malta's deeply rooted religious imprint continues to be evidenced by the fact that almost all Maltese are baptized in the Catholic Church immediately after birth. Thus the attachment of the Maltese to their religious heritage continues to be visible. Most people in Malta are brought up in a religious environment and from an early age are socialized into the values of the Catholic Church. Regular religious activities include going to mass (obligatory on a Sunday), saying prayers before meals and before going to bed, saying the rosary as a family, and going to communion and confession at least once a week. When children are 6 years old they start attending doctrine classes, which last until they are 11. These classes prepare them for their first communion and confirmation. Many young people become members of church groups and associations, and often the local youth center is housed within the parish buildings. However, the process of secularization has left an effect on the religiosity of Maltese young people. Industrialization, the housing boom, tourism, and the introduction of various forms of new media have brought about this process.

According to Ganado (1974–77), religion has been given a harsh blow. Over the past 30 years, young-adult attendance for Sunday mass dropped from 73 percent in 1967 to 56 percent in 1980 and 50 percent in 1995. The expression of Catholic identity among young people in Malta is certainly changing, and homogeneity is a thing of the past. While most young Catholics in Malta start from a common origin of a strong Catholic upbringing, many then take separate pathways influenced by the process of secularization.

However, one can also witness young people's interest in their respective village religious feasts, commonly known as *il-festa tar-rahal*. A recent study conducted by Abela and Cutajar (2002) shows that a significant number of young people participate actively both in the preparations required for the organization of the *festa* and also during the actual outdoor (social) and indoor (religious) activities, with more enthusiasm being shown toward the outdoor celebrations. Teenagers are at the forefront of putting up decorations within the church building and along the main streets of their village. Preparations start soon after the end of each annual *festa*. Others are involved in the manufacture of fireworks, which has now become a matter of great concern in terms of safety regulations. Although the manufacture of fireworks requires a license, which imposes both age limits and proficiency in pyrotechnics, it is not unknown that some young people are, in fact, breaking the law. Quite a few tragic accidents have occurred throughout the years.

CONCLUSION

In his introduction to *Maltese Society: A Sociological Inquiry* (Sultana & Baldacchino, 1994), sociologist Anthony Giddens describes the changes occurring under the impact of globalization as "a tangled web of tradition and modernity." Malta, that is, the Maltese Islands, is "part of a wider global society and the influence of the wider global order appears almost everywhere." In this respect, the traditional and transformational features of Maltese society can be located in its long experiences of dependence and the new, closer relationships with the people of the West in particular. Its geographical position and its small size have, respectively, contributed to multicultural and multireligious influences and to particular social features that constitute those particularities that make Maltese society what it is.

As has been shown in the previous sections, teen life in Malta can be seen as a reflection of the baggage of social, economic, and political experiences and changes that have molded Maltese society. Teenagers still show symptoms of traditional values, modern perceptions, and postmodern expectations. Family and religious values are rooted deeply in their overall behavior, economic stability and comfortable living are essential elements in their life course, and individualistic traits are shown in their attitudes toward religion, work, education, and current social issues. Although the specifics of the Mediterranean culture are still prevalent, young people are seen to be adapting easily to today's trends of mobility, lifelong learning, and "choice" rather than "linear" biographies.

Teenage life in Malta is not much different from that in other Western countries. However, the history, location, size, and climate of the island clearly contribute to making young people's lives in Malta particular and worldly-wise at one and the same time.

RESOURCE GUIDE

Nonfiction

Abela, A. (1991), *Transmitting Values in European Malta: A Study in the Contemporary Values of Modern Society*, Malta, Jesuit Publications.

Abela, A. (1994), *Shifting Family Values in Malta: A Western European Perspective*, Malta, Media Centre.

Abela, A. (1998), *Secularize Sexuality: Youth Values in a City Island*, Valletta, Malta, Social Values Studies.

Abela, A. (2000), *Values of Women and Men in the Maltese Islands: A Comparative European Perspective*, Malta, Ministry of Social Policy, Commission for the Advancement of Women.

Abela, A. (2001), *Youth Participation in Voluntary Organizations in Malta: A Comparative Analysis of European Values Studies*, Malta, Parliamentary Secretariat, Ministry of Education.

Abela, J., & Cutajar, D. (2002), *Young People and the Village Festa*, unpublished B.A. (Youth and Community Studies) dissertation, University of Malta.

Azzopardi, A. E. (1998), *Young People in Gozo: A Study*, Gozo, Malta, OASI Publication.

Azzopardi, A. E., Furlong, A., & Stadler, B. (2000), *Vulnerable Youth*, Strasbourg, Council of Europe Publishing.

Bezzina, C., Borg, M., & Clark, M. (1995), *ESPAD National Report*, Malta, Sedqa.

Boissevain, J. (1969), *Hal-Farrug: A Village in Malta*, New York, Holt, Reinhart & Winston.

Galea, A.M. (1998), *Young People's Perception of Entertainment*, unpublished research project (Youth Studies), University of Malta.

Ganado, H. (1974–77), *Rajt Malta Tinbidel*, vols. 1–4, Malta, Il-Hajja.

Ministry of Education (1999), *Creating the Future Together*, Malta, Klabb Kotba Maltin.

Pace, L. (2000), *Vegetarianism among Young People*, unpublished research project, (Youth Studies), University of Malta.

Sultana, R., & Baldacchino, G. (eds.) (1994), *Maltese Society: A Sociological Inquiry*, Malta, Mireva Publications.

Tabone, C. (1987), *The Secularization of the Family in Changing Malta*, Malta, Dominican Publication.

Tabone, C. (1995), *Maltese Families in Transition: A Sociological Investigation*, Malta, Ministry for Social Development.

Tonna, B. (1993), *Malta Trends 1993: The Signs of the Times*, Malta, Media Centre.

Tonna, B. (1994), *Malta Trends: A Report on the Signs of the Times for 1994*, Malta, Media Centre.

University of Malta (2002), *Guide to Higher Education in Malta: Handbook*, Malta, Publishers Enterprises Group (PEG) Ltd.

Vella, A.P. (1979), *Storja ta'Malta*, Malta, Klabb Kotba Maltin.

Zammit, E.L. (1984), *A Colonial Inheritance: Maltese Perceptions of Work, Power and Class Structure with Reference to the Labour Movement*, Malta, Malta University Press.

Zammit Mangion, J. (1992), *Education in Malta*, Malta, Studio Editions.

Web Sites

http://www.booksaboutmalta.com/

http://www.guidegozo.com/

http://www.insightmalta.com/

http://www.maltaonline.com/

Pen Pal Information

http://www.mylanguageexchange.com/Search-pen-pals.asp?selCountry=Malta

Chapter 8

THE NETHERLANDS

Wiel Veuglers and Amanda Kluveld

INTRODUCTION

The Netherlands is a rather small country in the northwestern part of Europe on the North Sea. The Netherlands became an independent state in the seventeenth century. In that period, called the "golden century," the Netherlands was an important trader and explorer of the world. Peter Stuyvesant founded New York, and in Lower Manhattan you still can find a few Dutch houses. The Dutch sailed over all seas and were ruling at that time in most parts of the oceans. The Dutch traded everything from tobacco to minerals, but also slaves from Africa to America. In the seventeenth century the Netherlands, in particular the western part, Holland, experienced a global era that attracted many travelers and refugees. The now famous canals and their typical houses were built. Cultural life was vividly portrayed in particular by painters such as Rembrandt and Frans Hals.

The creation of the Netherlands was the result of a war between Spanish and Dutch troops. This war was, moreover, a religious confrontation between the Catholic Spanish and the Protestant Dutch. The Dutch liberation had been led by William of Orange, and his family is still the royal family in the Netherlands. The territory of the Netherlands extended to the northeast and to the south. Most of the people in the south were Catholic, and a part of that south joined Belgium in 1830. Half of the Netherlands lies below the sea level, with dikes protecting the land. A great part of that ground below sea level has been gained by imploding. The Netherlands has partly been created by men themselves.

The Netherlands is a modern country with 16 million people. Trading is still important for the economy. And despite the smaller influence of religious nowadays, the Netherlands is a mix of Protestant and Catholic culture: Protestant mainly in the northern part, Catholic in the southern part. The living standard in the Netherlands is high, and unemployment is low. The political arena shows a mix of liberal, social-democratic, and Christian parties. Together they have created a strong state, good social services, and a liberal cultural climate. The Netherlands still attracts a lot of travelers and people who want to live and work in the Netherlands. The number of immigrants has grown strongly in the past few decades. Inhabitants of our former colonies Indonesia, Suriname, and the Dutch Antilles came to live in the wealthier mainland of the old royalty. In the 1970s, we invited many workers from Morocco and Turkey to our land, to do our low-skilled jobs. Many foreigners want to live in the Netherlands. The combination of a liberal cultural climate and the good social ser-vices contributed to the attractiveness of the Netherlands for people who wanted and still want to escape the political, cultural, and economic life in their own country.

The Netherlands has always been a member of the European Community. Recently we changed our currency, the guilder, into the euro.

Like in most Western countries, the proportion of youngsters is dimin-ishing. Almost 5 million of the 16 million inhabitants are under the age of 25. These young people make up 30 percent of the population. One generation ago they still made up nearly half of the total population. The decrease of the number of births and the increase in life expectancy caused the decline of the proportion of youngsters. Immigration has, however, slowed the decrease in the proportion of youngsters somewhat; 21 percent of youths under the age of 25 are immigrants and two-thirds of are non-Western immigrants.

Youngsters are an important social and cultural force. Adults realize that for sustaining society and for the individual welfare of the youngsters, youngsters should be educated and integrated in society well. According to the results of several research projects, most youngsters grow up with-out great problems, but for 10 to 15 percent this is not the case. Among them are many children of immigrants and low-skilled laborers. Despite the common feeling that youth are doing well, there is a growing concern about several tendencies in Dutch society:

An individualism that is becoming too utilitarian and less expressive
A lack of political interest among many youngsters
A decline in caring for others

A celebration of a hedonistic lifestyle, with a significant amount of
   drugs and alcohol
The growing use of violence

These developments are not unique to the Netherlands and are common
in most parts of the world, in particular in the Western world. We even
would say that these developments in the Netherlands are not stronger than
in many other countries, but we have to manage these developments too.

TYPICAL DAY

Dutch youngsters have to go to school until the age of 16, and even
after 16 many youngsters stay in school. At 18 students go to secondary
education. These schools are located in their own city or in their own
region. Most of the youngsters go on bike to school. The Netherlands is
flat, and sometimes they bike for 10 kilometers. Other youngsters travel by
public transportation like buses. Schools start around 8:30. Some students
drive cars when they are 18, but even then having a car is expensive.

After school they go home and combine free time and doing their
homework for school. On the average they have homework for 1.5 hour a
day, so students in the Netherlands have long working days, as their study
load is high. Officially they work 40 hours a week for school when they
are in the final classes of secondary education (16–18 years old). Many
of these youngsters have a part-time job, at an average of four hours a
week. They are, for example, assistants in supermarkets or distributors of
newspapers or commercial pamphlets. They have their dinner with their
parents early, between 6 and 7 p.m.

FAMILY LIFE

Although the number of family separations and single parents are
growing, most youngsters (86 percent) live in a family. Only eight percent
of couples with children are not married. Single-parent families climbed
from 8 percent in 1960 to 14 percent in 1998. The families became smaller,
however, with an average of 1.7 children in a family. Most youngsters
don't profit anymore from the benefits of growing up with many brothers
and sisters. They can't learn much from elder children or be mentors for
their smaller brothers and sisters. Their parents can concentrate on the
upbringing of only a few children. This moreover implies that they project
all their future plans on one or two children. The expectations parents
have of their children have risen enormously.

Family life has been changing too. Surprisingly, until recently not that many women were working outside the home in the Netherlands. But now they are catching up. However, a lot of them are working part-time. An interesting question is whether this has resulted in a growing participation of men in domestic work and in particular in caring for their children. Although a lot of Dutch men nowadays do shopping, cleaning, cooking, and caring for their children, women still do most of this work, and have, and feel, the primary responsibility for the management of family life and the upbringing of the children.

The relationship between parents and children has changed enormously. The Dutch sociologist Abram De Swaan speaks of a shift in families from a "relation of command" into "a relation of negotiations."[1] Children have their say in many family affairs; they debate with their parents and negotiate with them about the rules to follow. The relationship between parents and children became less hierarchical, and coercion has to some extent been replaced by dialogue. Children are very happy with this development. They think they have been taken more seriously. But at the same time, it demands a lot of them. They have to develop their own ideas, grounded in a well-balanced set of arguments; they have to communicate with their parents; and they have to accept the compromises in the agreements they make.

The changing relationships between parents and their children, becoming more horizontal, are visible in children addressing parents by their first names and by the age children leave home. In the 1970s children wanted to escape their family as soon as possible. The age that youngsters went to live by themselves sank strongly. Nowadays it has been rising again, in particular for boys. They leave home on the average at 23, girls at 21. The arguments for staying longer in the family are along the lines of "We may do at home what we want, our mum takes care of food and washing clothes, and we have a nice room by ourselves, often with all the modern electronic equipment."

Of course there are sometimes still conflicts between parents and children about curfews, motivation for school, the use and amount of alcohol and drugs, and more cultural-style-oriented expressions of clothes and music. Only a small number of youngsters have a socially risky lifestyle and are not "controlled" anymore by their parents.

FOOD

People in the Netherlands eat a lot of bread. A normal breakfast for youngsters consists of some slices of bread with cheese or peanut butter, together with a glass of milk. But besides these local favorites, many eat cornflakes or their healthy counterpart, muesli. For most youngsters, praying has been abandoned, sometimes replaced by watching MTV or another music channel. Often one of the parents is still at home when the kids leave for school.

Teens at lunchtime mostly eat slices of bread taken from home. School canteens don't offer meals to students, but they can buy snacks and candies. Bringing food from home saves money. Everyone knows the reputation of Dutch cheeses for being delicious and plentiful. The Netherlands manufactures many different and amazing cheeses. Older readers may remember a picture of Queen Beatrix dropping an entire herring down her throat, much to the delight of all the Dutch. She did this to open herring season. Fishing is a huge industry in the Netherlands, and Dutch herring is a delicacy. The correct way to eat a herring is to do what the queen did: tilt your head back, hold the entire fish by the tail, and drop it down your throat. Many were shocked when the queen was photographed eating this fish, but more felt she was making a strong statement about being part of her people.

SCHOOLING

Having a school diploma is very important for your future career. Research shows that in the Netherlands education has become even more important for success in your career. Although social class is still important in getting jobs, in particular by the networks it supports and the social and cultural capital appreciated in certain professional circles, education is a possibility to change one's life. Most youngsters are aware of the importance of a diploma; this doesn't imply, however, that they enjoy their schoolwork much.

In secondary education in the Netherlands there are different levels of education. The four most important are vocational education and the three levels of general education that prepare for a middle- or high-level vocational education or studies at a university. All four levels are of about equal size; The three levels of general education last four, five, and six years respectively. After that, most youngsters, in particular those coming from general education, continue their education at a higher vocational school or university.

In the first two years of secondary education, all students have the same subjects. Being a trade country and an internationally oriented country demands a high level of language teaching. All students start by learning English, French, and German (and of course their native language, Dutch).

More then 60 percent learn these languages for four or more years. Television, music, and computer games support the acquisition of English in particular. They also have classes in math, physics, science, chemistry, biology, information technology, and applied techniques. In the social domain they have history, geography, social studies, and religion. They also have arts and sports. Comparing with American education, in Dutch schools there are a lot of separate subjects, with mostly different teachers. Efforts to cluster specific sciences into general science have been blocked by the unions of the subjects' teachers and the universities. Students are confronted with many different subjects and teachers. For them school life is full of alternation, running to the next classroom with someone else teaching. In vocational education they choose a certain sector of economic life, for example construction, car engineering, plumber, nursing, trading, and so on. In general education they choose between four clusters of subjects: culture, economics, health, and techniques. All students in general education still have their four languages.

In international comparative studies Dutch students generally do very well, in particular with math, physics, and languages. Even though they study many subjects, their results for each of them are good. These good international results cannot, however, prevent public opinion from speaking about the low and still declining level of Dutch education. For youngsters it is frustrating that they have to work hard, concentrate on many subjects, and then still be accused of having intellectual weaknesses.

A few years ago the first author visited several U.S. schools. It is interesting to make more explicit comparisons between Dutch and U.S. schools:

In the Netherlands 70 percent of the schools are Catholic, Protestant, or based on a particular pedagogy like Montessori or Dalton. All the schools, however, besides religious education, have the same curriculum and are paid by the government. Students may choose the school they want to go to.

In U.S. schools students do more in the arts. In the Netherlands they do more academic work, in particular learning foreign languages.

Students have national exams at the end of secondary education for six subjects. When they pass this exam they can enter a university. Which academic studies they can do depends on the subjects. Universities don't have an assessment procedure for entering.

But this advantage has a particular disadvantage. The national exams
at the end of secondary school are considered so important that the
assessment uses more "objective" procedures like multiple-choice
than project work or essays. Also, the exams restrict the content
of the subject. It stimulates in students a calculated attitude of just
working for the exams. The exams produce an attitude that students are then blamed for themselves.

We spoke already about the four levels of secondary education.
Efforts to make Dutch education less selective (tracking) have
failed, and recently there is even an intensification of selective
procedures, an ideology legitimized by a concern for fulfilling
students' individual capacities and interests, but for students it is
more a question of selection than of choice.

Most schools in the Netherlands are quite safe places, but there is a
growing concern among teachers and parents about the growth of
bullying, the possession of knives, and fighting among students.
Schools want to be safer places; they first try to arrange this by
creating together with students a better school culture, but cam-
eras are becoming more normal and at some urban schools there
are now special security officers.

Dutch schools don't have great parking lots for their students.
Students may not drive until they are 18, and they often come
by bike.

Students in the Netherlands learn a lot, but they feel stressed by
the great expectations of their parents, the importance of a school certificate, the intensive study program, and the selection and tracking in
schools.

Modern society demands a lot of flexibility and self-regulation in all
domains of life. Education, and in particular secondary education, have
to prepare youngsters for this future role in society. The government has
started an educational policy to enhance self-regulated or independent
learning in schools. Students have to become responsible for their own
learning process. Most students like these new ideas about education, but
educational practice does not change that easily. The strongest obstacle is
the assessment structure. The Ministry of Education still wants to control
the output of education. Schools and students do not get the freedom to
determine what they want to learn and how. The paradox is that in educational discourse the student is seen as self-responsible and with many
choices, but in practice students have few choices, and self-responsibility
is more self-discipline.

SOCIAL LIFE, RECREATION, AND ENTERTAINMENT

Of interest to everyone is the leisure time, personal life, and sexual life of Dutch youngsters. Nearly everybody in the world knows stories about Dutch life and has strong feelings about it. It is important to look first at the images of certain aspects of Dutch life and then discuss different experiences. The Internet gives a lot of information about how Americans in particular think about Dutch life. Evert Ketting, of the Netherlands Institute of Social Sexualogical Research, says,

> A popular image of the Netherlands is that the country is the Sodom and Gomorrah of western civilization: it's a country where everything is possible and tolerated: drugs, prostitution, homosexuality and recently euthanasia. In short everything that God forbids.[2]

Ketting is right. Conservative thinkers from the United States especially tend to create this image of the Netherlands. There are a great number of Web sites dedicated to the liberal and sinful ways of the Dutch. All this is to warn the American people that one has to stick to good middle-class values, or else one will find oneself in a country like the Netherlands, in which it is of course impossible to raise one's kids, especially one's teens, in a proper and safe way.

In the discourse described by Ketting, the Netherlands acts as some sort of contrast nation for the United States when it comes to culture and values. There are countless examples. "What are you people? On dope?" the American sociologist Mike Males asks the Dutch on the Web site of *Youth Today*. Even more hilarious is the article entitled "The Low Country Sinks Lower" published by Tom Neven in the American magazine *Focus on the Family*, in which one can read,

> Consider that full nudity is common on Dutch television after 9 p.m. and that one can find pornographic movies on television during weekends. Consider that homosexual marriage is legal in Holland … Supermarket racks are full of magazines covering photos of nude women—all in open view. And hard drugs are consumed openly in so-called coffeehouses.[3]

In other words: One better stay away from the Dutch. Except for the image of Sodom and Gomorrah and the image of the brave little people with tulips and windmills, there is still another picture of the Netherlands. This is the image of the Netherlands used by more liberal thinkers in the United States. They think it's at least interesting to examine how the Dutch deal with subjects like sexuality and drugs in the life of their teenage children. They think the Dutch approach to these matters can actually help solve problems among teens in other countries. They like the Dutch society for its openness toward teen problems as much as the conservative family advocates hate the Netherlands for its lack of morality.

The Rights, Respect, Responsibility coordinator for Planned Parenthood of southwestern Oregon, Joanna Alba, thinks, for example, that the Dutch media campaigns on teen sexuality and prevention are quite progressive, because they are based on research to see what is effective and on a kind of humor teens understand. The most important thing about the way the Dutch deal with the subject of teen sexuality is, according to her, the fact that sexuality is dealt with as a normal part of life.[4] Journalist and essayist Judith Levine, author of the controversial (in the United States) book *Harmful to Minors*, agrees. She also thinks the 1990 Dutch law on sex between adults and children (in short: sex between adults and teens is legal as long as there is mutual consent; the child's parents can bring charges if they think the minor was coerced into sex) could be a good model for the United States. It recognizes children as sexual beings who can determine their future while not ignoring the fact that they are weaker than adults and still need legal protection.[5] Because teens are seldom forbidden to engage sexual activity, because they are free to talk about it with their parents and in school, and because of the media campaigns, the liberal thinkers conclude that Dutch teens have more mature attitudes toward sexuality and are more likely to use condoms. The Netherlands has the lowest abortion rate in the world.

If it works for sexuality, why should the liberal approach of the Dutch toward drug use not lead to the same good results? The United States has a lot of advocates of this statement. In his *Drug Legalization: Current Controversies*, Scott Barbour writes enthusiastically,

> The Dutch have no more drug problems than most neighboring countries which do not have a liberal drug policies. Further, by virtually all measures the Dutch have less drug use and abuse than the U.S.—from a lower rate of marijuana use among teens to a lower rate of heroin addictions among adults.[6]

Judy Wicks, an American advocate of liberal attitudes toward drugs, agrees. In the Netherlands, she knows, "hard-drugs are losing popularity and heroin is totally unfashionable with remaining addicts as well over forty years of age."[7]

Who's right? The conservative thinkers who see the Netherlands as Sodom and Gomorrah or their fellow Americans who think the liberal culture of the Netherlands is about as ideal as possible to raise one's children in a difficult age: the teens? Of course this question is impossible to answer; it depends on one's own beliefs and values. The low abortion and teen-pregnancy rates of the Netherlands is not a myth. Be assured that this dilemma is also important to the Dutch. The public and political debate focuses these days on moral values, parenthood, education, and the borders of liberal attitudes toward these. The image of the Netherlands abroad is often taken into consideration in the discussions on the subject. This does not always make things more clear. One must ask oneself, what is the role of sex and drugs in the daily lives of Dutch teenagers?

Dutch teens do talk about sex and sexuality with their peers, family, and teachers. Magazines for teenage girls and boys write quite openly about the subject. Teens write in questions and are always given the same answer: Do not do anything you do not want to do. Each person is free to do what he or she wants, and should not give in to peer pressure. As Evert Ketting states, "Live strictly and let live is an appropriate motto to characterize Dutch culture."[8]

So what do Dutch teens actually do when it comes to sexuality? According to the Dutch fertility and family surveys by Latten and De Graaf published in 1997, figures about the age of first intercourse are not available. But the survey did interview teens born between 1970 and 1974 at the age of 15 to 19. Of this group, 76 percent had kissed and 15 percent had had intercourse.[9]

More recent research by Brugman and Goedhart and others did include the age of first sexual intercourse. In a survey of 7,299 Dutch students aged 12–18, 3 percent of girls and 10 percent of boys aged 13, 8 percent of girls and 14 percent of boys aged 14, 18 percent of girls and 22 percent of boys aged 15, 35 percent of girls and 35 percent of boys aged 16, 49 percent of girls and 47 percent of boys aged 17, and 60 percent of girls and 49 percent of boys aged 18 and over had had their first intercourse.[10]

Compared with New Zealand, where the same research was performed, Dutch teens have their first sexual intercourse rather late. By 17 years of age, 49 percent of Dutch teenagers were sexually active, compared with 77 percent of New Zealand girls of the same age. According to the 1995 survey by Brugman and Goedhart, most girls born between 1977 and 1983 used contraception at first sexual intercourse: 43 percent used the pill, 70 percent a condom, and 13 percent no contraception.

These percentages can be explained by the fact that most girls used the pill and a condom, the so-called double-Dutch method. Less than 1 percent of 15- to 17-year-olds in the Netherlands get pregnant each year, compared with nearly 5 percent in Britain, which has the highest rate in western Europe, and 9.9 percent in the United States.

Teen pregnancy seems virtually eliminated as a health and social problem in the Netherlands, Simone Buitendijk of the Dutch Institute for Applied Scientific Research in Leiden told Reuters in 2001. With the lowest teen pregnancy rate in the world, the Netherlands also has the lowest abortion rate, although abortion in the Netherlands is legal and for teens even free.

According to Buitendijk, the secret of this Dutch success lies in the liberal attitude of the Dutch:

> In Holland teens know about sexuality and about procreation, how it works and what you should do not to become pregnant, their peers know and it's a very socially acceptable thing to prevent pregnancy.[11]

Another reason is given by Jany Rademakers of the Netherlands Institute for Sexualogical Research: "One key factor is that most parents talk with their kids about sex, early and routinely."[12]

The Dutch Green Party senator An Zwerver told the U.S. Senate that the Dutch government in no way promotes abortion. Instead, it prevents it by providing women with information on contraceptives. This education is an integral part of safe abortion services.[13]

Are the Dutch as open and educational toward the use of drugs like marijuana, cocaine, and heroin by their teens as they are about sexuality? To answer these questions, it is necessary to understand that drug abuse in the Netherlands is considered a health problem, and not a criminal problem.

It is not forbidden to use marijuana and hashish, and Dutch teens do use it. Cocaine and heroin are illegal to buy and sell, but recreational use is accepted. Information about marijuana, hash, and psychedelic mushrooms is distributed in retail stores called "smart shops." Teachers who teach the facts and figures about alcohol, nicotine, and other drugs also provide information. This is done by teachers with the assistance of the police, who tell teens about the legal consequences of using drugs, and health specialists, who discuss the medical aspects of drugs and healthy lifestyles.

The separation of hard and soft drugs has helped to keep people out of the drugs that really marginalize teens from society, Jan Huib Blans of the Jellinek Center states.[14] It is indeed interesting to see that the use of heroin, for example, is totally unfashionable. Teens are hardly using it. They consider it a drug for older losers. The use of soft drugs does not seem to be a gateway to heroin. Teens in countries surrounding the Netherlands are using more soft and hard drugs than Dutch teens.

Despite this rather loose attitude toward the use of soft and hard drugs (loose in comparison with the U.S. zero-tolerance approach), U.S. teens aged 12–15 are twice as likely to use marijuana as Dutch teens. Research compiled by the national Institute of Health and Addiction in the Netherlands found that less than 21 percent of Dutch adolescents have experimented with drugs. Those who do use drugs and find themselves in trouble can get help to overcome addiction. Judy Wicks, a U.S. writer, stated after visiting the Netherlands,

> At the heart of the Dutch philosophy is what they call an internal "locus of control." Children are taught from an early age that they are responsible for making the right choices concerning their own livers, rather than relying on regulations enforced by outside authorities such as parents, teachers and police.[15]

It's interesting to see that the philosophy described by her resembles the attitude of Dutch teens toward sexuality described by Ketting: Live strictly and let live. The slogan of the Jellinek Center, a Dutch organization that runs drug prevention, counseling, and treatment programs, appeals to this attitude: "Want to use drugs? First read the instructions."

So is everything concerning teens, sex, and drugs under control in the Netherlands? Are there no contradictions between the sea levels? Although the liberals are celebrating Dutch freedom, the answer must be no. The Netherlands actually deals with some serious problems concerning the health of its teens. And yes, these problems are certainly linked to sexuality and drugs.

The Dutch pride themselves on their low rate of teen pregnancy, liberal thoughts on sexuality, and low rate of teen drug abuse. But their excellent marks could vanish quickly. Care workers concluded in 2002 that teens have a shortage of basic knowledge on the functioning of their body, the use of the pill, and condoms. The number of venereal diseases is rising in the age group of 15 to 19 years. This can be explained in part by such factors as willingness to test and the fact that girls have more sexual contact from the age of 16 than boys. They have relatively frequently sexual contact with men who are considerably older then they are, and the chance they will be contaminated is because of this possibly larger.

Another problem in the Netherlands is the growth of teen pregnancy, for example in the capital, Amsterdam, among immigrants. Among Surinamese, Antillean, and Ghanaian girls, undesirable pregnancy occurs relatively frequently. Among Antilleans and Turks we find the most teenage mothers. Pregnant teens in Amsterdam often undergo an abortion. According to the *Nederlands Tijdschrift voor geneeskunde* (a Dutch illustrated magazine for medicine), the number of teenagers that bear a child is four times as high in Amsterdam than in the rest of the Netherlands. The Netherlands is no longer the country with the lowest number of abortions. Germany and Belgium seem to have passed the Netherlands, the Dutch press agency, ANP, declared in 2002. The abortion figure for foreign women and girls has been related to the country of origin, and is from 3 to 10 times higher than that of nonimmigrant women.

Another problem, often related to Muslim immigrants especially, is the declining tolerance toward homosexuality. Dutch teachers claim they are more and more reluctant, even afraid, to admit they are homosexual. In Dutch schools little information is given concerning homosexuality, and homosexual students and teachers say they do not feel safe at school. They are discriminated against, teased, and sometimes molested. Homosexual advocate organizations, such as COC, are requesting a dialogue with the Islamic community on this subject.

But Dutch teens can also learn a few things from their immigrant brothers and sisters. Immigrants, for example, live healthier lives. The food they eat is healthier because they eat more fish and less fat and use olive oil. They also use less alcohol and tobacco than their fellow teens. In the lives of teens born in the Netherlands, alcohol and tobacco abuse is becoming a more serious problem every year. According to the Nippo (the Dutch Institute for Pedagogical and Psychological Research), 30 percent of Dutch men aged 15–25 drink excessively (a minimum of 21 glasses of alcohol per week, or 14 glasses for women). Alcohol consumption is socially accepted, and teens are attracted to sweet mixed drinks like the Bacardi Breezer. Dutch teens combine the use of alcohol with smoking tobacco. The life expectancy in the Netherlands is still rising, but surrounding counties are doing better. The low country is not sinking because of sex and drugs, but because of the use of alcohol and tobacco by its teens. Sodom and Gomorrah seems to be much duller than its critics and advocates suggest.

Much like their German neighbors, Dutch teens love music. They are especially fond of house music, which has a techno beat. Naturally, like all teenagers, Dutch adolescents have many likes and dislikes in regard to music. Hip-hop has also become popular, and one can still find clubs that feature punk and new-wave music for kids to dance to. Teenagers often dress to reflect the type of music that they enjoy.

Since most teens speak English, they listen to American pop as well as British music.

Sports in Holland are also varied. Dutch teens are athletic and strong, and spend a lot of time outdoors. Many teens ice skate, and in-line skating is gaining in popularity. Because bikes are an essential mode of transportation, young men and women use their bikes daily. Football (soccer) is, of course, a major sporting activity, and most Dutch kids play football. School children and teens in the Netherlands also play a game called *blokjesvoetbal*, which translates in English as "block football," or *flesjesvoetbal*, which in English is "bottle football." Three to six kids play this game. Players guard one brick, and points are made by shooting a ball against the brick so that it falls down flat.

RELIGIOUS PRACTICES AND CULTURAL CEREMONIES

Religion has played an important part in the development of the Netherlands. In the sixteenth century, a war of independence was fought against Spain and it's Catholic king. This war defeated the Catholics and enabled the Dutch to reform their culture and religion. In fact, Catholics were treated very poorly after the war and were not allowed to worship freely or to hold political office. However, in the present, Catholics are welcome in the Netherlands, and masses are held in Dutch.

The dominant religious group in the Netherlands is the Dutch Reformed Church. While the Germans were forming the Lutheran Church in the sixteenth century, the Dutch followed John Calvin. Calvin was French and lived in Geneva, but became a great influence on the Dutch people who formed a type of Protestantism called Calvinism. For many decades, the Dutch Reformed Church was the only recognized church in Holland. However, in 1848, total religious freedom in all of the Netherlands was achieved. Today, although the Dutch Reformed Church is still dominant, many different creeds are practiced openly in The Netherlands.

CONCLUSION

Youth in The Netherlands lead a happy and productive life, in general. They enjoy a quality education, a comfortable lifestyle, and a great heritage. Unfortunately, not all youth are privileged, and Dutch educators and parents are concerned that as the world changes, so does the security and well-being of children and youth. In this case, Dutch youth are just as much a concern as youth in any other country.

NOTES

1. Abram De Swaan
2. Evert Ketting, "Is the Dutch abortion rate really that low?" in *Abortion matters: 25 years experience in the Netherlands*, Utrecht: Stimezo 1996, 5–14.
3. http://www.family.org/fofmag/pp/a0016298.html.
4. http://www.wecandobetter.org/jalba2002diary.htm (Teen Sexuality: Lessons from Europe, European Study Tour Joanna Alba Tour Diary, 20 August 2002).
5. Brian Robinson, "A harmful message? New book on child sex sparks uproar," http://abcnews.go.com/us/DailyNews/childsex_book020405.html; Judith Levine, *Harmful to minors* (Madison: University of Wisconsin Press, 2002).
6. Scott Barbour, *Drug legalization: Current controversies*. San Diego: Greenhaven Press, 2000.
7. Judy Wicks, "Pass the marijuana, please!" *Tales from the White Dog Café*, Winter/Spring 2001, http://www.whitedog.com/passthemarijuana.html.
8. Evert Ketting, "Is the Dutch abortion rate really that low?" In *Abortion matters: 25 years experience in the Netherlands*, Utrecht: Stimezo 1996, 5–14.
9. J. Latten and A. De Graaf, *Fertility and family surveys in countries of the ECE region: The Netherlands*, Amsterdam: UN ECE 1997, 12.
10. H. Brugman, H. Goedhart, et al., *Youth and sex*, http://www.lifeissues.net. writers/pry/abr-netherlands-00.html.
11. http://www1.excite.com/home/health/healthy_sex/article/0,17757,SA_1205,00.html.
12. http://www.fathersworld.com/fatherhood/article.cfm?template=fatherspla ce&article_id=830 (Patrick Boyle, "The sex talk, Dutch style").
13. http://anzwerver.nl/dagboek/archieves/000017/shtml.
14. http://www.cyc-net.org/today/today010808.html.
15. Judy Wicks, "Pass the marijuana, please!" *Tales from the White Dog Café*, Winter/Spring 2001, http://www.whitedog.com/passthemarijuana.html.

RESOURCE GUIDE

Nonfiction

Scott Barbour. *Drug legalization*, San Diego: Greenhaven Press, 2000.

E. Brugman, H. Goedhart, et al., *Youth and sex*. http://www.lifeissues.net.writers/ pry/abr-netherlands-00.html.

Abram De Swaan. *Human society: An introduction*, Amsterdam: Bert Bakker, 1996.

Evert Ketting, "Is the Dutch abortion rate really that low?" In *Abortion matters: 25 years experience in the Netherlands*, Utrecht: Stimezo, 1996, 5–14.

J. Latten and A. De Graaf, *Fertility and family surveys in countries of the ECE region: The Netherlands*, Oslo: UN ECE 1997, 12.

Judith Levine, *Harmful to minors*, Madison: University of Wisconsin Press, 2002.

Patricia Reaney, "Dutch offer winning formula to cut teenage pregnancy," Reuters, 3 February 2001, available at WV Free, http://www.wvfree.org/dutchstd.html.

Judy Wicks, "Pass the marijuana, please!" *Tales from the White Dog Café*, Winter/Spring 2001. http://www.whitedog.com/passthemarijuana.html.

Fiction

Hafid Bouazza, *Abdullah's Feet*. Brussels: Headline, 1998

Renate Dorrestein, *A Heart of Stone*. Penguin, 2003.

Arnon Grunberg, *Blue Mondays*. London: Vintage, 1998.

Arthur Japin, *The Two Hearts of Kwasi Boachi*. Toronto: Knopf, 2002.

Marcel Moring, *The Great Longing*. Toronto: HarperCollins, 1995.

Marcel Moring, *In Babylon*. London: Flamingo, 1998.

Margriet de Moor, *Duke of Egypt*. London: Pan Macmillion, 2005.

Margriet de Moor, *First Grey, Then White, Then Blue*. New York: Overlook, 2003.

Margriet de Moor, *The Virtuoso*. London: Viking, 2001.

Harry Mulisch, *The Assault*. Auckland: Knopf, 1999.

Harry Mulisch, *The Discovery of Heaven*. New York: Penguin, 2003.

Harry Mulisch, *The Procedure*. London: Viking, 2001.

Web Sites

www.hostelnetherlands.com/french/faq.php. Netherlands hostels, backpacking and youth.

www.un.org/esa/socdev/unyin/links.htm. Youth Web site links.

youth.unesco.or.kr/english/atlas/nation.asp?code=121. Youth policy in the Netherlands.

www.ict-edu.nl/content/nederlands/learn/middenframe_aides_schoolinfo_Netherlands.html. HIV/AIDS and youth in the Netherlands.

www.sws.soton.ac.uk/cwab/Session1/ICWs1WWW.htm. Introduction to Dutch youth.

europa.eu.int/youth/active_citizenship/index_nl_en.html. European Youth Portal: the Netherlands.

Pen Pal Information

http://www.opendiary.com/diarylist.asp?list=6&start=1&countrycode=NL&countryname=Netherlands

Chapter 9

PORTUGAL

José Machado Pais and Vítor Sérgio Ferreira
Translation by Richard Rogers

INTRODUCTION

The profiles of Portuguese teenagers are marked by a high level of diversity, which reflects the different life paths that young people take. There is, however, a certain universality in their experiences, situations, practices, and social values that typifies an important social and symbolic platform that confers upon them a relative degree of cultural and social identity as a social generation.[1]

To a large extent this generational awareness grew out of the social impact of an event that was of major importance to Portugal: the revolution that took place on April 25, 1974, and permitted the democratization of Portuguese society. The fact is that the transformations that led to or resulted from April 25 created a scenario that was propitious to the recognition of Portuguese youth as a social generation, both prior to the revolution, in the shape of the student movements that grew up in the aftermath of May 1968, as well as the movements against the colonial wars and the Salazar dictatorship; and after it, due to the liberalization of Portuguese society and the renewal of the ruling elites—something that gave young people the chance to participate in the democratic life of the country.

In addition to the extended cultural receptivity that was rendered possible by the new political conditions, the increase in the processes of globalization and urbanization also permitted the densification of cultural contacts and exchanges. New instances of information, socialization, and cultural awareness gained in visibility thanks to the expansion of the mass media—particularly a television that was now free from censorship—to increasingly wider sectors of the population, and also contributed to the intensification and acceleration of the circulation of ideas and knowledge. At the same time, the broadening of opportunities for access to the education system and the lengthening of academic paths furnished the April generation with a cultural training that was substantially superior to that of their predecessors.

The progressive improvement in living conditions enjoyed by virtually all Portuguese—in terms of income, consumption, and access to a wide range of services and facilities—and the process of economic growth that took place during the 1980s as a consequence of Portugal's entry into the European Community were decisive factors in the changes in the Portuguese people's value systems, which broke with the model that had characterized earlier generations. In other words, Portuguese society detraditionalized itself, particularly where people's private lives, cultural habits, and life ethics were concerned.

Indeed, it is above all in questions of taste in matters involving clothing and music, as well as in the greater value that young people attach to free time, the body, physical activities, and their sex lives, that it is possible to note the main areas of divergence between the different demographic generations.[2] These are aspects that thus take on considerable social visibility as an expression of the identity of today's young Portuguese and fulfill a reference and generational integration function that extrapolates upon mere proximity in terms of age. Inasmuch as they are common to all young people, these values end up acting as youth generational signs.

Recognition of the importance of lucidity, image, and pleasure in their daily lives does not, however, imply that young Portuguese are renouncing the work ethic. The ethics of consumption and work coexist—if only because without sources of income, there can be no narcissistic and hedonistic consumption. What has undergone substantial change is the way in which work is viewed. Among young Portuguese there has been a notable decline in the moral ethic of work as a duty: work is now considered to be more a right that society ought to guarantee than something that is really a social duty—that is to say, an obligation on the part of the individual toward society—to the point that it is the young Portuguese who are most concerned about unemployment. Threats of unemployment reinforce their materialist posture, albeit without limiting the development of other values that possess a connotation of postmaterialism, such as tolerance or the defense of multiculturalism and the environment.

This coexistence of attitudes of both a materialist and a postmaterialist nature is an indicator of an ethical stance toward life and society that can be termed *defensive postmaterialism* and is reflected in the assumption of typically postmaterialist values, without thereby necessarily implying the abandonment of attitudes that are traditionally linked to materialism, such as concern about (un)employment and economic growth. What we are in the presence of is a defensive strategy pursued in a context in which professional and economic insecurity run the risk of being perceived as something that might become a lasting state of affairs.

TYPICAL DAY

What activities do Portuguese teenagers engage in during the course of a day, and what proportion of their time to they devote to each one? According to a survey that the National Statistical Institute (INE) conducted in 1999 on a representative sample of the Portuguese population aged 15 and over,[3] practically half of a teenager's average day[4] (around 11 hours) is dedicated to activities of a personal nature—such as sleeping, eating, and personal hygiene. The main period of sleep takes up 8:14hrs each day, which means that teenagers are not much sleepier than the population aged between 25 and 54 (8:08hrs) and that they sleep quite a lot less than Portuguese aged over 54 (9:11hrs). However, they do tend to take longer siestas (2:08hrs) than the rest of the national population (1:30hrs)—probably when they come home from school.

The time that teenagers make available for their various daily meals (breakfast, lunch, dinner, and tea and snacks) is not very different from that which the rest of the Portuguese population devotes to them— around 1:54hrs. This indicates that they take their meals with the rest of their family—a practice that has not yet disappeared in Portugal. The same is true of the time they spend on personal hygiene—about 0:50hrs a day—which is again very close to the national average (0:48hrs).

However, those teenagers who already work tend to invest more time in their professional occupations than does the average Portuguese (7:54hrs versus 7:32hrs). Besides spending more on their primary professional activity (7:40hrs versus 7:20hrs), compared to the rest of the working population they also tend to devote a more significant part of their time to the exercise of a secondary one (4:43hrs versus 3:34hrs). All this comes on top of the approximately 1hr they spend traveling to and from work every day. Among those who go to school, it is the youngest who devote the most daily time to tasks related to their studies, both in class (5:51hrs) and doing homework (2:16hrs), and while going to school and back (1:09hrs)—which means that on average more than 9hrs of a Portuguese teenage student's day are taken up with school-related activities.

Around 1:55hrs are spent on domestic work and looking after family each day, compared to a national average of 3:52hrs. This set of activities includes tasks such as preparing meals, doing housework, caring for clothes and shoes, looking after domestic animals and pets, cultivating or maintaining kitchen gardens, and looking after and helping adult family members. Women—particularly mothers—continue to be responsible for routine family tasks, even when they work outside the home. The only domestic activities on which the time spent by young Portuguese is relatively greater than the national average for the remaining age groups are vehicle maintenance (0:43hrs) and child care (1:41hrs). They devote most of their remaining time to entertainment and cultural activities (2:12hrs), watching television (2:04hrs), playing sports (1:58hrs), engaging in other pastimes and games (1:40hrs), socializing with family and friends (1:36hrs), and listening to music (0:55hrs).

In rural environments, however, where many children are used to performing agricultural and domestic tasks, the management of a teenager's day is organized in other ways. For example, the following is the normal layout of a weekday in the life of a 14-year-old boy who is still in school and belongs to a country family that raises livestock:[5]

8:00 A.M.: Get up; wash face; get dressed and eat
9:00 A.M.: Feed the cattle; chop firewood (when there is frost in the fields)
10:00 A.M.: Look after the livestock
12:30 P.M.: Eat lunch; watch television
1:00 P.M.: Go to school
6:00 P.M.: Fetch grass; muck out the stables; feed the cattle
8:00 P.M.: Eat dinner
9:00 P.M.: Watch television
11:00 P.M.: Go to bed

Similarly, in an urban context there are specific segments of young people whose daily time is organized in ways that differ significantly from the common pattern. Let's take a look at the time budget of a drug addict who parks cars and whose life is ruled by the consumption of heroin and the corresponding need to raise the funds needed to buy it:[6]

12:00 P.M.: Get up; take drugs
1:00 P.M.: Park cars
4:00 P.M.: Take drugs
5:00 P.M.: Park cars
7:00 P.M.: Take drugs
8:00 P.M.: Park cars

11:00 P.M.: Go home; take drugs
1:00 A.M.: Go to bed

FAMILY LIFE

More than 80 percent of Portuguese teens live with their family of origin,[7] mostly (74 percent) in its core form (mother, father, and brothers and sisters), although a considerable percentage of young people (7 percent) also live with extended family groups (core family plus relatives)—a model that is relatively more frequent in the lowest strata of Portuguese society. At the same time, the proportion of teens who live in single-parent families (with only their mother or father) is also starting to become substantial—a situation that to a large extent is resulting from the liberalization of divorce in Catholic marriages following the April 25 revolution in 1974.

Although young people are leaving the parental home at an increasingly later age, in most cases departures continue to be motivated by marriage. In other words, as a rule people leave their original family in order to found a new one. Whereas in 1980 young men who married for the first time averaged 25.4 years of age and young women 23.3 years, since then it has been possible to note a progressive rise of the age at which both sexes marry: in 1986 the average age at which men married for the first time was 27, while women did so at the age of 24.1 years.[8] Consequently the great majority of teenagers in Portugal are still single (98 percent) and childless (92 percent). However, if we look at the evolution of the rates of childbirth outside wedlock among the Portuguese population aged between 15 and 19, there has been a very clear rise over the last 40 years: from 3.3 percent of births in 1960 to 10.4 percent in 1996—an indication of an extension of the traditional pattern of illegitimacy, which essentially occurs among young parents and is potentially stigmatizing.

In Portugal family life is increasingly being lived without the constant presence of the mother, which was traditional until the 1970s. The fact is that the rise in the number of working women is probably the most significant factor in the evolution that the structure of the workforce in Portugal has undergone in recent decades. The proportion of women who worked outside the home practically doubled between 1960 and the mid-1970s, from 17 percent to 33 percent, and has progressively continued to increase until the present day, albeit at a more moderate rate. In 1997 it stood at 43 percent.

This large-scale entry into the active life by Portuguese women initially began as the result of the need to replace male workers who had emigrated or gone to serve in the colonial war. This substitute employment occurred both in agriculture and in industrial sectors such as clothing and electronics, which are dominated by intensive, cheap labor. Thereafter the number of women who entered the job market continued to increase, due not only to factors of a strictly economic nature, but also for reasons that involved women's rejection of both a life in which they were shut away in a domestic universe and financial dependence on their husbands.[9]

Despite the changes, the family continues to be one of the main instances for both the socialization and controlling the social life of Portuguese adolescents—a function in which the figure of the mother is especially significant. When they are asked to assess the degree of influence that certain factors exercise on their decisions about the clothes they wear, for example, 62 percent of young people aged between 15 and 19 recognize that their mother's opinion plays an important part. However, when their emotional life begins to include dating, we witness a transfer of the position of reference opinion maker in relation to the construction of their visual appearance to significant others, such as friends of the opposite sex or boy/girlfriends.

At the same time, when we look at the reasons cited by Portuguese adolescents who rarely or never go to bars and/or discotheques (48 percent and 43 percent of young people aged between 15 and 19, respectively), we find that the main explanations for not going out in the evening are derived from the fact that their family does not like or allow it. In the case of young people between the ages of 15 and 17, family opposition is quoted as the reason by 57 percent of respondents. Coming of age tends to lead to a pronounced loss of family power when it comes to exercising control over young people's lives, inasmuch as from the age of 18 onward the main factor that dissuades people from going out to this kind of nightspot is their own perception that they are places that are full of people and confusion.

Family control over going out in the evening prior to attaining the age of majority at 18 is particularly manifest among young women, who, generally speaking, not only go out less than their male counterparts, but also start doing so later. Whatever the case, it is between the ages of 15 and 17 that young people most often begin to frequent bars and discotheques, albeit with a relatively limited degree of nocturnal mobility. One of the most common family control strategies is the parental requirement to be home by a given time. For the youngest (aged between 15 and 17), this deadline is often set at midnight. With each hour that passes thereafter there is a substantial fall in the proportion of adolescents who must return home after nocturnal outings. The most frequent threshold for a slowdown in the extension of the time at which young people come home is once again situated between the ages of 18 and 20.

Another aspect of family control over youthful outings in general (not just at night) concerns the information that young people give their parents about where they are. In general, Portuguese adolescents keep their parents informed when they go out: 60 percent of adolescents always or almost always tell their parents where they are, and 28 percent tell them some of the time. There is, however, a marked gender difference in this respect—while 33 percent of young males recognize that their parents always or almost always know their whereabouts, this percentage almost doubles among their female peers (60 percent).

However, while parental supervision of children does seem to exist in this domain, the same cannot be said about sexual relationships. Of the 42 percent of young Portuguese aged between 15 and 19 who said that they had already engaged in sexual relations, 19 percent had become pregnant without wanting to or feared that they had already caused a pregnancy, and the great majority (81 percent) had not told their parents (neither their mother nor their father, individually or together) about it. The lack of communication in this respect is serious, given that the sexual initiation of the majority of Portuguese adolescents occurs between the ages of 15 and 17 (64 percent), or even earlier (19 percent).

FOOD

Young Portuguese display substantial respect for the daily meal chain: the great majority state that they never (58 percent) or rarely (32 percent) miss either lunch or dinner. The exceptions occur mostly among those who enjoy higher rates of academic attendance and higher social status, live in an urban environment, and are most dissatisfied with their figures—elements that permit us to suggest the hypothesis that this type of behavior largely reflects a conscious strategy for controlling their bodies.

When it comes to eating habits, the ingestion of foodstuffs with a high sugar content (cakes, chocolates, ice cream, and so on), sodas (colas, orange-ades, and so on), and fast-food-type meals (hamburgers, pizzas, french fries, and so on) is quite entrenched among Portuguese teenagers, but declines with age and the completion of the various stages that comprise the process of transition to adulthood. The consumption of sweets/desserts and sodas primarily occurs either weekly (50 percent, 39 percent) or daily (29 percent, 37 percent), whereas that of fast-food-style meals is mainly either a monthly (36 percent) or a weekly (32 percent) practice.

The regular intake of sweet foods is quite strongly rooted in the Portuguese gastronomic tradition and traverses practically every type of Portuguese youth and social situation. Daily consumption only falls a little with advancing age and an increasing perception of the danger attributed to the ingestion of foods that contain a lot of fat, salt, or sugar. This perceived risk leads around 60 percent of young Portuguese to consider that it is either very or quite dangerous to eat foodstuffs with a lot of fat, salt, or sugar—a percentage that is higher among young people of the female sex, those who live in urban environments, and those who are socially and academically advantaged.

The fact that the social differences that can be seen in the perception of the danger associated with the intake of such foods do not result in an effective reduction in the regular consumption of sweets reveals the continuing influence of strong gastronomic traditions on the current generation of young people. Although aware of the inherent risk in abusive consumption of this kind of food, the majority of young Portuguese do not go without their daily sweet. In this they may be influenced by ancestral Portuguese cultural tradition, in which great value is attached to popular, conventional sweetmeats. Even today a variety of desserts that used to be prepared in the country's former convents and monasteries are still much sought after (and indeed go by some very suggestive names: Heavenly Rasher, Nun's Bellies, Abbot's Cake, Mother Abbess's Cake, Angel's Mumps, Saint Catherine's Sighs, and so on).

Practically absent from the consumer habits of young Portuguese are energy drinks (of the Red Bull and Isostar type). Despite the intense advertising that has been directed at them as a target group, 58 percent of Portugal's teen population never drink them, while 28 percent of young people rarely do so and only 13 percent do so with any degree of regularity. The latter group includes young people whose lives are more demanding and wearing from the point of view of performance and physical effort: young worker-students at higher academic levels, young people who go to discotheques more regularly, and those who assiduously practice one or more sports. In these cases the consumption of energy drinks plays an instrumental role in adapting or heightening bodily performance in contexts and social situations that are potentially characterized by more demanding levels of physical requirement.

Wine is another foodstuff that Portuguese teens do not often consume: 53 percent of teenagers said that they had not once drunk wine during the past year, while another 29 percent did so less than once a month. This situation contrasts with practices under the Salazar regime, when the prevailing forms of socialization were oriented toward the consumption of wine, to a large extent as a conscious means of stimulating the country's viticultural output. The importance that this type of socialization possessed is revealed by a motto that was quite widespread under the regime: "Our land's wine feeds a million Portuguese." Indeed, one of the alimentary habits that was instilled in weaker children was based on the traditional "tired-horse soups," which consisted of a plate of bread soaked in red wine and sugar. It was also customary to quiet babies who cried a lot by dipping their pacifiers in a chalice of port or unfermented wine. These days beer (lager) has clearly replaced wine among young consumers of alcohol. Around 30 percent of Portuguese teens drink beer at least weekly, and only 16 percent said that they had not drunk any during the past year.

SCHOOLING

The transformations that have taken place in Portuguese society and its education system over the last three decades have had a major effect on the offer of and society's demand for academic training, particularly in relation to the growing mobilization and aspirations of young people in relation to education. In the 1980s and 1990s the extension of compulsory schooling and the improvement in living standards, together with the expansion of the academic network at every level of learning, the growth of policies designed to democratize access to formal education, and the changes in forms of family socialization and the structure of the job market, led to a significant broadening of school attendance among the youth population and consequently to later professional insertion on the part of young Portuguese.

Since the 1970s the number of students registered in the second and third cycles of the basic education system—the sole path to conclude nine years of compulsory minimum schooling[10]—has not ceased to rise in Portugal and has virtually quadrupled over the last 10 years. Despite the higher concentration of students who are registered in these initial educational cycles, in recent years we have also witnessed a tendency toward accelerated growth in the demand for secondary education.

When seen against this background, it is understandable that 71 percent of Portuguese teenagers aged between 15 and 19 are students, mostly at the secondary (49 percent) and higher (36 percent) levels. Notwithstanding this, 13 percent of teenagers possess extremely low levels of academic qualification (sixth grade or less). Even more serious is the fact that two-thirds of these underqualified teenagers have already left the school system without even completing their compulsory minimum education. Half are rotating through the job market, while the rest either help family members without being paid for their work (8 percent) or are unemployed (7 percent). It is also among this group of young people, who possess very low academic qualifications and find themselves in more precarious and vulnerable social situations, that we find those who enter the job market at the earliest ages, including 30 percent who do so prior to the minimum permissible working age of 15.

These data reveal the extent that the phenomenon of leaving school early and unqualified—that is to say, before completing their compulsory minimum education and/or before reaching the age until which school attendance is mandatory—still obtains in Portugal. It is thus at the most elementary levels of education that we find the bulk of the process of social academic selection. Compulsory education continues to be beyond the reach of many young people, above all those who come from social backgrounds that are marked by the reproduction of traditional forms of agricultural or industrial labor, as well as by poverty and social exclusion. The data reflect the dimensions of a problem that successive political plans for education reform continue to prove unable to eradicate.

Even so, some recent studies on the Portuguese university system have revealed a very significant expansion of both the expectations that young people possess when they enter the higher education system and their effective attendance rates, together with a tendency toward the feminization of university-level studies. The fact is that since the April 25 revolution girls have enjoyed higher levels of academic attendance than before—levels that are now higher than those of their male counterparts, who are substantially more given to leaving the education system. This trend toward the feminization of learning is especially true of higher education and suggests a generalization among young Portuguese women of strategies aimed at the accumulation of academic capital with a view to potentially ensuring improved conditions for their future professional insertion.

In Portugal obtaining a higher education degree or diploma constitutes the materialization of a major private and public investment and crowns a long academic career, which will have lasted for at least 16 years. It represents a major public investment to the extent that the state is the primary protagonist in the offer of education, particularly up until the 12th grade at school, as well as the principal owner of universities with a good reputation, even following the boom in private universities that has occurred since the mid-1980s. The latter continue to be the second choice of students who are unable to gain access to the public universities because they lack high enough grades. At the same time it is a major private investment because students' parents remain responsible for the high costs of keeping their children within the education system.

SOCIAL LIFE, RECREATION, AND ENTERTAINMENT

Portuguese teens' free time is strongly marked by a convivial form of hedonism: when they are asked what they most like to do with their leisure time, 57 percent of Portuguese between the ages of 15 and 19 say that hanging out with friends is their first option, followed at some distance by the intention of having as much fun as possible (21 percent). Young people who live with their parents are those who invest most in social relations outside the domestic space, particularly in nocturnal spaces, and "hanging out" and "having fun" are precisely the characteristics that young Portuguese associate most closely with evenings/nights.

One of the places in which teenagers in Portugal choose to socialize is the café. Going to the café is a daily or almost daily practice for 60 percent of Portuguese teens and at least a weekly one for another 22 percent. Going to bars or discotheques with a certain degree of regularity is also a practice that is engaged in by more than half of young people up to the age of 19 (around 57 percent and 52 percent, respectively). Going to such places is a clear opportunity for intensifying relationships, and being with friends is by far the main reason (46 percent of adolescents who go out at night) for doing so. Another important motivation is related to the opportunity to dance, which is cited by 19 percent of adolescents. The explicit expectation of meeting new people (15 percent of young respondents) is also significant—above all when we bear in mind the weight attached to socializing that we have already noted above—and is expressed by substantially more males than females. The convivial object of nocturnal sorties is also evident in the company that young people keep when they go out to bars and discotheques. The most customary format (53 percent) is to go in groups of friends that include members of both sexes, and 24 percent of Portuguese teenagers also take advantage of bars and discotheques as places for dating.

Going out in a group made up of members of the same sex or on one's own is considerably less commonplace (12 percent and 2 percent, respectively), and both are principally male options. Indeed, one persistent distinction in youth sociability in Portuguese public spaces is that which divides young people by sex—an element that in turn indicates the continuing existence of stereotyped gender-based asymmetries. Whatever the environment they live in, girls display a lower degree of participation in sociability networks outside the domestic space. However, this sexual differentiation is significantly less accentuated in urban contexts than it is in rural ones.

Among young people, nightlife is often associated with more sophisticated and aestheticized investments in their visual bodily image. Even
though when it comes to the composition of their daily visual appearance, Portuguese adolescents already attach quite a lot of value to aspects
such as "originality," "difference," and "comfort,"[11] when asked whether
they possess clothes or accoutrements that they especially use to go out
in the evening, approximately one-third say that they do—a proportion
that tends to increase along with the frequency with which the same
respondents go to bars or discotheques: virtually half of the young people
who regularly (daily or weekly) frequent bars or discotheques own special
accessories that they use on those occasions.

However, we should not think that Portuguese adolescents only conduct their social lives in collective public spaces and that home is a forti-
fied redoubt or an individual refuge that serves solely for passive forms of
leisure. Particularly in the case of students who live with their parents,
the domestic space is quite permeable to sociabilities that go beyond
their own family, be it in the shape of telephone contacts or in that of
interdomiciliary visits.

Talking to friends or to one's boy/girlfriend on the (fixed or mobile)
telephone is a regular practice for around three-fourths of Portuguese
adolescents and even a daily one for about one-third of them. This
proportion rises exponentially among those who are in a relationship.
Given the extent of the use and ownership of mobile phones in Portugal,
this instrument constitutes a device that intensifies the porosity of the
domestic space, particularly where young people are concerned. Having
friends come over or being invited to friends' houses are also quite
common practices for about two-thirds of Portuguese teens (64 percent
and 69 percent, respectively).

Receptive domestic activities, such as watching television and listening to the radio or music (CDs, cassettes, and so on), occupy a leading
position among the most common pastimes engaged in by Portuguese
teens: 94 percent of young people between the ages of 15 and 19 watch
television every day, while 75 percent listen to the radio and 62 percent
listen to music on a daily basis. Once again, and in parallel with that of
collective public spaces, this fact reveals the domestic space's importance
as a key hub in young people's use of their free time.

Other receptive domestic activities, such as reading from any one of
a number of support formats, are generally less common, although the
frequency with which they are engaged varies between different social
profiles. Around half of all Portuguese teenagers read newspapers and
magazines on a daily or weekly basis—the daily practice of this pastime

is more common among young people who already work and above all among those who are attending higher education. At the same time, the reading of periodical publications is also marked by gender differences: young males prefer newspapers, and the proportion who read them daily is similar to that of those who do so weekly; whereas young females tend to opt for magazines, which they read on a weekly basis.

Although less frequent among Portuguese teens (only one-fourth do so daily or at least weekly), reading books (other than schoolbooks) tends to become more frequent as academic qualifications increase. It is a nonexistent habit among almost half of young people who only possess a basic level of education, for whom daily reading is a residual practice. This scenario is reversed among young people who have completed or are on longer academic paths. Among those with higher education, daily or weekly reading is the most widespread recreational activity and is engaged in by around half of all the young people who have attained this academic level.

While still on the subject of activities that take place at home, we find that besides being relatively rare among Portuguese teens as a whole, computer-related (such as surfing the Web or playing computer games, for example) and artistic (writing or painting, for example) occupations require both qualificational and symbolic (where amateur artistic practices are concerned) and/or material (when it comes to using computers, for example) resources that are unevenly distributed within the Portuguese social structure and constitute an area in which social class is clearly a distinctive operator. Despite their rarity, these types of domestic activity are nevertheless a paradigmatically youthful form of leisure, to the extent that it is teenagers who display the greatest receptivity to this kind of use of time. Here we should point out the recreational use of computers, which is the domestic leisure practice that has experienced the greatest increase over the last decade,[12] from 5 percent to 21 percent—a proportion that, despite this rise, is still substantially lower than that of young people who never use computers (43 percent).

Moving away from the domestic sphere, besides going to the café each day and going out in the evening on a regular basis, a substantial proportion of Portuguese teenagers also quite regularly use their free time to enjoy nature by going to the beach in the summer months (80 percent), simply taking a walk outdoors (61 percent), or going out to window-shop (83 percent), make personal purchases (64 percent), or go to the cinema (64 percent)—activities that are currently packaged together in the mall format, which is now widespread in Portugal.

Skatepark in Ovar, Portugal. Courtesy of Frederico Pinto.

Sports are also a regular activity for around half of all Portuguese teenagers (56 percent), but one that clearly declines as they progress in the transition to adulthood. Twenty percent practice some form of physical exercise daily or almost daily and another 31 percent do so at least once a week, while only 5 percent do engage in sport, but less often than this. Gender continues to be one of the variables that most influence sporting habits in Portugal, inasmuch as not only do sports penetrate the male youth universe to about twice the extent that they do the female one, but young men tend to engage in a larger number of sports and to do so more regularly.

Of all the available formats, soccer takes the lead with almost half (43 percent) of Portuguese teens who play any type of sport as its practitioners, followed a long way off by various kinds of gymnastics (28 percent) and swimming (5 percent). Gender differences emphasize the predominance of the practice of soccer among the male segment of the youth population (72 percent), compared to the female segment (18 percent). The latter is dispersed among a wider range of sports, and here gender contrasts are more marked in the practice of the various forms of aerobics (19 percent of women versus 1 percent of men) or other gymnastics (37 percent versus 7 percent), swimming (20 percent versus 6 percent), and other team sports excluding soccer (23 percent versus 13 percent).

Finally, the social and cultural conditions experienced by young people are also reflected in significant distinctions in the practice of sports. Soccer is predominant almost to the point of exclusion among young males who only possess basic education and the lowest social status, for whom other forms of sport are residual in nature. As we move up the academic and social structures of the youth population, we find that the almost exclusive and central nature of the practice of soccer loses ground to a certain sporting eclecticism, which is patent in the relative prominence that certain types of more individualized sports, such as keep-fit gymnastics, are gaining.

A large part of the daily routine of Portuguese teens is dedicated to listening to music. The great majority (86 percent) often put music on as soon as they get home, and the percentage who habitually listen to it while they are working or studying (76 percent) or during their daily travels (68 percent) is also quite high. Listening to music while doing nothing else is a practice in which 69 percent of young Portuguese indulge—the same proportion as frequently watch music programs on television. This is indeed a cultural practice that is particularly dominated by the younger segment of the population, inasmuch as the daily presence of music in its various formats falls off considerably as people move toward their 30th birthday.

The reciprocal relationship between musical tastes and friendship networks is clear to see when we look at the similarity of preferences shared by close friends. Around three-fourths of Portuguese teens believe that their friends' musical tastes are very or quite close to their own. It is above all among students that music is most closely associated with bonds of friendship, and the possession of higher academic qualifications tends to correspond to a greater degree of overlapping between musical taste and relationships between friends.

This means that the academic universe has a strong influence on the reciprocity between taste-related cultural zones (namely musical taste) and social relationship zones (namely of the types that involve friendship). This interpretative framework takes on a more precise outline when one observes certain specific practices that reflect this articulation between taste and conviviality. Listening to and talking about music, singers, and groups with friends, for example, are practices that are widespread among teens, more than 80 percent of whom participate in them. Friends' opinions are indeed one of the main factors that young people take into account when they buy albums. Swapping albums with friends is not quite as common, but is nonetheless a frequent practice that involves 62 percent of teens, among whom students are the group who most often circulate music between members. Against this background it is no surprise that parents are rarely colisteners, doing so with no more than 15 percent of young people.

Music is experienced in a manner that is not only convivial, but also hedonist. Around three-fourths of Portuguese teens frequently listen to music at loud volumes and dance to the sound. At the same time, their musical tastes also tend toward a search for a sensorial and hedonist experience in which preference is given to music that is "happy and entertaining" (29 percent), that has "a good beat to dance to" (20 percent), or that "makes us vibrate and feel strong emotions" (12 percent). Still, we should note that boys attach greater importance to the sensorial and rhythmic aspects of the musical experience than do girls, who are motivated more by its melodic and textual suitability—that is, by music "that is pleasant to hear and relaxing" and "that contains a message."

The same distinction between the sexes is also apparent in two of the musical styles that are preferred by young Portuguese, who are divided in an almost symmetrical opposition between boys who like rock and girls who enjoy romantic music. In general terms Portuguese teens' favorite musical styles are rock (44 percent), pop (31 percent), romantic music (27 percent), the new trends in dance music (house, techno, drum 'n' bass, and so on) and Brazilian music (18 percent each), and, finally, metal (heavy metal, trash metal, and so on, with an expressive 17 percent). The aficionados of rock, pop, the new dance music, and metal are primarily teenagers, in proportions that fall as age increases. The opposite is true of preferences for romantic, Brazilian, and a variety of types of Portuguese music, which become more popular as people grow older.

RELIGIOUS PRACTICES AND CULTURAL CEREMONIES

Even though a large majority (77 percent) of the Portuguese population believes that today's young people are less interested in religion than the older generations,[13] the fact is that although this generational difference does exist, observation reveals that it is not as deep as all that. The vast majority of Portuguese teens (86 percent) reproduce the religious orientations of a country that is traditionally Catholic, although nearly half admit that they do not practice their religion.[14] Catholicism nonetheless continues to be dominant among the younger generations, albeit with a marked divide between practicing and nonpracticing Catholics. A family socialization that is more intense among younger members means that the teenage age group (15–19) contains a higher proportion of young people (38 percent) who are active and participate in Catholic religious life—a percentage that falls by about 10 points in the age groups between 20 and 29. Other religious beliefs are residual in nature—less than 2 percent of respondents. The proportion of respondents who express a nonreligious position, including indifference, atheism, and agnosticism, is fairly substantial, however (12 percent).

Against this background, it is possible to say that in overall terms the existing structure of religious preferences in Portugal tends to be reproduced among the latest generations, although a slight tendency toward secularization can be noted in the small decrease in the proportion of young people who say that they are Catholics, compared to that of the total percentage of the population who express the same position (estimated at around 91 percent). This may be seen in both the increase in the ratio of young nonbelievers to all persons who do not profess a religious affiliation in Portuguese society as a whole (estimated at about 6 percent), and the predominance of nonpracticing young Catholics compared to those who do actually practice their religion, and reflects an absence of religious practice (rare attendance at religious ceremonies and infrequent prayer) that is tending to combine with a series of beliefs that are replacing traditional forms of religiosity, such as an interest in astrology and reading horoscopes, palmistry, telepathy, UFOs, aliens, witchcraft, spiritualism, and so on.

Having said that, in general terms the traditional Portuguese cartography of the distribution of religious identification is also reproduced among the young. The tendency toward secularization maintains a prominent position in the country's capital, Lisbon, where the various forms of nonbelief possess the largest number of adherents (26 percent) and where Catholicism is simultaneously most nominal (only 10 percent of young people in the Lisbon region say that they are practicing Catholics). It is in the northern regions of the country that we find the highest indices not only of Catholic belief, but also of active involvement by young people in religious ceremonies. We should not forget that it is in these regions that there exist the highest proportions of rural classes (small farmers and rural proletariat), whereas Greater Lisbon is home to an overrepresentation of the upper classes and the petit intellectual and executive bourgeoisies—precisely the class categories that are most given to nonreligious positions.

Similarly, the gender differentiations in religious life continue to exist, with young women displaying a higher rate of participation in religious events. The fact is that that which distinguishes boys from girls is not so much religious identification—in both cases overwhelmingly Catholic—but rather their position in relation to religious practice, in which the great majority of young male Catholics do not participate. In any case, whatever a young person's gender or social and geographic origin, the general rule is that young Portuguese do not overtly renounce the country's religious tradition. As a result we continue to see the significance of this affiliation in certain forms of youth behavior, particularly going out in the evening. For example, when we analyze the factors that discourage nighttime sorties by young people, one of the most important of which is the perception that bars and discotheques are places that are full of people and confusion, we find that this is a reason that is particularly emphasized by young Catholics and is more prevalent among those who practice their religion than those who do not. Besides this, it is the families of young Catholics that tend to exercise a tighter control over their children's evening outings and that either do not let them go out in the first place or restrict the time by which they must be home: indeed, it is practicing young Catholics who come home earliest (26 percent by midnight and 60 percent by 2 A.M.), while it is those young people who do not possess any religious affiliation who clearly stay out later at night (59 percent of these young people come home after 3 A.M.). What is more, the parental requirement to be home at night by a predefined time continues to be exercised until a later age by the families of practicing young Catholics.

If we look at the existence in Portugal of cultural ceremonies that are specifically destined for young people, one example that we find is the debutante balls—private parties that economically well-off families organize in order to celebrate their daughters' 15th birthdays. We should not ingenuously look upon these balls as merely implying a change in social status. The debut is designed to announce to society—or rather to high society—that the debutante is beginning to reach marriageable age and to establish good prospects for a match. Still, debuts are not a marriage market, but rather a "private school" for sensibilities and tastes, at which young ladies are taught the rules that govern that market. By taking part in debutante balls, young people internalize taste criteria that provide them with the capacity to make a "good choice"—in other words, they learn to attach value to their own milieu and to recognize its boundaries. The effects of the various forms of family socialization are also very evident in these cases.

CONCLUSION

As a social category, youth is a world that tends to crystallize a certain homogeneity via whatever is said or thought about it, both in people's daily conversation and in the words of politicians and the media. However, the youth category is not made up of a homogeneous group; on the contrary, it materializes a heterogeneous social reality that is crisscrossed by multiple divides in which, as we saw earlier, the effects of inherited cultural capital, family socialization, and gender categorizations are still strongly felt.

The fact is that, as we have seen, being young in Portugal today is a diversified, dilated, and complex social condition. From the end of the academic path (be it voluntary or involuntary, early or later on) until full- or part-time, definitive or intermittent socioprofessional insertion; from the moment of leaving one's family of origin until the constitution of a new residential unit, whether or not it is associated with new forms of conjugality and progeny; and in the ever more diverse ways of occupying free time themselves, although in general the processes that mediate the condition of being young are tending to last longer, they take on different shapes and combinations, possess different durations, and take different periods of time to materialize, depending on the groups and social contexts to which the young people of a given generation belong.

Nonetheless, on both the social and the symbolic plane, in today's Portugal there is a certain generational convergence in the different ways of being young—a convergence that is being brought about by factors such as the widespread availability of education that followed the April revolution, the high level of youth exposure to the media (quite standardized) and the information that is exchanged between and disseminated by the various youth conviviality networks. These factors have been relativizing and transculturalizing young people's identities in Portugal and have also been contributing to some degree of massification of the forms of consumption that serve as a reference point for Portuguese youth.

In the face of this process, in Portugal the younger generations have gradually been coming to constitute an important reference framework for the older ones—a process that has permitted a certain intergenerational horizontality of values. Among the older generations there is a degree of permeability to some youth values. Youthful tastes are passing to older people. Some young people initiate their parents in new technologies and music. It is as if the processes of socialization had turned around: it is no longer just the children who are being socialized by their parents; be it with enthusiasm or with resignation, the latter end up adhering to some of the values that are primarily held by young people—the so-called youth values, which, to a large extent, entail hedonism, conviviality, and having a good time.

The capacity to influence the adult world that young people are displaying is made possible by the more relational and democratized model (as opposed to an authoritarian one) that currently governs the relations between parents and children. Without losing its importance as an instance of socialization and social control, today's family is moving toward a respect for the individuality and independence of each member and particularly that of teenagers. Far from the time when corporal punishments were the rule as a means of exercising parental authority, today parents limit themselves to verbal reprehension or grounding, while simultaneously shouldering—whenever possible until quite late—the obligation to provide their children with financial assistance in their future lives.

NOTES

1. K. Mannheim, *Le Problème des Générations*, Paris, Nathan, 1990 (1st edition, 1928).

2. José Machado Pais (Co-ord.), *Gerações e Valores na Sociedade Portuguesa Contemporânea*, Lisbon, ICS/SEJ, 1998.

3. *Inquérito à Ocupação do Tempo—1999, Principais Resultados*, Lisbon, INE, 2001. It should be noted that the times listed are for those members of the population who actually engaged in the activities in question.

4. Here constituted by the population aged between 15 and 24 and resident in Portugal, inasmuch as of the various age groups for which data has been published, this is the one that is closest to the group known as teenagers. Thanks to the fact that we were able to gain direct access to the databases concerned, in the remaining chapters we will respect the definition that is actually implicit in the term *teenager* and will use the data provided by survey respondents aged between 15 and 19.

5. Graça Alves Pinto, *O Trabalho das Crianças*, Celta, Oeiras, 1998.

6. José Machado Pais, *Ganchos, Tachos e Biscates. Jovens Trabalho e Futuro*, Oporto, Ambar, 2001, p. 332.

7. As per the data provided by the National Youth Survey in 2000 and published in José Machado Pais & Manuel Villaverde Cabral (Co-ords.), *Condutas de Risco, Práticas Culturais e Atitudes Perante o Corpo*, Oeiras, Celta, 2002. Unless stated otherwise, all the statistical data presented hereafter are from this survey, which was conducted by Lisbon University's Social Sciences Institute (ICS) within the ambit of the work of the Permanent Youth Observatory (OPJ). At the same time, from this point on, Portuguese teenagers are represented herein by the young people aged between 15 and 19 years who responded to the survey.

8. Alexandra Lemos Figueiredo, Catarina Lorga da Silva, & Vítor Sérgio Ferreira, *Jovens em Portugal: Análise Longitudinal de Fontes Estatísticas (1960–1996)*, Oeiras, Celta, 1999.

9. Anália Torres, "Casamento em Portugal—entre o sim e o porque não?" *Dinâmicas Multiculturais, Novas Faces, Outros Olhares*, vol. 2, Lisbon, Instituto de Ciências Sociais da Universidade de Lisboa, 1996.

10. The Portuguese education system is currently divided into three main stages: basic education—which is considered compulsory and entails three cycles,

the first lasting for four academic years, the second for two, and the third for three, thus constituting nine years of minimum compulsory education covering a common core of subjects; secondary education, which includes three academic years and already assumes that students will opt for a particular area of studies; and finally higher education, the duration of which depends on the course in question. Access to the latter is conditioned not only by the average grades obtained in the subjects taken during the secondary phase, but also by those obtained in the national exams taken at the end of the 12th (and final) year at school, plus a grade for each subject that varies depending on the course and establishment to which the student is applying.

11. The clearest social reflection of the consecration of these values in the choice of a young person's image is the recent success enjoyed by "casual wear," particularly in urban contexts. Casual wear is a relaxed and creative style, the producers of which seek their inspiration in street fashion, albeit often renewed and added to by the symbolic addition of a designer label. As a result, although the "comfort" value has never lost its dominant position among adolescents, it is now being somewhat sacrificed to criteria like "brand," "style," and "fashion."

12. Based on data from two surveys of Portuguese youth that the Instituto de Ciências Sociais da Universidade de Lisboa conducted in 1987 and 2000.

13. José Machado Pais (Co-ord.), *Gerações e Valores na Sociedade Portuguesa Contemporânea*, Lisbon, ICS/SEJ, 1998.

14. According to the results of the 1997 National Youth Survey, as published in José Machado Pais & Manuel Villaverde Cabral (Co-ords.), *Jovens Portugueses de Hoje*, Oeiras, Celta, 1998.

RESOURCE GUIDE

Alexandra Lemos Figueiredo, Catarina Lorga da Silva, & Vítor Sérgio Ferreira, *Jovens em Portugal: Análise Longitudinal de Fontes estatísticas (1960–1996)*, Oeiras, Celta, 1999.

Inquérito à Ocupação do Tempo—1999, Principais Resultados, Lisbon, INE, 2001.

K. Mannheim, *Le Problème des Générations*, Paris, Nathan, 1990 (1st edition, 1928).

José Machado Pais, *Ganchos, Tachos e Biscates. Jovens Trabalho e Futuro*, Oporto, Ambar, 2001.

José Machado Pais (Co-ord.), *Gerações e Valores na Sociedade Portuguesa Contemporânea*, Lisbon, ICS/SEJ, 1998.

José Machado Pais & Manuel Villaverde Cabral (Co-ords.), *Condutas de Risco, Práticas Culturais e Atitudes Perante o Corpo*, Oeiras, Celta, 2002.

Graça Alves Pinto, *O Trabalho das Crianças*, Oeiras, Celta, 1998.

Anália Torres, "Casamento em Portugal—entre o sim e o porque não?" *Dinâmicas Multiculturais, Novas Faces, Outros Olhares*, vol. 2, Lisbon, Instituto de Ciências Sociais da Universidade de Lisboa, 1996.

Chapter 10

SPAIN

Carme Garcia and Ainhoa Flecha

INTRODUCTION

Spain is located in the south of western Europe, occupying almost the entire Iberian Peninsula, plus two archipelagos (the Canaries and Balearics) and two cities in the African continent, Ceuta and Melilla. It has an approximate area of 504,750 square kilometers. Almost half of this area is on tablelands, and there are five big mountain ranges that cross over it. Spain borders France in the north, Morocco in the south, and Portugal in the west. The waters that bathe our coasts belong to the Cantabrian Sea, the Atlantic Ocean, and the Mediterranean Sea. This strategic situation explains why Spain has traditionally been a place for encounters among different cultures, having various influences on our traditions, which are characterized by openness and acceptance. In the south, the Straits of Gibraltar have been a bridge between cultures from Africa (until the fifteenth century, a part of our territory was under Muslim authority), the East (for example, at the end of the Middle Ages the gypsies came from India arriving in Spain), and the West (the ships that were to arrive in North America departed from here). In the northwestern part of the country there is, for example, a certain cultural unity of Galicia with other more northern regions with a Celtic tradition. In the north, the chain of mountains that separate Spain from France, the Pyrenees, have traditionally been a thoroughfare rather than a barrier, thus becoming a place for cultural exchanges of all kinds. At the same time, the eastern sea connects us with the Mediterranean tradition, which is reflected by the Roman and Greek sites, the Mediterranean diet, and the contact with the eastern commercial and cultural routes.

Spain has a very important historical and contemporary cultural richness, which is reflected in ancient celebrations (like the Semana Santa—Holy Week—in Sevilla), an important tradition of craftsmanship with a wide variety of local schools, spectacular sites considered part of the human heritage (the Altamira caves or the Alhambra in Granada), monuments from all eras, hundreds of high-quality museums (like the Prado Museum, the biggest art gallery in Spain), and renowned artists and writers from different ages (Cervantes, Velázquez, Gaudí, Lorca, Picasso, and so on). Spain is currently part of the most advanced European circles of music, art, and culture.

Spain also has a tremendous natural richness, thousands of kilometers of beautiful beaches, and a variety of habitats, species, and so on. This natural richness is currently threatened by polluted seas, atmospheric contamination, desertification, and deforestation, due to a great extent to fires and ground erosion. It is important to note that environmental awareness is growing among teens. This is visible in campaigns specifically addressed to them regarding recycling and rejecting the consumption of fish that have been caught before procreating. Spain's cultural and natural wealth is so attractive that the country receives millions of visitors every year. In fact, Spain is the third-most-popular tourist destination in the world, after the United States and France. This is the reason why there are more and more teens that focus their professional goals on the tourist sector.

Spain is part of the capitalist and global economic system, and although it is heavily influenced by the periods of prosperity and recession in the European Union, in which it has been a member since 1985, it is currently undergoing a rapid rate of development. Nevertheless, one of the main problems for those teens who aim to get their first job is an unemployment rate of 11.3 percent, one of the highest in Europe, which is even higher in the case of women. The most important economic sector is services (tourism, leisure, and so on), followed by industry (textiles, metallurgy) and an important agriculture sector (citrus fruits, olive trees) that is internationally recognized because of the quality of its products.

The 40,499,791[1] inhabitants of Spain are distributed into 17 *comunidades autónomas*, each one with a government, a president, and a specific political and administrative structure. These are Andalusia, Aragon, Asturias, the Balearic Islands, the Canary Islands, Cantabria, Castile–La Mancha, Castile y León, Catalonia, Community of Valencia, Basque Country, Extremadura, Galicia, Madrid, Murcia, Navarra, and La Rioja. There are also two autonomous cities out of the peninsula: Ceuta and Melilla. In all these regions Spanish is the official language, although it coexists with other languages in some of them: Catalan in Catalonia, Valencian in the Community of Valencia, Balear in the Balearic Islands, Euskera in the Basque Country, and Galician in Galicia.

Spain has been a parliamentary monarchy since the constitution[2] came into being in 1978. Despite the autonomy of the *comunidades autónomas*, this document guarantees the unity of the state, and this is why it is questioned by those who want more independence. Formerly, Spain was governed by the dictator Francisco Franco. In 1939, he won a bloody civil war, in which many citizens (Americans as well as Europeans) could not stop Franco from coming to power. He died in 1975, after four decades of repression. Since then, Spain has been going through a process of transition toward democracy, which is completely consolidated today. The chief of state is King Juan Carlos I, who belongs to the dynasty of the Bourbons, and the democratic transition took place during his mandate. The fact that Spain is a monarchy does not confer executive, legislative, or judicial power to the king. Legislative power is reserved for Parliament and executive power for the government; the president is ultimately responsible for the decisions made in the Council of Ministers. The parliamentary system has general elections once every four years. The president since 1996 has been José María Aznar.

In the shift from Francoism to democracy, the panorama has changed a lot for Spanish teenagers. Their current life options were unthinkable only two generations ago, so that it is difficult for many of them to imagine the conditions in which their parents or grandparents used to live. For example, military service was compulsory until 2001, thus obligating all young men (women were not allowed) to leave their studies, jobs, and homes in order to live in military barracks for many months. For many teens, it is difficult to imagine that their fathers were forced to do military service for more than a year. Approximately one decade ago, there were many young people who refused to go into the army, running the risk of imprisonment, which made that situation unsustainable. It forced the authorities to offer a *prestación social sustitutoria*, or social services for those who refused to do military service, and later they abolished it altogether.

Spain is considered to be an advanced and modern society, which has known how to take steps toward international cultural, social, and economic currents, as well as to maintain a plural identity.

TYPICAL DAY

The main routine of Spanish teens consists of school (compulsory from ages 6 to 16), lunch- and dinn ertime, and spare time, which is usually spent in leisure or doing the homework. Paid work is completely forbidden until age 16.

Education organizes young people's time from September to June, from Monday through Friday. Schools are normally in students' neighborhood, except in the case of some private or boarding schools. School usually begins at 9 A.M. Before school teens carry out the usual rituals of preparing for the day, like showering, dressing, and having breakfast. They either walk to school or are driven by car by a family member or in a car pool. Except for at private centers or some rural schools, there is no bus service. Around 11 there is a break, during which many students have a morning snack. Between 12:30 and 1:30, teens usually have the main meal of the day. Despite the myth of the *siesta* in Spain, it is only institutionalized on the weekend and on holidays, and it is not enjoyed by everybody. Modern life (unfortunately) makes it impossible for many people to partake of this healthy habit.

In the afternoon, schools are usually open from three to five. After school, teens usually go to hang out with their friends directly or virtually, watch TV, go to the gym, surf on Internet (often chatting), or, for the more studious, do their homework. Having an afternoon snack is a widespread habit that helps people stave off their hunger until dinnertime, which almost never takes place before 9 P.M., and on holidays begins at 10 P.M. or even later.

In the weekends, teens often go with their families to visit relatives or to see monuments, museums, villages, and so on. Some spend their time in Scouts or similar centers (in Catalonia there are secular groups called *esplais*). Some participate in cultural or leisure associations, or nongovernmental organizations that contribute to environmental awareness and protection, overcoming social exclusion, and so on. There are many teens that take part in their favorite sport—usually football (soccer)—with their school's team. And like thousands of teens all around the world, they go with their friends to the cinema (where most productions are from the United States); to eat something in a fast-food restaurant (Dunkin' Donuts, McDonald's, Burger King, Kentucky Fried Chicken); to buy clothes from brands like Diesel, Levis, and Quicksilver; or to have fun with their skateboards. They often spend time chatting in the park in the afternoon while they eat *pipas* (sunflower seeds) or *quicos* (toasted corn). The older ones will probably go to discos, which are part of the coolest circuits of European music. Some discos open in the afternoon and do not offer alcoholic drinks.

Some teens vary their weekend activities depending on the season. In spring, they often go to the park to play football or skateboard in

Street art, Madrid, Spain. Courtesy of Laura Layera.

the public spaces. In the summer, going to the beach is a widespread practice, as are visits to theme parks or simply walking on the street with a soft drink or an ice cream. In the fall, temperatures are not very extreme, but because of the rain, people tend to do indoor activities like playing video games or surfing the Net. In winter, it is usual to go skiing, iceskating, or to a *granja* (like a bar, but warmer, where people usually eat something) to drink hot chocolate with *churros*. Clearly there are a wide variety of options depending on the season of the year, the age of the individual (the older they are, the later they arrive at home), the region (in the south of Spain people spend more time outdoors, because of the warmer weather and because the cities are smaller), or the level of social commitment. Some activities are more individual, others are more collective, and still others have a benefit for the community as a whole.

FAMILY LIFE

The typical Spanish family is nuclear (mother, father, and children). However, we should point out that this model does not represent all Spanish teens, who have very different biographies. There are single-parent families, divorced families, families with adopted children, and so on. This is why some schools in our country have decided to change the name of the Asociación de Madres y Padres de Alumnos (Students' Mothers and Fathers Association, or AMPA) to the Asociación de Familiares de Alumnos (Students' Relatives Association, or AFA). Also, it is important to highlight that new kinds of families (gay or lesbian, for example) are appearing. Although they are still a minority, they are becoming more and more visible in a normal way. Despite everything, many of these families that are part of daily life are not recognized by the government, unlike what is happening in other European countries. It is true that some positive initiatives are taking place, like the more recent Ley de Parejas de Hecho (Law for Common-Law Partners), which recognizes that two people living together can be considered a couple despite not being married, or belonging to the same sex. However, this law does not give them the same rights as the traditional families.

The traditional Spanish family has undergone a very important change with the historical events that has led to democracy and, day after day, to greater equality. The patriarchal family, in which the man works outside of the home and the woman carries out the domestic work, has changed a lot. It is difficult for women in Spain to participate in the labor market at the same rate as men; however, it is quite usual for teens to have mothers that work outside of the home. Therefore, it is possible to find situations in which the man is unemployed (it is not a very unusual situation in our country) or retired, while the wife's (who is normally younger than her husband) job is the main source of income at home. This situation is the cause of many rapid role changes, especially in the new generations.

In Spain, due to the delayed entry into a social service system in comparison with northern European countries (with continued low pensions, a lack of infrastructure to help the families, and so on), the nuclear family has created networks of solidarity that substitute certain services that are not provided by the government. Therefore, it is quite common for teens to live together with their grandparents and sometimes other members of the family. Also, in the Mediterranean tradition (Italy, Spain, and so on) there is a very warm idea of the home, with family celebrations where many family members (grandparents, uncles, aunts, nephews, cousins, and more) participate. It also has a positive impact on the care of the elderly. Many mothers have not renounced working, but because of the still existing division of gender roles, they have also had to care for these new family members. This situation has led many women to assume a heavy burden. It is true that there is an increasing equality between men and women with regard to domestic tasks, but it is also true that there is still a long way to go. This is especially obvious with the care for elderly members of the family.

Women that do the domestic work usually deal with caring for the children's education and the home on their own. Employment and participation in social and educational activities will cause a fairer distribution of domestic responsibilities and an increase in women's autonomy. In general, this division of roles also affects teenagers, so that boys and girls deal with domestic work in an unequal way, although this is changing radically. Nowadays, it is more and more usual for teens to feel that they have a familial responsibility (cleaning their room, washing the dishes, shopping, and so on), but it is still true that there is not a completely equal distribution of responsibilities between girls and boys.

Different factors affect this traditional model of the family. Social class can be a factor in determining whether domestic work is an issue, because, for example, there might be domestic help in wealthier families. However, this does not guarantee that homes are not patriarchal. It is possible to find gender inequalities in wealthy families as well. Instead, it is possible that an unemployed father and an employed mother can contribute more to the transformation of the traditional family, since he might have to do the domestic work and take care of the children. Culture is another important factor. Ethnic minorities incorporate new family behaviors that also have to be taken into account. Some of them, like the solidarity of the Romaní community, their respect for the elderly, and their cooperative way of working, are very positive and potentially transformative. At a time when Spain is suffering a very important decrease in birthrate and an increasing number of teens are coming from noncommunitarian immigration, it is necessary to reflect on the family models we want, the models that current teenagers will have in their future. Family is a pillar of society, but it is changing. The main thing is that we will be the protagonists of this change.

Teenagers' daily life is also influenced by other possibilities that their parents did not have. For instance, it is usual to have motorcycles (up to 50 cubic centimeters) with a driver's license that can be easily obtained at the age of 14. A driver's license for motorcycles and cars with a higher cylinder capacity can only be obtained by those older than 18, after passing a strict theoretical and practical exam. Many teens also have cell phones as well as an incredible ability to codify phrases and write SMS messages at high speed. Nowadays, the information and communication technologies, along with TV and other appliances, have a big role in teens' lives, more than that of their parents.

FOOD

Traditional Spanish food is a cultural institution. It is part of the so-called Mediterranean diet, which is based on a balance among vegetables (salads, legumes, fresh and dry fruits, and so on), meat (especially poultry and small amounts of red meat), fish, milk products, and eggs. Its origin comes from thousands of years ago, bringing together influences from Roman, Greek, Arab, South American, and other cultures that have taken part in Spanish culture. Bread and pasta are very important, as well as small amounts of wine (although in general it is not considered all right in families for teenagers to drink a whole glass during the meals). The main source of fat is olive oil, a natural fruit juice that conserves all the qualities of olive. Among the most popular dishes is the *paella* (a rice and seafood dish), *tortilla de patatas* (scrambled eggs with fried potatoes that many teens eat in their sandwiches), *gazpacho* (mixed vegetable soup), and *cocidos* (a stew that is generally made with poultry, meat, and vegetables). Doctors recognize that this is a very balanced and healthy diet, although modern life makes it more and more difficult to have the time required to prepare some of these dishes. Some dishes (tortillas, pastas, and so on) are very popular among girls and boys.

This kind of food is common to most homes, defended by the most famous cooks, and present in the daily menu of most restaurants, the big meals of holiday celebrations (birthdays, Christmas, and so on), and elementary and high school cafeterias. The products of the Mediterranean diet can also be found in supermarkets, even in those belonging to big multinational companies, as well as in small grocery shops. However, the most traditional space to buy these products is the *mercados*, or markets, which are set up outdoors once a week (especially in small villages), or permanently set up in big indoor spaces. They are organized in "streets" that are lined by different stands: bakeries, dried fruits, salted fish, and so on. It is a real sight to see the fresh fruit carefully piled, the shoppers catching the eye of possible buyers, the fresh seafood, and more. Some *mercados* are very beautiful, like that of La Boquería, in Barcelona, made from a steel structure from the modernist period.

On the other hand, the Spanish, especially teenagers, also like fast-food restaurants very much. However, there is a Spanish tradition that shares certain characteristics with fast food. We are referring to *tapas*, which can be eaten quickly and while standing up. These are small portions of food that are part of the Mediterranean diet and have their origin in the thirteenth century. In some southern areas, *tapas* are free when you have a drink. *Tapas* help people resist the time between the lunch at one or two o'clock and the dinner at eight or nine, especially when it is delayed on the weekends. On Saturday and Sunday, some people have *tapas* for breakfast too, so they substitute the snack they usually have during the week.

SCHOOLING

The Spanish educational system provides compulsory education from ages 6 to 16, although most families send their children to school at the age of 3. Primary education is compulsory and is divided into three different periods called *ciclos* (from ages 6 to 8, 8 to 10, and 10 to 12). Secondary education is constituted by two *ciclos* (from 12 to 14 and 14 to 16). The end of this period also means the end of compulsory education, and most students get their secondary education degrees, which allows them to continue studying at *bachillerato* (16–18), or high school, and leads to higher vocational training or college. In order to enter college, everyone must take an exam called the *selectividad*, which lasts two days and is feared by teens, since it is an evaluation of all the academic contents and aptitudes acquired throughout school. If students cannot get the degree for secondary education, they have the option to enter a *programa de garantía social* (vocational training), which includes basic and professional training.

Although public schools provide free education, close to 30 percent of all schools are private and state-assisted centers (private schools that receive official economic subsidies from the state). Most of the latter (20 percent of the total) are Catholic state-subsidized centers.[3] Most private schools are located in big cities, thus excluding students in rural regions or with special characteristics. Therefore, private centers rarely receive boys or girls whose families have economic problems or those belonging to ethnic minorities, except in very exceptional cases. Most schools and high schools are coeducational, but some private and boarding schools can be only for girls or boys. Teenagers do not usually wear a school uniform, except in some private centers.

The school year begins in September and lasts for nine months. There are three main evaluation periods, when teachers evaluate the knowledge acquired by students and their behavior, effort in exams, homework, and class participation. In general, we can say that there are compulsory and optional subjects, so that each student can choose his or her own school schedule. Methods and content are normally very different for teachers who have been out of school for a while. A good example is the content given in history class, in which some aspects of Spain that never used to be dealt with are finally recognized today. This is the case, for example, with the conflictive relationship with America or the existence of very diverse nationalities in Spain. On the other hand, classes prove to be very different depending on the Proyecto Educativo de Centro, or the School Educational Project, agreed upon in the school. Therefore, classes can be more teacher-led or more participatory, more focused on rote memory and grades or more focused on the process. There are vacations in the summer (from the end of June to mid-September), at Christmas (almost two weeks), and at Easter (around 10 days between March and April). High schools are usually open only in the mornings, but there are some that open in the afternoon or the evening. After school, students often do extracurricular activities (sports and leisure, generally) linked to the school, do their homework, or attend foreign-language classes (mainly English).

Although coeducation is very widespread in Spain, gender inequalities do exist in school, like with sports, certain behaviors, and even preference for subjects. This is one of the reasons why there is a clear influence of gender on the preference of degrees: the scientific-technical degrees normally have more male students, and humanities are often chosen by a majority of girls. But this tendency is currently beginning to shift, especially on the part of girls, who are moving into spaces formerly occupied only by boys. This tendency is not as significant in the other direction. That is, it is more likely that a girl would decide to study chemistry than that a boy would choose to study nursing.

SOCIAL LIFE, RECREATION, AND ENTERTAINMENT

Traditionally, the Spanish have been friendly people and have put a lot of importance on social life. In small villages, greeting people is very important, and it is easy to begin a conversation with a person you do not know on the bus, or to be accompanied to the place you are looking for. Although these good habits are not present in the cities in the same way, some foreigners who come to Spain are amazed by our warm social behavior. When two friends meet, it is normal that they give each other two kisses on the cheek or hug. Shaking hands is considered to be too cold. Generalizing a bit, we can say that it is easy for feelings to be visible with laughs, gestures, hugs, and so on, especially among teens. This is why it is easy to make friends despite not speaking Spanish.

The social circles of Spanish teenagers are wide, with periodic celebrations with many people, such as family, classmates that follow the same

track even until college, and the neighborhood where they have friends
and play in the street. Another interesting aspect is that many residents
of our cities come from families living in small villages, where they often
go on holiday. For this reason, it is normal for teens and youngsters to
maintain friendships until adulthood with people they only see once or
twice a year.

After the highly repressive Franco period, Spanish people are experi-
encing sexuality in a more open way. So, for example, homosexual groups
have become more normal, and premarital sexual activity has undergone a
notable increase. This has also brought about the fact that sexual contact
occurs at an earlier age and an increase in unwanted pregnancy, which
sexual education has been trying to meet by socializing the use of contraceptive measures like the condom. This is why these issues often appear
in school curricula. Some regional governments have proposed measures
like distributing condoms in high schools and making specific classes for
teens. Although these initiatives have created many debates, they have
been carried out. As a result, teens tend to be more careful about sex, and
to think more about who they want to share their lives with.

Normally, teens' circles of relationships are defined by the spaces in
which they live their lives (school, family, neighborhood, and so on). In
these spheres they find the elements that they can identify with (fashion,
sports, music, and so on). It is normal for boys and girls to go out together,
if they know each other from their neighborhood, the school, or a youth
club. There is no prejudice in this respect. It is also possible for boys and
girls to go out separately, if the group of friends are from a sports team, for
example. However, boys' and girls' behavior also reflect some inequalities in the socialization of gender roles. This can be seen, for instance
(depending on the region), in that a boy might be expected to be tougher
in the sports he plays, or that he will have to take the initiative to ask a
girl out on a date, while the opposite might be frowned upon.

There are also many Spanish teenagers who have a transformative
social mentality, who regularly participate in nongovernmental organizations and social movements or who have committed attitudes. Examples
are very diverse. For example, there are teens that openly declare themselves to be gay or lesbian, attend the various spaces set up specifically for
young people, or participate regularly in social organizations. The same
can be said with regard to environmental movements, feminism, and
other issues regarding the struggle against exclusion and inequalities. At
the same time, many teens show that they have reflected on tradition.
Some return to it proudly and others critically, and still others try to
recover a part of the history that Francoism had denied. This is why, for

example, teens that live in regions that have their own language usually speak Spanish as well as the language of their region. They also take part in some initiatives for the recognition of their identity.

There are many places for teenagers to establish relationships. Because of Spain's particularly nice climate, teens often like to sit and chat for a while on street benches or in parks, in public outdoor swimming pools, in front of schools, and so on. Public squares are very typical here. We make use of at least two streets, where a widening provides a space for grass, or we reserve a space in an island of buildings with or without vegetation, benches, fountains, and so on in order to chat, go for a walk, or hang out. Other meeting points are avenues or *paseos*, streets that normally have trees and benches that are inviting. It is also probable that the younger kids choose indoor spaces in order to chat with their friends. At the same time, the Internet, SMS messages, cell phones, and cybercafes where they can play long games on the Net are also all the rage. These meeting points are generating forms of communication and expression for spreading fashion and socialization of values and behaviors. Music, fashion, and leisure places are spaces that provide the opportunity for social identification, recognition, and developing relationships.

Although there are notable differences in teen fashion between boys and girls (which can seem a bit daring, due to the need for teenagers to explore their gender image), they sometimes have a similar image, with T-shirts, pants, hats, or other accessories. Boys, at the most, get their hair dyed or wear an earring, which used to be only for girls a few years ago. Piercings and small tattoos are currently very popular among young people. Also, complaints about the small sizes fostered by fashion brands and shops that specifically cater to teens have been appearing in the mass media. This has brought about actions by Spanish models and designers, in which they oppose this type of fashion and have been avoiding the use of models who are very thin. Anorexia is a significant problem for some girls and, more recently, also for some boys. Of course, social class can have an influence on identifying with a given urban image, or when acquiring certain brands that will lead teens to adopt a certain image. In general the image of Spanish teens is very similar to those from other Western countries due to the great influence the mass media, movies, leisure industries, music, and fashion have on boys' and girls' need for exploring and affirming identity.

The most popular sport in Spain is soccer (called football here). Big teams bring together hundreds of thousands of people every match. At the doors of the stadiums, after the training sessions, there is usually a crowd of teens who want to get a signature or take a photo with

The Gothic Quarter, Barcelona, Spain.
Courtesy of Laura Layera.

their idols: Ronaldo, Ronaldinho, Beckham, Raul, Zidane, and so on. There are even specialized publications and picture-card collections addressed to teens. Oftentimes, the sports press counts on the support of the youngest spectators. Soccer video games are also very popular. Even the small local teams can have loyal supporters. This is a basically masculine sport in Spain, unlike in the United States, although there are some girls' teams in our country that are acquiring more and more importance. Basically boys play football in schools and high schools. The proportion among boys and girls is much more balanced in other sports, like basketball, volleyball, or track and field.

Many teens practice outdoor sports in Spain: tennis, swimming, track and field, and so on. Cycling is especially important in the Basque

Country, where we can find great cyclists like Joseba Beloki or Iban Mayo. However, there are small cycling clubs all around the country in which teens, mainly boys, take part. It is not difficult to find them in one of the many B (bicycle) roads that cross over the mountains. In the winter, many teens go skiing. Given that there are important ski slopes in the country, even in southern regions, it is not necessary to go too far in order to practice this sport. In general, skiing has traditionally been a sport for families from higher socioeconomic backgrounds, although the scope of practitioners is widening. In fact, many schools and high schools offer it to their students at reasonable prices. Anyway, youngsters are renewing the practice of skiing with new and more urban (paradoxically) modalities like snowboarding (which is very similar to skateboarding), with specific clothes and more fashion accessories. Getting back to urban centers, going to the gym or the swimming pool is a common activity for many girls and boys who want to relax after their academic day. There is significant choice of public gyms and swimming pools, some with very good facilities, so that there are even waiting lists. Some people decide to attend private gyms, which usually prove to be a little expensive for most. Martial arts are in high demand in these gyms. There are also private clubs only attended by wealthy families where teens can play golf or do water sports. The latter are normally quite elitist and practiced by only a few in Spain.

We have been explaining how in Spain, social life, expressing feelings outwardly, friendship, and so on are very important, maybe because of the Mediterranean tradition we mentioned earlier. Along with this, there is also a great openness to new tendencies, favored in many cases by the generations that suffered isolation directly or indirectly during the dictatorship. Generally speaking, we can say that teens' forms of entertainment are very influenced by these principles.

Apart from spending time in outdoor spaces, squares, and public parks, or going to the cinema or to fast-food restaurants, music is an important nucleus of the Spanish teen's entertainment. Musical preferences show a mixture of tradition and modernity. New musicians inspired by traditional music from different places of Spain are a rage among young people. Ojos de Brujo or Mártires del Compás, inspired by Andalusian *flamenco*, are having great success. Others, like Estopa or Rosario, are inspired by the Catalan *rumba*. In Galicia, a new generation of musicians like Carlos Núñez, Hevia, and Cristina Pato are inspired by Celtic music. In the Basque Country, Kepa Junkera uses traditional instruments like a small accordion and a horn and combines them with new sounds. Partly thanks to these fusions, young people are showing a renewed interest in traditional music, which people listen to in huge concerts, bars, or radio stations, which also offer other music from around the world.

Many radio stations and some TV channels are specifically addressed to the young population, including hits produced in the Anglo-American world. MTV has a large audience among those who have cable TV. Record companies have teenagers as their main targets and try to appeal to them with concerts, big parties, and so on. Even some radio stations connect with foreign radio stations in order to listen to a specific DJ session. So today's music fashions flow quickly and simultaneously from many countries, so that many youngsters from the United States would not be amazed by the clothes worn by teens in Spain.

Spain is a country with a big nightlife. Night leisure hours are strictly defined by law. There are afternoon dance clubs that are open from 7 P.M. to midnight. Some require you to be over 18, because alcoholic beverages are served, unlike others addressed to an under-18 crowd, although smoking is always allowed. Tobacco smoking is widespread among teenagers, both boys and girls, but there are more and more cases in which teens reject tobacco, even entering into conflicts with their smoker parents. Between 7 P.M. and 3 A.M. many music bars open their doors, mainly to an over-16 crowd. Discos are opened from midnight to 5 A.M. The so-called after-hours open around 5 A.M. and close at 9 A.M. Only those over 18 can attend these places.

There are certain tourist areas, like Ibiza, that have generated a club culture, producing its own fashion and electronic music, maybe the most recognized on a European level. In the summer, people also hold rave parties, more or less spontaneously (many of them are prohibited), and outdoor concerts, as well as the so-called advanced music of those musicians we wrote about before and other internationally recognized artists.

Nightlife is strictly controlled by law in order to avoid car crashes, overall produced by the excessive consumption of alcohol and drugs. The increase in consumption of Ecstasy and cocaine among some young people is a special cause for concern. In Spain, these drugs, like cannabis, are forbidden. In order to overcome this problem, the government has launched aggressive advertising campaigns addressed to young people, while some associations get into these spaces to distribute information about the risks of drug consumption.

RELIGIOUS PRACTICES AND CULTURAL CEREMONIES

Although most Spanish people declare that they are Catholic (80 percent),[4] 56 percent assert that they are not really religious, or not at all. This apparent contradiction should be understood in terms of the

Catholic tradition we have had in Spain for many years, and also because of the heavy religious impositions after the civil war during Franco's dictatorship. For this reason, with the arrival of democracy, the constitution immediately aimed at assuring religious plurality with article 16, which defines Spain as a secular and nonconfessional state.

It is a significant piece of information that most young people who were born around the fall of the dictatorship declare that they are only a bit religious, or not at all (concretely, 75 percent of those born after 1978). In general, beliefs are restricted to the familial and private sphere, and they appear in varied situations. Therefore, most couples get married in the Catholic church (64 percent) and most children are baptized (79 percent). Another example is people's names, which had to refer to the calendar of saints' feast days or to different aspects of religion (María, Milagros, José, Pablo, and so on) until very recently. Nowadays, many people still celebrate their birthdays as well as their saint's day. These and other cultural expressions have been fostered more by social conditioning than deep religious beliefs. Things are changing today, and parents usually choose other names for their children. In daily religious services, usually there are not any young people, although some of them attend Sunday mass. Despite everything, there are many youngsters that have great faith, as we could see in the multitudes gathered during the visit of Pope John Paul II to Spain.

A particular aspect of the Catholic faith among young people is the so-called Camino de Santiago. This is a walking route that thousands of pilgrims (most of them quite young) take every year through the north of Spain, to the cathedral of the city of Santiago de Compostela. Along the road, people pass by a range of villages and churches that predate us by almost a thousand years. Originally, the journey was a form of penitence, but today it fluctuates between the public demonstration of faith and, most of all, the recreational aspect.

There are also Protestant and Islamic minorities as a consequence of immigration. There have been some racist outbreaks recently, for example, against the construction of mosques, although they are not supported by most of population. In Spain, social organizations and movements have established a democratic regime and citizenship participation, which brings together a multicultural tradition and a strong will to modernity.

CONCLUSION

Many features of Spanish teens' way of life are explained within the framework of a traditionally welcoming and generous culture (as a very graphic example, Spain has the highest rate of organ donation in the world), always open to exchange with other cultures. This is reflected in the warm behaviors and interactions among people and in the cultural manifestations we have mentioned, in many cases influenced by contributions from other peoples.

Some of the features we have explained are closely related to the maturity of the so-called democratic transition. Despite the possible mistakes in this process, the steps from dictatorship to democracy have been taken solidly and in a relatively short time (it has almost been three decades since the death of Franco). Nowadays many teens live in a totally different social and cultural situation from that experienced by many of their relatives. Maybe because of all this, many of the things we have explained involve a great will for freedom, openness to new behaviors, and transformation. The high participation in social movements and the transformative conscience of many teens and adults should be understood in this sense. Teens will grow with the possibility of being owners of their own destiny, which was not possible in Spain for many years.

NOTES

1. Instituto Nacional de Estadística [National Statistics Institute]. 1 January 2000. Available at http://www.ine.es.

2. The text of the constitution is available at http://www.congreso.es/funciones/constitucion/indice.htm.

3. Data from. 2001. Informe España 2001 [Report Spain 2001]. Madrid: Fundación Encuentro.

4. The following data were gathered by the Centro de Investigaciones Sociológicas (Sociological Researches Center): CIS. 2002. Religión y sociedad. Datos de Opinión, vol 29. Available at http://www.cis.es/boletin/29/index.html.

RESOURCE GUIDE

Nonfiction

Alvarez Junco, J. (Ed.). 2000. *Spanish History since 1808*. New York: Oxford Univ. Press.

Brenan, G. 1995. *The Spanish Labyrinth*. New York: Cambridge Univ. Press.

Carr, R. (Ed.). 2000. *Spain: A History*. New York: Oxford Univ. Press.

Fuentes, C. 1999.*The Buried Mirror: Reflections on Spain and the New World*. Boston: Houghton Mifflin.

Gibson, I. 1997. *Federico García Lorca: A Life*. New York: Pantheon Books.

Gillespie, R., Rodrigo, F., & Story, J. (Eds.). 1995. *Democratic Spain: Reshaping External Relations in a Changing World*. New York: Routledge.

Michener, J. A. 1984. *Iberia*. London: Ballantine Books.

Vicens Vives, J. 1970. *Approaches to the History of Spain*. Berkeley: University of California Press.

Williams, M. 2004. *The Story of Spain*. New York: Golden Era Books.

Fiction

Cela, C.J. 1990. *Journey to the Alcarria*. Madison: University of Wisconsin Press.

Cervantes Saavedra, M. 1992. *The Adventures of Don Quixote* (translated by J.M. Cohen). London: Penguin.

García Lorca, F. 1987. *Poem of the Deep Song*. San Francisco: City Lights.

Valle Inclán, R.M. 1993. *Lights of Bohemia*. Warminster (Wiltshire): Aris & Phillips Ltd.

Web Sites

http://www.aspiringspaniard.com/

A top-notch interactive guide to Spain offering information on all Spanish things, from traveling to history and food.

http://www.learn-about-spanish-and-spain.com/

Information about Spain in easy-to-use categories, from food and recipes to travel and health care.

http://spanishculture.about.com/

All kinds of information about Spain: recipes, food, culture, history, and more.

http://www.tourspain.es/Portal/ES/Default.htm

Complete and useful information about everything necessary for traveling in any region of Spain.

http://www.typicallyspanish.com/

A complete search engine for anything to do with Spain.

More Information

Instituto Cervantes in the United States

A worldwide nonprofit organization created by the Spanish government in 1991. It is the largest organization in the world concerned with the teaching of Spanish. It works with other institutions in organizing cultural activities such as lectures, book presentations, concerts, art exhibitions, and more.

Instituto Cervantes Albuquerque (USA) Inc.
National Hispanic Cultural Center of New México
1701 4th Street SW
Albuquerque, NM 87102
Tel: 505-246-2261
Fax: 505-246-2613
E-mail: dirabq@cervantes.es

Instituto Cervantes Chicago (USA) Inc.
John Hancock Center
875 Michigan Avenue, Suite 2940
Chicago, IL 60611
Tel: 312-335-1996
Fax: 312-587-1992
E-mail: chicago@cervantes1.org

Instituto Cervantes New York (USA) Inc.
122 East 42nd Street, Suite 807
New York, NY 10168
Tel: 212-661-6011, ext. 6
Fax: 212-545-8837
E-mail: classprogram@cervantes.org

Spanish Embassy
2375 Pennsylvania Avenue NW
Washington, D.C. 20037-1736
Tel: 202-728-2335
Fax: 202-728-2313
Spanish Institute

An organization founded in 1954 for the understanding of the Spanish culture, past and present, and its influence in the Americas through a variety of programs.

Spanish Institute
684 Park Avenue
New York, NY 10021
Tel: 212-628-0420
Fax: 212-734-4177
Web site: http://www.spanishinstitute.org/

Pen Pal Information

Consejería de Educación y Ciencia de la Embajada de España en Estados
Unidos y Canadá

http://www.spainembedu.org/intercambio/

Correspond electronically with students and teachers.

Sección del Instituto Cervantes

http://www.inetworld.net/eac/penpal/

A good way to make friends on email.

Chapter 11

SWEDEN

Anna-Maria Ahlén

INTRODUCTION

Secretly the following lines live within many Swedish teens, today as well as for the last several decades. They are comforting in this phase of transition:

> Yes, of course it hurts when buds are breaking.
> Why else would the springtime falter?
> Why would all our ardent longing
> bind itself in frozen, bitter pallor?
> After all, the bud was covered all the winter.
> What new thing is it that bursts and wears?
> Yes, of course it hurts when buds are breaking,
> hurts for that which grows
> and that which bars.[1]

This also illustrates two aspects of the Swedish culture: closeness to nature and the notion of suffering in life.

The country is situated in the north of Europe on the Scandinavian peninsula. In the south it has fertile soil, whereas in the north are high mountains, and a large part of the country is covered with forest. By size it is one of the biggest countries in Europe, but when it comes to population, with its approximately 9 million citizens, it becomes one of the smaller ones. One could imagine that with such a large territory the Swedes would be spread out all over the country, but to the contrary, about 85 percent live in urban areas (more than 1 million of them in the capital, Stockholm), and 90 percent live in the southern part of the country. One could imagine that most parts of Sweden would be difficult to inhabit and culture since most of it is at the same latitude as the tundra in Alaska, Canada, Greenland, and Siberia. It is thanks to the warm Gulf Stream, which has its origin in the warm streams of Florida and North Carolina and wanders through the Atlantic Ocean up to the Nordic Sea, that the climate is warm enough.

Sweden is a kingdom, but the head of the state, King Carl Gustaf XVI, has only representative and symbolic power. Instead the governing power lies with the citizens, who in general elections elect the parties of Parliament. At the present there are seven parties in Parliament. After an election they negotiate about forming a government and then vote for prime minister. The prime minister leads the government's work and appoints the ministers. If Parliament is not satisfied with the government, they can decide to defeat it by a no-confidence vote or remove a minister. But the power of Parliament has decreased: since 1995 Sweden has been a member of the European Community and subject to its legislation.

Financially, Sweden has a solid market economy. Companies such as ABB, Ericsson, Electrolux, Saab, and Volvo started as Swedish companies and are by now multinational companies, with international ownership based in an international market. The steel industry is also part of the economy, as is the production of paper pulp, of which much is exported for printing daily papers, and it had a leading position during the 1990s.

Sweden is working actively within organizations such as the UN on improving the environmental situation of the planet. Great improvements in Sweden have also been a result of this work. For example, the capital, Stockholm, is situated on many islands, and its water is so clean that one can eat the fish from it and swim in it. When you are walking past Parliament in the heart of the city, you can often see people fishing in the streams below.

Closeness to nature is something precious to the Swedes: they can walk or camp anywhere in nature thanks to the legal right of access to private land. It is a right for everyone to be in nature and pick flowers, berries, and mushrooms. One can bathe at private beaches if they are not part of a garden, and one is even allowed to make a fire if it won't endanger the surroundings. But with these rights also follows the responsibility not to inflict any damage to nature and never leave any garbage there. One is not allowed to enter or cross a private garden. But more about the Swedes' closeness to nature later.

Let us now examine ways in which the world would be a much more boring place without the Swedes. The Swede that has had the most impact on the natural sciences is Carl von Linné, who found a way to categorize flowers and other plants in the eighteenth century that is still valid today. Even though Sweden has a very small population, Swedes have invented many things that make life easier in modern society, such as the zipper, the safety match, the ball bearing, the AGA stove, the home refrigerator, the adjustable wrench, the tetra pack, the computer mouse, and the self-moving vacuum cleaner, among others.

And how dull the U.S. music industry would be today without the Swedes. What? Yes. What would Britney Spears, Celine Dion, Westlife, and the Backstreet Boys do without the Swedish hit songwriters Max Martin and Jörgen Elofsson, among others? And some of the best rock videos of Madonna and Robbie Williams—just to mention two of many—are directed by Jonas Åkerlund. Several Swedish groups and artists are selling rather well in the United States today, for example, the Cardigans, the Hives, Soundtrack of Our Lives, the Hellacopters, Millencolin, and Sahara Hotnights. During the 1990s Ace of Base was bigger in the United States than at home. And during the 1980s Roxette was number one on the U.S. hit list for quite some time, as was Björn Skifs in the mid-1970s. Not to mention ABBA, which started this triumphal procession around the world in the mid-1970s.

Today, Sweden is actually the third-biggest export country for rock and popular music in the world, after the United States and Great Britain. How come? There are several aspects of the Swedish education system and culture that are suggested as an explanation for this, but that will be explored further on in the chapter.

The U.S. film industry has also some great Swedes working within it: the director of *Gilbert Grape* and *The Cider House Rules* is the Swede Lasse Hallström. His film *My Life as a Dog* is also a wonderful story about a boy's life in a Swedish village. The director Ingmar Bergman's film can be bought on DVD in the United States. Some Swedish actors also include, for example, Peter Stormare, and legendary actresses such as Greta Garbo and Ingrid Bergman never die.

Most Swedes have Swedish as their native language; in the north of Sweden there are also native speakers of the Sámi languages, Finnish and Meänkieli, which are official languages in Sweden together with a gypsy language and Jiddisch. But through immigration, which has increased since the 1960s, there are now many languages spoken in Sweden and taught in the schools, since children of foreign origin have the right to an education in their native language.

Immigrants or children of immigrants make up more than 1 million of a total population of about 9 million, so more than 10 percent of the population has an immediate immigrant background; most of them come from the neighboring country of Finland, but otherwise they come from all over the world, some because they got married to a Swede, others for work or as refugees. But between 1850 to 1930, one-fifth of the Swedish population emigrated to the United States and Canada.

Sweden has not been involved in a war for about 200 years. But before it became a kingdom, different leaders wanted to create a great Swedish state that would rule all the territories around the Baltic Sea. And all the countries surrounding the Baltic Sea have for a longer or shorter time been included in the Swedish kingdom. The first king of the present royal family, Bernadotte, was a French general of the emperor Napoléon, and he became adopted by a childless king. He became king in 1818. Why a Frenchmen? The Swedes hoped that with one of Napoléon's generals on the throne they would once again be able to conquer some of the countries around the Baltic Sea, especially Finland, which Sweden had lost to Russia in 1809. But Bernadotte thought otherwise; he was tired of war and realized that Russia was too powerful as an enemy, one it was better not to enter into war with. In one of the offices of Bernadotte he had a copy of the U.S. Declaration of Independence. It is supposed to be one of the only copies from that time left in the world.

When Bernadotte became the king, he was also a ruling king, although with less power then his precursor, but today the royal family has lost all its power; actually, they are the only adult citizens who are not allowed express their political opinions. What happened in the 180 years that could explain this shift of power?

Historically, the Swedes have to a large extent been peasant freeholders and workers. This has developed a culture of responsibility-taking for the land and the people, no matter what their social background. In the old days the inhabitants in the parishes took care of the poor, and during harvest everyone that could do a little work was employed. An idea that has evolved into the Swedish welfare state and has been steering social life and the political activities regardless of whether the ruling party is right-wing or left-wing (the Social Democratic Party has been in government during most of the twentieth century) is to give each child similar possibilities no matter what financial or social situation the child is born into. They should have the right to health care, basic education, a university education, and social security all through their life.

In the nineteenth century industrialization took off and the factories needed skilled workers, so education had to be widespread, and the creation of an elementary school system in 1842 also went hand in hand with the ideas of the Age of Enlightenment. During this time there was also starvation in Sweden, and large groups emigrated to the United States. Among those who remained, the workers started to unite in trade unions to negotiate better working conditions and salaries. They realized that knowledge about society, legislation, and the political system was necessary to become successful. Informal education became the key to this. They did this by forming groups and learning together. This developed into the folk high schools and study associations. Solidarity between the workers was strong, and many intellectuals supported them. In the 1930s what has been referred to as the Swedish model developed, which meant striving for good relationships between the different agents in the labor market. The social policy was improved by increased care for the elderly, a housing policy that allowed workers to get good housing, and an employment policy.

The democracy in Sweden is not only something that is shown in elections; there are also many democratic processes in schools (where sometimes even half of the board members are students), companies, and trade unions, and many Swedes participate in several democratically run NGOs. An important concept in Sweden is the right of public access to official records. This means that anyone has the right to see all matters and even all correspondence (even e-mail) that are sent to and from the government, parliaments, local governments, public authorities, and other official organizations. This makes Sweden a very transparent society that invites its citizens to participate in the society-building processes as well as monitor them closely. Even in the companies there is an unusually strong tradition of openness when compared with U.S. companies when it comes to control and participation in how the company is run both by the employed and the stockholders.

Unemployment in August 2004 was about 5.5 percent, but then we must consider that there are many adults involved in educational activities instead of being officially unemployed. Sweden also has quite a lot of people that have retired due to sickness, before the general pension age of 65 years old, but more and more people are now continuing working after this age.

TYPICAL DAY

In a way there are just as many ways to be a teenager in Sweden as there are teenagers in Sweden. But then a text like this would be impossible. So instead of getting all the shimmering and glimmering of teenagers as individuals, the text will focus on some simplifications of what can be common for larger groups of teenagers in Sweden. But of course the situations vary depending on the financial and ethnic position of the family.

One thing they all have in common is going to school: this steers the days for teenagers no matter what their social, ethnic, or cultural background, since really very few drop out of school before they have reached the age of 18, but they are only obliged to attend school until they are 16 years old or have finished the nine-year comprehensive school.

Between 6:30 and 7 is a common time to wake up to get ready for school. These morning rituals are largely similar to those in the United States, since there are similar living standards. They take a shower, brush their teeth, and decide what to wear—often an important issue, since many teens belong to different subcultures that express themselves through the way they appear. They have a quick breakfast and then dash off to school. How they get to school varies depending on how far it is and what season it is. Some have far to go, and they travel by school bus or the regular public transportation system, which is free of charge. If it is not too far and the weather is fine, taking a bike is the most popular way to get to school, or they can walk. Very few go to boarding school—there might not be more than three boarding schools in the whole country— often those who have parents that work abroad.

The school day usually starts around 8:10. The days are filled with classes, and the students are moving around between different classrooms depending on what subject they have, since the different subjects have their own classrooms.

Around noon there is lunch. A cooked meal is served in the dining hall free of charge in the nine-year compulsory school, and in the upper secondary school, which is equivalent to high school, the lunch is free of charge in some municipalities while in others the parents pay a sum each semester for the lunch.

The best thing about school is the breaks, some would say: this is the time students spend with their friends, chatting about life and love, playing cards, studying, listening to music in an MP3 player, eating snacks, and so on. The school day ends around 3 or 4 P.M. When the school day has ended, they go home by themselves or with a friend and have a snack. Many are engaged in activities such as taking different types of classes in the evening or playing a sport. This is often suggested by the parents, and sometimes the teen actually feels forced to do this, to live up to the parents' great expectations.

It is common that they have chores to do at home, which often gives them a higher monthly allowance. But this is also negotiated between the teen and the parents, to get the right balance between workload and

The Flumeride is one of the most popular attractions at the Amusement Park Liseberg, Goteborg, Sweden. Courtesy of Goran Assner. Used with permission of Image Bank Sweden.

pocket money, which is also good training in negotiations and useful for the future. In the evening they do homework, spend time with friends, or use the computer for chatting or playing Internet-based role-playing games. And some time each day is also spent in front of the television. They also enjoy spending a lot of time in their rooms doing nothing. The time to get to bed varies, but they usually go to bed around 10 or 11 in the evening.

The school year is divided into two semesters: the autumn semester starts in the middle of August and ends in December, just before Christmas, and the spring semester starts in January and ends the first week of July.

FAMILY LIFE

What is a family? In Sweden, as in many countries, the concept of a family is changing from the nuclear family to other constellations of families. A family could also be a single parent with the child, or a child growing up with the grandparents or in a foster home. Even though the parents do not live together, they usually have shared custody, so many

Swedish kids find themselves living one week with the father and his new family and the next with the mother and her new family, but in their later teens they are more free to decide who to live with. Not unusual is that their separated parents starts new families and have new kids, perhaps with partners who have children of their own, so identifying brothers and sisters is a lot more complicated than saying that it is those who have the same biological parents.

To get the finances of the family balanced, both parents have to work. The high living expenses also make it more difficult for single parents. And the financial possibilities of the richer are getting better, but the poorer families find themselves in more difficult situations. Younger teens never work, and it is quite rare to find older teens working during the weekdays; a few might deliver commercial handouts in the mailboxes of homes in the afternoon, but during the weekend this would happen only if they were lucky enough to find a job. During the summer and Christmas vacations it is common to find them working. They save the money to buy their own TV and stereo, pay the bills for their mobile phones and driving lessons, travel, and buy clothes. It is regarded as good that they work; they learn to handle their own budget and get used to working life, so one finds teens from all financial backgrounds working, but perhaps it is easier for the kids of wealthier families to find better-paying jobs.

Before a couple has children they share the household duties and have a similar level of income, even though women tend to earn a bit less than men in general, but after children are born the responsibilities change: the women start to do more inside the home, such as caring for the children, cooking, cleaning the house, and washing clothes, and the men do less. And then it is not unusual that the women cut down on their jobs to work 30 hours a week instead of 40, to manage everything at home. Then, when reaching pension age, women are often put in a financially weaker position, since the pension is decided only by their life income.

The kitchen TV was introduced during the 1990s, and it is becoming more and more popular, but nevertheless many teens bring dinner to the TV room. In the busy families it is common that family members only have a meal together on the weekends, and even then it is rare to find a family with teenagers dining together at home. Family life in Sweden is formed in relation to the processes of working life.

In Sweden it is illegal to have sex with someone under the age of 15. Age 15 is also the age of criminal responsibility, but there are still special rules for punishments of people under 21. At 16 teens are allowed to negotiate contracts of employment and do what they want with the money they earn. At 18 they are allowed to vote in general elections, sign contracts, get a driver's license, and order alcohol in restaurants; however, they are not yet allowed to buy alcohol at the state-controlled company for the sale of wines and spirits, and alcohol is not sold anywhere else. Not that many get their driver's license at 18, since it is very expensive, and it is not really necessary to have once since public transportation in general functions well in the urban areas. But in the rural areas it is more important to have a car to be mobile. And it is also expensive to have a car: it costs a lot to buy as well as to own it, there are taxes, car-insurance costs are higher for teens (especially for boys, since they have a high risk of being in accidents), and gas prices are about three times higher than in the United States.

Leaving the teens and becoming 20 is something that many teens really look forward to, because then they can buy alcohol, but when that becomes possible a bit of that desire gets lost.

FOOD

Ask a typical Swedish teenager what typical Swedish food they like, and they would undoubtedly say, "Pizza, hamburger, pasta, pancakes," and then think for a while and say, "Meatballs, that I like, and then there's raw spiced salmon and pickled herring, but I don't eat that very often, and of course *smörgåsbordet*—I was about to forget it!" During the last 30 years, the everyday food in Sweden has changed a lot; new eating habits are following in the steps of globalization, both in terms of what dishes the meals consist of and how they are prepared. Much of the traditional food that before was eaten as everyday food has now become something luxurious and eaten on rare occasions or in restaurants, since it takes a long time and a lot of skill to prepare and cook.

The pizza place, Chinese restaurant, and hamburger place all have their places even in the smallest of Swedish towns. Actually, the pizza place is also found in small villages and is often the only restaurant and takeout place of that village, although the traditional hot-dog stand also has its place, not to mention some of the gas stations that sell a lot of fast food, often around the clock. In the big cities there are restaurants with food from just about any place in the world.

What is served in restaurants also affects what is eaten at home. Cookbooks from all over the world have become popular, but often they are bought or given as gifts, looked through, and placed on the bookshelf, where they remain. Exotic food usually enters the homes as spice mixes or ready-mades that get cooked in the microwave.

If the family has a car, the food is most likely bought in a big supermarket; otherwise there are plenty of food shops that are open every day of the week in the cities and villages. There are a great variety of products, but still not as much as in the United States, since the population is much smaller and spread out over the country.

What about hunting? During the autumn it is popular among some of the rich, landowners, and people in the north to hunt elk and deer. Traditionally hunting has been a male experience, but more and more women are getting licenses to hunt and forming hunting groups. However, it is one of the most expensive ways to get meat, since it is expensive to get a license and a territory for hunting if one is not a landowner.

Even though the fast-food market is expanding, the opposite is also happening. Especially among young people there's a great awareness of the quality of the food, and they try to get food that has been produced in an ecologically sound way and in a way that is fair toward the workers. There are an increasing number of vegetarians, and a variation of that with those who eat egg and fish and those who are very strict about the vegetables they eat.

Both men and women cook. Interestingly, the garden grill is considered male territory, but otherwise the women do most of the everyday cooking, even though the men are catching up, and men especially do more of the cooking for dinner parties. But there are also an increasing number of teens that show interest in gourmet cooking—being a chef has become a dream profession for more and more teens.

Breakfast often contains toast or rye bread with cheese, some Swedish version of salami or liver pâté, yogurt with cornflakes or muesli, orange juice, and hot chocolate and/or tea.

The teenagers' lunch is served in school and is a cooked meal; often just one dish is served, but in some schools there are a variety of dishes to fit the lifestyles and religious practices of the students. They also offer a lot of vegetables and salads as a complement to the served dish. This lunch is not always "cool" enough for the teens; instead they like to eat fast food or even candy, which they pay for themselves, instead of the healthier school lunch.

Dinner could be some microwave ready-made or a cooked meal, but it is seldom that the whole family has time to gather for a meal during the week. Christmas food especially is very traditional; some musts on the Christmas dinner table are baked Christmas ham and boiled rice pudding, and for the sweets, saffron-flavored buns and a spicy kind of gingerbread biscuits. It is also popular to build gingerbread houses of this pastry. During the fasting before Easter, the Swedes like do to anything but fast: during this time of year a special bun called *semlor* is sold, which is a wheat bun with almond paste inside and whipped cream on the top.

The typical summer food is pickled herring, with sour cream, chives, and fresh potatoes boiled with dill; anything that can be grilled is also a popular summer food. When having a cozy time on the sofa in front of the TV watching a film or having a small party, U.S. snacks are a must, such as potato chips, flavored peanuts, and soft drinks.

In recent years there has been an increase among kids of different types of food allergies and illnesses, such as diabetes, that affect what food they can eat. And just as in the United States and elsewhere in the postindustrial world, there is a problem with increasing fatness among children and teens, which will create health problems during their life. There are also more psychological problems related to eating and controlling the body, such as anorexia, especially among teen girls but also a growing among of boys. Boys more often are subject to a problem where they feel the need to have bigger and bigger muscles.

SCHOOLING

An issue that is continuously debated in Sweden is whether students should have school uniforms. They are allowed to wear whatever clothes they want in school, have their hair however they want, and use makeup however they want, with the exception that they are not allowed to use racist symbols. But there is an ongoing debate about whether there should be school uniforms, since in some schools students that do not have clothes from specific designers or of a specific type get bullied or are left without friends. Students are still free to decide how to look in Swedish schools, but it is obligatory to go there.

Everyone in Sweden has to go to the nine-year compulsory school when they are between 7 and 16 years old, although children can start when they are 6 if the parents request it. Homeschooling is nonexistent. After this, 98 percent of them continue on to upper secondary, even if it is not compulsory. There is really no alternative for them—it is unlikely that anyone will get a job without an education from upper secondary.

The students together with their parents are allowed to choose which school they want to attend; studies show that social class to a large degree influences their choices. The schools can be national, municipal, or private/independent; 94 percent of the students attend municipal schools. There are also a few private boarding schools where there are high school fees as well as boarding fees; usually those schools have students from the nobility or financial elite or with parents working abroad. They are also subjected to the national curriculum. All private or independent schools have to be approved by the Swedish National Agency for Education, which can close down a school if it does not follow the curriculum and legislation. The schools are adjusted for receiving disabled children—they have the right to the same education as nondisabled children, and the right to the support of technical equipment and/or a personal assistance for compensating their disability.

All education throughout the public school system is free of charge; there are no school fees, nor charges for teaching materials, school meals, health service, or transportation arranged by the municipality or public transportation to the school. In upper secondary it is still free of charge to attend the programs, but there are fees for lunch, books, and writing materials, but health care and transportation is still free of charge. Some students go to the same school for the entire nine years, but it is more common that they change schools when turning 13 and starting the seventh grade, and then again when starting upper secondary. All the schools and classes have students of both genders. But for gym, it is common that boys and girls have separate classes when they reach their teens. In some schools they are also experimenting with separating them for math classes, since that appears to be a subject that boys are dominating in.

Everyone that has passed compulsory school is allowed into upper secondary, and if they have not passed in some subjects they have the right to special education in those subjects. In some municipalities they have summer schools so that the students can catch up. Upper secondary is divided into 17 three-year national programs, of which 13 are vocational. All of them provide a broad-based education and result in the general eligibility required for entering a university or other institutes of higher education. The idea is that all teens should have the general qualifications for entering a university when they have finished upper secondary, including those who attend vocational programs. There is also the individual program for those who were not admitted into the national programs. But it is debated whether this should be closed down or not, since some believe that everyone should attend a program, but others think that there have to be alternatives for those who do not have the qualifications and/or don't want that.

In terms of homework, some educational scholars believe it is crucial for learning, while others say that there should be no homework, and instead there should be time within the school day for repetition—the Swedish school system is balancing between these two standpoints. In several of the compulsory schools the classes often ends around 2:30, and then there is time until 4 when students get help from teachers with homework or get extra help to catch up after illness or if they are behind in a subject.

But in upper secondary homework is important for succeeding, and for preparing students to learn how to learn and plan part of their learning processes themselves. At the end of upper secondary they also do project work on a topic they are interested in, in relation to their program, which could be on either an academic or vocational area. Another aspect of learning that is much emphasized in the Swedish schools is group work, to support the students' learning and working together.

Parliament decides on curricula for schooling in Sweden; within this goal-oriented framework each municipality or private school is free to decide how its schools should be run, and there are no national guidelines on the choice of content or what methods are to be used. Instead there are national tests in the core subjects; in grade nine in the compulsory schools as well as for the upper secondary schools there are national tests in English, mathematics, and Swedish. Those tests provide support for the teachers to establish grades. These national tests are offered for each subject at the same time all over Sweden.

The teachers have a lot of power when grading, but also a lot to take into consideration, from how the students perform in the classes to how they do on tests. The grades are goal- and criterion-oriented, and there are three passing grades: passed, passed with distinction, and passed with special distinction. Additionally, the teachers in compulsory as well as upper secondary schools meet individually with each student and his or her parents to discuss achievements and how to improve.

The teachers usually have three to four years of university education, with a special focus on teacher training for teaching at compulsory schools; the teachers at upper secondary have university educations in the subjects they teach together with teacher training for the theoretical subjects, and vocational education together with teacher training for the teaching in the vocational programs. It is still possible that some of the teachers do not have teacher training education; however, they will get less pay.

In upper secondary many students experience great stress because they will do whatever they can to get great grades, since that determine what university education they will be accepted into. Sixty-five percent of students complete upper secondary within the stipulated three years, and after some additional years 73 percent have completed their exam.

The government has the goal that 50 percent of all students should continue on to higher education within a couple of years of finishing upper secondary. There are also an increasing number of youths that continue on to higher education among students of working-class or

Celebrating secondary-school graduation. Courtesy of Bengt af Geijerstam. Used with permission of Image Bank Sweden.

immigrant background, and especially girls from those groups believe that education can improve their life. Boys from those groups, on the contrary, often hope to become sports heroes or rock stars.

National statistics on grades shows that girls have better grades as a group than boys. Perhaps this is a reason why there are many more female students as undergraduate students at the university—there are about 60 percent women and 40 percent men at the undergraduate level.

SOCIAL LIFE, RECREATION, AND ENTERTAINMENT

Want to phone a best friend? One has to make sure to have a booking in the agenda before to know that she or he will be there and have time to talk to you. Especially among high-performing upper secondary students in urban areas, life is sometimes hectic. It's regarded as a sign of a successful lifestyle if the daily agenda is fully booked. And it gives the illusion of having control over life. But for the majority of teens life is more laid-back. However, the uses of information and communication for socializing with friends are important. The mobile phone is crucial in this communication; most teens in Sweden have at least one. And sending and receiving many SMS messages is a part of the daily routine for most teens, an activity that sometimes doesn't even stop during classes. It seems as if the idea is that you don't exist if you are not a part of this communication. The mobilephone bill takes up quite a large part of the budget for many in their late teens. Parents don't usually pay the teens' mobile-phone bills, which sometimes could put the teens in very difficult financial situations if the bills become too large. But parents are at the same time happy that their teens have a mobile, so that teens can contact them if they are in trouble or so that parents can get in contact with them if they do not come home as planned.

Teens are very independent in choosing friends, dates, and boy and girl-friends, and parents do not object unless the friends have severe problems with drugs or alcohol or are young criminal offenders. However, teens choose their friends among those they go to school with and those they meet in their spare time and when going out, so their social space does to some degree overlap with their geographical and class space—whom they make friends with depends on where they live and where they go to school, and that is to some degree dependent on what social position or social class their parents have, a pattern that is more or less universal.

Many teens are members of websites where they get chat friends; some of these will lead to real friendships, but most are anonymous contacts.

Schools always arrange dances a few times each year. And there are often youth centers in the school building or close to it where teens can go in the afternoon and evening if there are no parents at home, or they might go there anyway to hang out with friends, flirt with the opposite gender, arrange dates, have a lemonade, and so on.

Relationships with the opposite sex or the dream of such relationships is of course always an important part of teen life. There are a variety of ways of expressing it, and there are

> teens who have no relationship, some because they are too shy, some because they feel like waiting, and some because of reli-gious or cultural practices
> teens who date
> teens who have a steady partner
> teens who live together with their steady partner in one of the homes of the parents
> teens who do not want to commit to a relationship and are exploring their sexuality

Sweden has one of lowest rates of teenage pregnancies in the world. Why? Is it because there teenagers are kept away from knowledge about reproduction, dating, and premarital sex? Many teenagers are sexually active, but they have safe sex; sex education has been an obligatory subject in Swedish schools since 1935, and there are tax-financed counseling organizations as well as NGOs that advise about relationship issues and contraceptives, give away condoms, and so on. And there is information in mass media, in both youth magazines and TV programs.

There are a lot of fun rituals when finishing upper secondary. This includes a lot of partying and drinking. It is common that each class creates some kind of jacket or T-shirt with some print or proverb that the class has created that they wear during spring semester. Often students arrange dinner parties in their home or in a restaurant or some other hall for their classmates or friends. So the spring before graduation is full of partying. When getting close to the end of the semester, there are champagne breakfasts with classmates and some of the teachers (somehow they are able to get sparkling white wine even thought they are not old enough to buy it). When the big day is coming, the students dress up in their best dresses or suits, since there are no specific graduation gowns in Swedish schools or universities. Instead they have caps with different colors depending on the program. The day that the cap is put on formally, families and friends gather in the schoolyard with placards of the student as a young child that they hold up so the student can find them. Then they bring the student home to a continuing party in some kind of fancy vehicle—they seem to be competing with one another for the most spectacular one, some leaving school in a wagon covered with leafy branches, a luxury car, a classic car, or even a helicopter. And some have nothing, thinking all this is too spectacular. In the evening it is common that the students drive around sitting in a large open-side wagon, visiting parties or other fun places.

There are many different types of recreation that teens are engaged in, from hiking in nature to all kind of sports, workouts, and dancing to all kinds of cultural activities such as playing rock music, singing in choir, acting, painting, and so on. And some find their recreation in baking, cooking, or sewing clothes, and others in front of the computer.

The love for nature and hiking is something that Swedes are brought into at an early age, and many enjoy it all through their lives, from holidays with family or friends doing walking tours that last for several days in the Swedish mountains to long walks in the forests fishing, mushroom picking, and so on.

Physical activities can be more or less organized; some play street baseball or bicycle with neighboring teens, while others play in soccer or ice hockey teams, with both girls and boys, even though there are more boys in this. But as a matter of fact the Swedish national teams of women's ice hockey and soccer have taken medals in World Cups and Olympics in recent years. And some of Sweden's best male ice-hockey players end up in the NHL on U.S. teams. But there are also quite a few that are engaged in more individualized games, such as track and field sports, especially since there are some great Swedish athletes now that inspire the youth. Tennis is popular, and golf is getting popular thanks to superstars like Annika Sörenstam. Other teens do not have this competition focus, but like to do workouts, yoga, aerobics, and so on. Girls are traditionally attracted to horseback riding and dancing, from ballroom to classical and modern ballet. But with the increased interest in show business, more boys than in earlier generations show interest in dance.

There are a lot of possibilities for teens that are interested in cultural activities. There are educational associations that arrange classes in everything from dance to language, painting, photography, and so on. These associations also support teens that want to start music bands, by giving them money for instruments, providing music lessons, and lending rehearsal rooms to them. For those interested in music there is also the municipality-organized music school, which provides lessons in all types of instruments for a low cost from when the kids start school until they finish upper secondary. That institution is often a part of the explanation for why Sweden has so many rock groups.

Some of the organizations that work to provide teens with sports or the possibility for cultural expressions do this to get them off the streets and prevent them from entering a possible criminal career. The interest in party politics is decreasing, but there is instead an increase in interest in participatory movements and specific actions with a political twist.

Swedish teens enjoy the same things as U.S. teens. They wear the same type of clothes from the same brands and listen to the same type of music, in similar ways. They see the same films; U.S. films are very popular in Sweden, especially among teens, which they see both on DVD and in the cinema. There are less TV channels broadcasting in Sweden, although they now have several programs that are produced especially by youth for youth, but there are also many U.S. and English soaps and series as well as channels for those families that have a satellite dish. And of course MTV is a must.

Partying is something that becomes more important the older the teen gets. Even though there are strict regulations for buying alcohol, it is not unusual to see drunken teenagers during Friday and Saturday evenings at private parties or in the streets.

RELIGIOUS PRACTICES AND CULTURAL CEREMONIES

Rather than going to church or any other religious space, many young as well as adult Swedes seek their religious experiences in the winds whispering in the large forests, in the ripple of rivers, in the dark mirror of a forest lake, in the symphonies of the birds, when the sun breaks through the dark clouds, or in the melting of the ice and snow:

> Yes, it is hard when drops are falling.
> Trembling with fear, and heavy hanging,
> cleaving to the twig, and swelling, sliding—
> weight draws them down, though they go on clinging.
> Hard to be uncertain, afraid and divided,
> hard to feel the depths attract and call,
> yet sit fast and merely tremble—
> hard to want to stay
> and want to fall.[2]

So, the experience of a higher existence is reflected in the rebirth cycle of nature. Even though many teens are not practicing any religion, they have an interest in existential issues. Films such as Star Wars and The Matrix have a part in forming teens' existential life, since they trigger them to raise questions about their existence, what the world consists of, and how to understand the complexity of life.

It is not unusual that a Swede would claim to be an atheist or to have a belief in a higher essence but does not connect it to any formal religion, even though they belong to the church. About 80 percent of the population belongs to the Lutheran Church of Sweden. The second biggest religion is Islam.

Since Sweden is a multicultural society with freedom of religion, there are all types of religions and existential movements that some teens are exploring, such as new age, yoga, tai chi, and karate, as well as the many different churches of Christianity, Hinduism, Buddhism, Taoism, indigenous people's religion, and so on. Those groups are not only in the big cities, but also in many of the smaller towns.

School teaches about all religions and philosophies. One would even find some teens going to philosophy classes in their spare time.

A part of discovering the self and the world is done through traveling. In their late teens they often travel in Europe with friends; attend language schools during the summer in England, France, Spain, or Germany; and some spend a year in a U.S. college. When they have finished upper secondary and worked for a few years, it is not unusual that they work to save money for traveling the world as a backpacker for several months or up to a year.

CONCLUSION

According to some youth researchers, having fun in the present is the most important priority for Swedish teens. Many dream of becoming famous, by, for example, reaching a dream profession in the media, especially a TV host, professional sports star, or chef: a lot of Swedish chefs makes great food shows, unlike the one on the Muppet show—that guy does not even speak Swedish. Many view their identity as a project they can change and play with. Living as if life is eternal, yes, they would say, "If I die ... " and relate to school and working life as projects, where they can change as they want.

But the other side of that coin is the feeling of dissatisfaction and discontent with oneself, one's body, and one's life. The consumption of antidepressive drugs increases; 10,000 teens and children in Sweden take antidepressive drugs, and the amount has doubled since 1999. The number of teens that take illegal drugs is also increasing.

It becomes important not to lose touch with the miracle of life:

> Then, when things are worst and nothing helps
> the tree's buds break as in rejoicing,
> then, when no fear holds back any longer,
> down in glitter go the twig's drops plunging,
> forget that they were frightened by the new,
> forget their fear before the flight unfurled—
> feel for a second their greatest safety,
> rest in that trust
> that creates the world.[3]

NOTES

1. The first verse of "Yes, Of Course It Hurts" by the Swedish poet Karin Boye, in translation by David McDuff, http://www.halldor.demon.co.uk/tree.htm.
2. The second verse of "Yes, Of Course It Hurts."
3. The third and last verse of "Yes, Of Course It Hurts."

RESOURCE GUIDE
Nonfiction

A brief guide to Sweden is *Sweden and Swedes* by Claes Britton, a booklet published by the Swedish Institute. It introduces Swedish cultural history, design, music, gastronomy, and the welfare state and business sector, among other things.

Swedish design is great. Learn more about it in *Swedish Design* by Lotta Jonson, a book published by the Swedish Institute.

Sweden has some interesting customs at Christmas, Easter, family tradition, and of course the uniquely Swedish tradition of Lucia: read about them in *Maypoles, Crayfish and Lucia—Swedish Holidays and Traditions* by ethnologist Jan-Öjvind Swahn, a booklet published by the Swedish Institute.

What way to get to know the Swedish culture is better than tasting it? Read *Smörgåsbord: A Swedish Classic* by Kerstin Törngren to find out more about Swedish food. *Smorgasbord* is one of the few Swedish words that has been included in the English language. Here you will find both the history of the smorgasbord as well as recipes. The booklet is published by the Swedish Institute.

Fiction

The poem that frames this chapter is written by the female poet Karin Boye. Read more about her at the site of the Karin Boye Society: http://www.karinboye.se/.

Within everyday life lies a mystery. Maria Gripe is one of the most popular authors of youth books in Sweden, and several of her books are in English, including *Agnes Cecilia*.

A tale about the old days in Sweden, written by the first women to receive the Nobel prize for literature, Selma Lagerlöf, is *The Wonderful Adventure of Nils Holgerson,* in which we follow a boy that has been transformed to the size of a doll and travels through Sweden on the back of a wild goose. Read more about Lagerlöf at http://nobelprize.org/literature/laureates/1909/lagerlof-bio.html.

Astrid Lindgren is the author of children's books that are loved around the globe and have been translated into over 70 languages. She has written stories about the strongest girls in the world, perfect if you want to read something Swedish to small siblings or when babysitting: Pippi Longstocking, Emil in Lönneberga, the Brothers Lionheart, and Karlsson-on-the-Roof, among others. Read about her and her characters at http://www.astridlindgren.se/eng/.

In Mikael Niemi's story *Popular Music from Vittula* we follow the struggles of Mattis, a boy growing up in the "vodka belt" in the north of Sweden, in a place where the Swedish and Finnish cultures are mixed. In Sweden this book is much appreciated among teens as well as adults, and it received a prize in 2000 for the best Swedish novel. Read more about it at http://www.swedishbookreview.com/article-2002-2-niemi.asp.

The love story *Heart's Delight* by Per Nilsson has received several international prizes for the best youth literature.

Read more about Swedish books that are translated into English at http://www.swedishbookreview.com/.

Web Sites

http://www.exms.com/

http://nobelprize.org/

http://www.royalcourt.se/

http://www.skolverket.se/english/

http://www.sr.se/rs/

http://www.svt.se/

http://www.sweden.se/

Pen Pal Information

http://www.chili.se/

http://www.kamratposten.nu/

Even though the magazine is written in Swedish, it is possible to send a note in
English to get a pen friend. Send it to

Regular Mail

Brevlådan

Kamratopsten

S-5 44 Stockholm

Sweden

E-mail: brevladan@kamratposten.nu

http://www.lunarstorm.se/

Chapter 12

TURKEY

Mustafa Sever

INTRODUCTION

Turkey is located in the area where three continents meet. Many countries share borders with Turkey: Georgia, Armenia, and Iran to the east; Bulgaria and Greece to the west; and Syria and Iraq to the south. Turkey, because of its location, has geographical and political significance, as it represents the gate of the West opening to the East. The significance of Turkey as a cross-continental passage is highlighted in the many water bodies surrounding it: the Mediterranean Sea to the south, the Black Sea to the north, and the Aegean Sea to the west. Turkey stretches over an area of 814,578 square kilometers, which is slightly larger than the state of Texas. Three percent of the country is in Europe, whereas the rest is part of Asia. This is a unique reality that no other country in the world shares.

Turkey has 68.7 million inhabitants, and 99 percent are Muslims. The coastal regions have the highest population densities. The population in Turkey is very young; almost 60 percent of the population is below age 30. Turkey is an ethnically diverse nation populated mostly by Turks, Kurds, Arabs, Jews, and other ethnic groups. Although Turks are predominantly Muslims, the state is officially secular. Turkey was founded after the collapse of the Ottoman Empire in 1923; modern Turkey follows the model of the European nation-state. The monarchy was replaced by democracy and the political system and social affairs were secularized. The system of government is a republican parliamentary democracy, which was founded by Mustafa Kemal Ataturk in 1923. Elections are held every five years, and politics is practiced by multiple parties of different political orientations.

The executive branch in Turkey is composed of the president of the republic and the Council of Ministers. Turkey is divided into provinces based on geography, economic conditions, and public service requirements. Provinces are further divided into administrative districts. All citizens over 18 years of age have the right to vote, form political parties, be elected, and engage in all sorts of political activities.

Turkey's economy is liberal and market-driven, and private enterprise is encouraged and sanctioned by the law. The country's leading manufacturing industry is textile and clothing production. The other big sectors are processed foods, iron and steel, and automobiles. Due to its climate, historical background, and seas, tourism is another important service for the Turkish economy.

Employment is highly influenced by the fact that two-thirds of the population live in the cities. So a considerable part of the Turkish people are employed in industrial, commercial, government, and service professions.

Military service is compulsory for all males who reach the age of 19 unless they are still pursuing their studies or have excuses that are sanctioned by regulations.

TYPICAL DAY

What is typical of teenagers in Turkey? Although this question might have simple aspects to it at the surface level, trying to understand the specifics of not only teenagers in Turkey but the country itself leads us to view the situation in a different manner. Understanding cultures could be determined either by an outsider's view or an account given by an insider. In both cases, we might run the risk of simplifying the conditions of a cultural context in order to introduce as general an outlook as possible to people who are interested in knowing something about the culture. Look, for example, at the vivid picture that Jenny White shares with her readers about a single observation of a street in Istanbul:

> Men lean against the wall in front of the shops, chatting and smoking. Women advance purposefully, trailing children and toting plastics bags of purchases. Many of the women wear large, colorful headscarves that draped forehead shoulders, bosom. Others are dressed modestly in long skirts and loose shirts, their hair uncovered. (2002, p. 63)

At a deeper level, answering the question raised above would seem more complex when we ask ourselves if the history of Turkey, or say by comparison that of the United States, can be in any way described as typical. One would naturally attempt to find similarities when trying to locate what is typical about a certain culture. This might be a safe road to take if one is after easy, but not somehow authentic, knowledge about a given culture. And when we talk about culture as a historical reality, then it becomes more difficult not to consider the element of difference that marks both culture and its diverse divisions, teenagers included. When you say the word *Turkey*, some people might associate it with the exotic past of the Ottoman Empire—Islam conquering Christian Europe and introducing different modes and styles of life. But in studying the history of Turkey more closely, it becomes more obvious how the country has undergone different stages and orientations.[1] Take, for example, what happened in 1923. Right after the end of World War I, with the weakening of the Ottoman Empire, Mustafa Kemal Ataturk introduced a major change into the life and culture of the Turkish people (Mardin, 1994). His project mainly aimed at modernizing Turkey by applying Western and secular methods that would shift the country from one historical reality, in which Islam and tradition were prominent, to another, where Westernization became an essential feature in domains as varied as language, law, the rights of women, and the system of government. Now, you would ask, where do teenagers figure in this? As a matter of fact, Ataturk paid specific attention to teenagers, and to women, as the vehicles toward the modern Turkey he perceived. Because his project was intended to be a fresh beginning for a Turkey very different from the nation that had been ruled by the sultans for hundreds of years, children and teenagers, being the future men and women of the nation, were looked upon as being the representation of this new beginning. That is why Ataturk dedicated April 23 as the new republic's national day of children[2]—the young citizens of the new Turkey were seen as the promising force in realizing the goals of modernization he had in mind.

Obviously, this new emphasis given to teenagers helped introducing various changes in their daily lives and specific cultures. However, this was not a simple change: whereas urban elites willingly adopted the project of modernization in regards to the different aspects of their lives, including those of their teenage kids, other parts of the population continued to adhere to conventional principles, like those who lived in the countryside or those who belonged to working and poor classes. Therefore, the change brought about by the project of modernization was not typically received or applied across different sectors of the Turkish people. This would continue to be true in later stages of the history of the nation, in the sense that difference rather than similarity is to be observed even at the present time. Let's try to look at this issue of difference in relation to practical realities of Turkey.[3] As in the United States, you may expect that social class would play a role in this difference. That is true of Turkey, but we also have to think in terms of location, that is, the division between the urban and rural parts of the country. Now, you should not be thinking that this makes things harder to understand: as a matter of fact, we should look at this as one way of understanding cultures in how they differ from others rather than in how they intersect on common grounds. This makes our journey a little bit more complex, but it adds to it many dimensions of exciting exploration of conditions that we might not be familiar with as individuals growing up in a certain country.

When one discusses difference it becomes harder to be satisfied with a description of a cultural setting for Turkish teenagers as *typical*. Of course, if one wants to know that Turkish teenagers wake up in the morning and go through some rituals like brushing their teeth, having breakfast, and saying goodbye to their parents before heading to school, then we are talking about some typical patterns not only among Turkish kids but almost among the majority of kids in the world. However, the aim in this chapter is really to get to know stuff about Turkish teenagers that might be different from how U.S. teenagers, for example, go about their daily social and cultural lives. For this specific reason we have to see how different economic, geographical, cultural, and social conditions influence Turkish teenagers differently.

So it is both important and logical to see how teenagers, like any other age group of the population of a certain nation, would be influenced by the conditions their country may come to encounter at one point or another. Take, for example, what happened in Turkey during the 1980s. The military took over power and tried to control many aspects of public life, including the reversal of the earlier teenage involvement in politics as a radical practice across the spectrum of Turkish political parties.[4] In that period, one can notice how the workload at schools increased dramatically. This meant that young citizens under this new military rule had less time to dedicate to activities outside their curriculum, specifically political activities that empowered their characters as individuals seeking the well-being of their teenage culture and their society at large.

Soon after the end of the military-rule era, along with the technological and economic changes that liberal policies of opening Turkey to global markets brought along, we can see how this impacted Turkey in general and teenagers in specific. Let's remember that location in Turkey, probably as in the United States, plays a role in helping people understand how difference is a matter of life rather than the exception. It is true that Westernization has not been a novelty for Turkey, but the further opening of the society to foreign economic and cultural styles has created a reaction specifically among those who saw this as an attack on everything Turkish in the traditional sense of the word. Among those have been "Islamic youth," who saw in the Islamic religion an affirmation of what they perceive as the true identity of the Turkish people (Saktanber, 2002).[5] In addition to these, different teenage affiliations can also be seen among young people who come from privileged urban backgrounds who associate with Western lifestyles and values. But it should also be noted that the youth who, with their families, decided to migrate from the countryside to the cities and have thus populated the outskirts constitute another category that can be called the teenagers of the *gecekondus*. (Following Kongar's definition, "the gecekondu is officially defined as 'the dwelling unit on somebody else's site which was built without obtaining the approval of the landowner and built in a way which is not approved by the general legal provisions for buildings and construction'" [1976].) This is an another important category, because it is estimated that 50 percent of the urban population live in *gecekondus*[6] of all sorts (Baharoglu & Leitmann, 1998).

Two teenagers from the same city who wake up to the same morning rituals, like washing their faces and having breakfast with their families, might leave their homes for two totally different purposes. One would go to school as expected of people at the same age in many parts of the world; but the other would head to the streets trying to sell *simit*[7] in order to support his poor family. Obviously, the same day would not be typical for both kids. For each, *typical* would mean something different. What makes a typical day typical for each of the two is not their preference of different lifestyles but rather the material conditions in which they are born. So the poor kid, not of his or her own choice, would find the reality of leading a typical day at school spent smoothly in the classroom or on the playground hard to grasp. On the other hand, for the more affluent kid, it is typical to come home from school to share some of the funny stories of the day with his or her family around the dinner table as a good meal is being served.

A typical day in the life of a Turkish teenager is not limited to these two kids. Let's see how difference prevails in relation to specific details, as is the case with getting to school. In the United States for example, the bus is expected to be the means for transporting teenagers between their homes and their schools. In Turkey, however, teenagers in rural areas would walk many miles to school, or they would spend considerable time on a bus that goes from one village to the next before it gets to one central school in a district of dispersed villages. Walking is the way to get you to school for yet another portion of Turkish teenagers, that is, teenagers who live in the *gecekondu* areas. This is only one part of the many hardships the residents of *gecekondus* of modern Turkey have to endure: some *gecekondu* neighborhoods lack basic services like electricity and running water.

FAMILY LIFE

Similar to the difficulty we have encountered in specifying a single typical tendency in the life of Turkish teenagers is the difficulty of specifying a typical family life. The reason for this, as has been indicated earlier, might be socioeconomic factors, geographical locations, and religious and social lifestyles. In Istanbul, for example, it is frequent that both fathers and mothers work outside the house. This is especially true of the middle and upper classes in urban Turkish situations. Surprisingly, in the countryside, where one would expect labor to be more distinctly gender-based, women work hand in hand with men outside the house on the farm, on jobs that are equally physically demanding. With reference to the focus of this chapter, children and teenagers are usually a part of the agrarian labor force on lands owned by their families. Thus, after schools, teenagers in the countryside divide their time between their homework and helping their families on the farm. However, in some urban settings where conservative lifestyles are followed and valued, women might not work outside the house at all. These fine distinctions also affect the children. In many cases, girls are expected to assist their mothers with house chores, while such demands are not placed on boys, who are expected to pursue tasks that affirm their masculinity.

The distinction between work conducted inside the house or for the family and that which requires teenagers to work outside the house and for somebody else is also significant. Some Turkish parents, even those whose socioeconomic conditions would naturally benefit from extra incomes generated by children, refuse to allow their children to work outside the house while they are still at an age of schooling. This has to do with elements of dignity that organize the hierarchy in the family, which defines it as the responsibility of the father specifically to provide for his family until they are capable of becoming independent. This responsibility is coupled with the conviction that education is essential and that better education will lead to better employment. On the other hand, child labor is a very important social concern in Turkey due to the fact that child workers between 6 and 14 years old represent 4.2 percent, and 15–17-year-olds 28 percent, of the employment for all age groups (State Institute Statistics [SIS], 2001).

The family in Turkey is not only a unit for providing better conditions for its members but also an affirmation of solidarity. This is obvious with the emphasis given to the primacy of having all family members eat together at the dinner table. However, this picture may not reflect the eating practices for all Turkish families. After a long day at work or school, Turkish families highlight familial ties by getting together and listening to others as well as exchanging stories and advice. Both men and women share these meals with their children, a rule that is usually not violated unless some guests are around in the households of conservative Turkish families, where sexual segregation becomes a practice; for example, men would eat with male guests and women and children would eat with female guests.

The family plays a major role in Turkish society today. Thus, when it comes to issues of drinking and smoking among teenagers, we have to think about the family and not only about the state regulations in studying how teenagers behave. The legal drinking age in Turkey is 18. However, in some families, if drinking is tolerated, children can have some drinks now and then even before they reach the legal age. In other families, where conservative values are prevalent, children even beyond 18 might not feel comfortable drinking or smoking in the presence of their fathers in particular. Outside of the context of the family, state regulations in regards to purchasing alcohol or cigarettes for people who are underage are not that strictly applied. Because of the labor divisions within Turkish families, such as that children frequently buy items for their parents, and these can be alcohol or cigarettes, it is rare that shopkeepers ask for IDs, simply because of the assumption that these items might be purchased for an adult.

According to the European Union (2003) annual report, although there is a steadily increasing tendency toward using heroin and cocaine in recent years, drug abuse is viewed as a relatively small problem in Turkey. This situation might be related to traditions and customs, as well as the multigeneration family structures that tend to observe teenager's behaviors very closely.

Eighteen is also the legal age for obtaining a driver's license. However, because of the high prices of cars and gas, very few teenagers actually own a car. In most of the cases, teenagers would drive either their parents' cars or those of very close friends. This is one major difference between rich kids and their poorer counterparts. But given the high rate of traffic accidents in Turkey, even some rich parents would not be happy with their kids driving on the crowded streets of big cities and their highways.

The fact that Turkey is increasingly open to Western, and specifically American, influences might explain some of the changes that have occurred among teenagers in Turkey with reference to the image they would like to project of themselves and their lifestyles. Like other parts of the world, some aspects of the lifestyles of Turkish teenagers could be described as more Americanized. This is specifically true when we talk about how some American English phrases and expressions have found their way into the daily language of Turkish kids, in what might be described as affirming their "coolness." These influences also appear in the increasing adherence to fast foods instead of traditional Turkish dishes, as well as in following the latest in Hollywood productions.

FOOD

Some people claim that they can identify the person by the foods he/she eats. This is somehow true when one thinks of Turkey, a country the size of Texas, surrounded by four different seas, that displays a wide environmental and geographical diversity. So one simple answer to the question about food preferences in Turkey might lie in what a certain region might produce or in how affordable it is for people to buy a certain type of food. In other words, people eat foods they can afford to buy, no matter how traditional these foods are. For example, in coastal areas fish is cheaper than in the inner parts of Turkey, which influences the cuisine in that area. Another factor in the food variation in the Turkish cuisine might have to do with the history of the nation itself. Modern-day Turkey is the successor of the Ottoman Empire, which at some historical points impressively stretched over wide geographical areas across Africa, Asia, and Europe. This helped in the inclusion of many varieties of cuisine into the cultural boundaries of the empire, something that has lived beyond the end of the empire into the many different items that one can see at a typical Turkish dinner table. Because of this wide diversity, it might be useful to name some. Turkish people like to eat different kinds of kebabs such as *adana, urfa, antep,* and *sish* kebabs as well as the tender lamb dishes of central Asia, the steaks of western Europe, and the delightful appetizers, soups, and vegetable dishes of the Aegean and Mediterranean, along with the sweet pastries of the Ottoman court, topped with a small cup of strong Turkish coffee.

The diversity in Turkish cuisine has been furthered by the introduction of fast-food culture, which is more appealing to younger generations. When kids go out with their friends, they usually frequent fast-food restaurants, something that does not really appeal to parents, who might prefer a healthier diet for their kids. And healthier foods are usually associated with foods that are cooked at home, usually by women, which might suggest how gender roles are negotiated in relation to cooking and

Karum Shopping Centre, Ankara, Turkey. Courtesy of Gokhan Okur.

providing meals for the family. But in some instances men can also prepare meals, especially if they have work schedules that are more flexible than those of their wives or if cooking is a hobby for them.

One interesting phenomenon that seems to be common among different sectors of Turkish society is that families, rich or poor, urban or rural, conservative or liberal, rarely eat out. One reason for this might be that dinnertime is family time, when families get together in the privacy of their familiar spaces. Having a meal at a restaurant in a space shared by others might be seen as intrusive.

Usually people go to several types of markets to buy foods. The most typical is the bazaar, which is frequented by people either daily or weekly, depending on the city or town. Bazaars gives the opportunity for people to shop for fresh foods. However, in the last decade, Turkish people were introduced to superstores and malls such as Metro, Kipa, Tansas, Carrefour, Carrousel, and so on. These huge shopping centers usually serve upper-middle- and middle-class families, given their being located in suburban areas or in the heart of the upper-middle-class neighborhoods, usually accessible by privately owned cars (Durakbasa & Cindoglu, 2002).

SCHOOLING

Usually, the academic year begins in the second week of September and ends at the end of the second week of June. All public schools are free and open to everybody. A typical school day in Turkey at the elementary level starts with the pledge performed by students of different grades. This pledge is usually committed to serving the motherland and the well-being of the citizens of the nation. Afterward, children, who all wear the same type of uniform, go into their classrooms, where they learn by listening to the teacher and performing some tasks. Students usually get break periods between sessions. All over Turkey, it is compulsory that children attend eight years of schooling regardless of their socioeconomic or geographical backgrounds, and also regardless of the type of school they attend, be it public, private, or trade school. The socioeconomic factor plays a major role in determining who goes to what school type, and the school type also influences the kind of education that children receive. For example, in public and trade schools, the emphasis is on developing survival skills among students. But private schools, which are usually modeled after Western-style educational institutions, tend to encourage the development of analytical skills that are usually tied in with promoting students as potential future leaders. This explains the different patterns of teaching: while at public schools lecturing is the norm, teachers at private schools tend to give more learning responsibility to students by increasingly involving them in learning through problem solving and specific task accomplishment.

Examinations are usually the means to determine the progress of students through a higher stage of their schooling. This is specifically the case at the end of the period of compulsory education. After completing eight years, children have to pass special examinations that are held nationwide in order to attend "special or bilingual" schools. But the most challenging examination, after completing high school, is the University Entrance Exam, which is administered once in a year in June by the Student Selection and Placement Center (OSYM). Although every year approximately 1.5 million teenagers enter this exam, only a small part of them are able to see the door of university campuses. On the other hand, students have to devote considerable time to prepare for this challenging exam. One can argue that many of the senior high school (*lycee*) students cannot do anything other than preparing for this exam.

While most Turkish parents value the education of their children throughout different stages of schooling and college education, socioeconomic factors might interfere. For example, a father who cannot afford the cost of attending college for his children might encourage them to enroll in vocational schools instead. This is seen as a means of assisting parents in shouldering the financial challenges of life in a market-driven economy, but also as a tool for building survival skills that would assure a decent life after children become independent from their parents.

Public schools are open and free to all children from all walks of Turkish life and society, which enables children from lower economic statuses to achieve some level of education and literacy. This goes hand in hand with the government's policy that mandates at least eight years of compulsory schooling. Parents who have the financial means to pay for the education of their children usually choose to send them to private school. Private schools do not only mean institutions that are modeled after modern Western educational systems. Some schools that adopt the principles of Islamic lifestyles also fall under this category: these are schools that have same curricula as those mandated by the state, but they involve some aspects of Islamic school culture and lifestyles.

A typical expectation of what goes on in a given classroom is that the setting would be specific to one group of students who are at the same level of their schooling education. Whereas this is true of most urban classrooms in Turkey, in some rural areas of the country, where small villages are scattered around with only a small student population in each, making it impractical for schools to be built in each of the villages, schools are usually built in a central location and attended by children from the surrounding villages. This not only means that children either have to be bused over considerable distances or walk many miles to get the school, but it may also lead to crowded schools without necessarily having a proportionate number of teachers. Therefore, one teacher might be in charge of several grades, and these are assigned to one classroom to enable the teacher to handle different groups of students simultaneously.

Socioeconomic factors and geographical location influence the schooling experiences of Turkish teenagers. But other elements seem to affect the choices and outcomes of schooling among teenagers. One of these is the state-endorsed secular policies that ensure the secularization of

Turkish society, education included. This state secularism sometimes clashes with aspects of life and culture that are Islamic: most of Turkey's population is Muslim, and it has been claimed that the headscarf is a religious symbol and must be banned in secularist institutions. The secularist government and its various organs, such as the Council for Higher Education (Yuksek Ogretim Kurumu), set up strict standards for women in headscarves. Women wearing headscarves have not been allowed to enter public institutions such as schools, courts, and some government service buildings since 1998. These "secularist standards" have particularly affected female students coming from conservative Muslim families. Many of them have had to drop out of school.

SOCIAL LIFE, RECREATION, AND ENTERTAINMENT

The social life of teenagers in today's Turkey is as diverse as their schooling experiences. This is simply because social life in Turkey is determined and influenced by the different realities of its citizens, such as religion, tradition, custom, education, geographical location, socioeconomic status, and individual and collective preferences and choices.

The primary space for Turkish teenagers to meet their age peers is the family: family get-togethers are not exclusive to the immediate family but quite often involve siblings of different ages from the extended family. But beyond the private space of the family, teenagers in Turkey meet other teenagers in spaces that might look very similar to where U.S. teenagers usually meet. The school, the playground, social and cultural clubs, sports clubs, and coffee shops are some of the places where you can see Turkish youngsters socializing with and meeting other teenagers. Although not all these spaces might exist in Turkish rural areas, alternative venues, especially those that are socially sanctioned where tradition and religion are significant, provide opportunities for Turkish youth to get together. For example, in weddings in small villages almost everybody gets invited to take part in the ceremonies, which allow teenagers, in the presence of their older siblings, to meet their fellow teenagers. This might also happen on holidays, religious or social, that involve either collective celebrations or extensive visits from one house to another.

Although dating among teenagers might be viewed negatively and even discouraged among conservative families, the concept is well accepted in urban parts of Turkey, where teenagers usually have the liberty of dating people of their own choice. The fact that teenage dating is a more accepted and frequent practice in cities then in the countryside does not necessarily imply parental sanctioning. Sometimes teenagers, especially girls, choose not to let their fathers know about their dating. This might be due to the prevalent social recognition of the father as the central figure, who ought to be respected if not feared, and this might be argued to be true across the social and cultural spectrum in Turkey. Even if premarital relationships are implicitly tolerated in some families, teenagers usually choose not to explicitly make their dating practices known to their families, as this might be seen to negatively affect the image of the family as a unit of dignity in its social interaction with other families in the community.

Dating among teenagers in Turkey takes on practices and concepts that are different from how teenagers in the United States, for example, would go about dating. Instead of direct initiation of a relationship that might come from either the male or the female, in Turkey, dating among teenagers shares many common features with how men and women in general interact in the public space of the society and culture, where indirectness appears to rule. Usually, it is male teenagers who take the first step if they would like to date a certain female teenager. But this requires lengthy and sophisticated techniques, where indirectness is the norm. For example, in the United States a boy might take a girl out for dinner on their first date; in Turkey, however, this might have to wait until the seventh or eighth date, simply because the male and female are socialized into cultural notions that you get closer to your date by being indirect, as directness is sometimes associated with being too intrusive or hasty.

Culture also figures to be important when it comes to behaviors among Turkish teenagers. Traditionally, the father is the figure of authority in the family, and respect toward this figure is not only expected but demanded from children. For example, teenagers or even adults who smoke would prefer not to do so if the father is present, in order not to overtly challenge his authority. This might extend to more extreme cases, like the way children sit in the presence of their father, as this is expected to follow a certain discipline in some Turkish families. So doing anything that might socially affect one's family negatively in public is looked down upon: for example, children and parent alike are expected not to share what happens inside the privacy of their homes with outsiders, especially if what is happening involves some problems or family feuds. In short, social and cultural norms determine what behaviors are acceptable for not only teenagers but other parts of the population as well, such as women. However, things might look differently where tradition and religion exist to varying degrees. However, when Turkish teenagers are in their own cliques with other teenagers, one might see different types of behavior that might not necessarily respond to the standards implied when they are in a social context that involves adults or siblings.

The project of modernizing Turkey that Ataturk started in 1923 has brought about various changes in Turkish society and culture, a reality that has recently intensified with the increasing integration of Turkey into the global economy and its continuous attempts to join the European Union. This change might be felt, for instance, in areas such as dress codes among teenagers. Blue jeans, for example, are commonly worn by teenagers from urban, rural, and ghetto backgrounds to some degree or another. On the other hand, other elements of social life seem to have undergone lesser change. Sex might be one of these. In many parts of Turkey, especially where Westernization and secularization have been countered by tradition or religion, premarital sex in general is still considered a social taboo. Teenagers are usually expected by their families to abstain from sexual practices until they get married at an older age. What is essential here is the common principle valued by many in Turkey, which is honor. Preserving the face or the name of the family is dependent on adhering to norms that the society and culture at large deem appropriate and encouraged. Thus premarital sex, which contradicts the teachings of Islam, would be seen as an impediment to the honor of the family as a whole in the eyes of the community. Unfortunately, because of existing gender inequalities in several parts of the country, female teenagers appear to fall under greater pressure in complying with this social and cultural condition than their male peers. Male teenagers might experience sexual relationships with a greater degree of ease than females because even when the parents know, the honor of the family seems to them not to be at the same risk as when the same act is brought about by a female.

By contrast, the taboo status given to premarital sex seems to have loosened in urban areas of Turkey, although one must not generalize. Dating in these areas is somehow more tolerated, which in itself makes premarital sexuality among teenagers more acceptable. But, this is not the typical pattern in Turkish cities. If we look at teenage sexuality in *gecekondus*, things become more similar to what has been said about teenage sexual practices in rural and conservative parts of Turkey. Here honor is also important, and teenagers are expected to maintain the face of their families in a consistent way. These different examples show once again that there are few similarities in the life and practices of teenagers in Turkey that one can generalize and talk about as a typical norm.

When teenagers become adults and are willing or ready to marry, their different backgrounds also determine how they go about marriage. In the rural parts of Turkey prearranged marriages are still a social practice in some instances; but in other cases, individuals might have a bigger say in choosing their marital partners, even though choices might be limited by how much influence customs and religious values have. On the other hand, the more urban spaces of interaction available to Turkish youth in large cities make it possible for them to have more choices when it comes to marriage. Parental interference in determining who and how to marry might be minimal. When it comes to marriage within the context of urban ghettos or *gecekondus*, both patterns can be seen. So some individuals would go along with the choice of prearranged marriage, whereas the conditions of others might enable them to choose their own would-be spouse.

According to Yurdadon, "modern competitive sports were practiced and introduced to Turks, mainly, by European diplomats during 19th century. From the beginning, development of sports in Turkiye has been problematic and influenced by the national economic, political and social problems" (2002).

Kids played some forms of games in the streets until the late 1980s. It was a common picture that as a car approached, kids had to stop the game and wait for the car to pass. Around that time government and municipalities started a new trend that aimed at creating more recreational areas and parks, including spaces for some kinds of sports like basketball and soccer. Many areas are designed for sports and sports-related activities. One can say that soccer is Turkey's national sport and is played everywhere. Some of the well-known teams are Fenerbahce, Galatasaray, Besiktas, and Trabzonspor. Although soccer is the most popular sport in Turkey, basketball, volleyball, handball, and wrestling, which is considered the ancestral sport, are also popular.

Sports are divided along gender lines. For example, soccer has always been the most popular of all among the boys, as it is the most popular sport in the whole country. Girls usually do not participate in soccer. Rather than participating in organized sports, they prefer some forms of games. Although there is a league of women's soccer, usually soccer is considered to be a boys' sport. But that is the only exception. Other sports such as basketball, volleyball, swimming, skiing, and track are performed equally by both, and in some of them girls excel.

School teams are available as early as primary school. When it comes to high school, competition becomes more challenging. Good players of school teams form the foundation of club teams. These boys and girls participate in club and school tournaments at the same time. High school team sports usually include basketball, volleyball, and handball, which, however, are less popular than soccer and wrestling. Although the most popular sport in the country, soccer is not organized well at primary and high schools. Usually soccer is conducted by clubs. Also, the other sports, like skiing, swimming, and track, are conducted by clubs and competition is induced by the clubs.

Usually the best-known players are those who are in soccer and basketball. On a national level, these two games have achieved some international success. Turkey came in third in soccer in the World Cup of 2002 and second in basketball in the European Championship of 2001.

As mentioned before, soccer is the most popular sport in the country. It is an industry of hundreds of millions of dollars. Competition among the three big clubs of the country is very intense. This takes its toll on supporters: game violence is not uncommon in Turkish stadiums, and tight security measures are usually taken before and throughout the matches.

Turkey is a peninsula and has four seas surrounding its north, south, and west borders. But it is very hard to say that sailing is a popular sport among teenagers, due to its high costs of maintenance. Wealthier kids can afford to practice sea sports around the many sea resorts along the long and diverse shores of the country. For poorer teenagers, sea sports might be simply limited to swimming.

Eating out, hanging out with friends at coffee shops and social clubs, dancing, listening to music, going on picnics, and so on are some types of entertainment for Turkish teenagers. Turkish youth listen to different kinds of music, domestic and Western. An Istanbul boy might do his homework while listening to U2, while a village girl might help her mother around the house with some folk music playing in the background. The 1960s were very important years for the history of pop music not only for Turkey but for other parts of the world as well. Turkey was influenced by this pop fire, and pop songs were sung in their original language for a long time until some Turkish composers wrote Turkish lyrics for famous songs. Economic problems, pessimism, and unhappiness, especially among people who live in ghetto areas of big cities, created another form of music called "Arabesque." This new music was the mixture of pop, folk, and traditional themes in content as well as Arabic rhythms and music structure in instrumentation. As the country experienced more social and economic problems, the Arabesque music became more popular.

Where mingling between males and females is more tolerated, boys and girls can dance with each other in public in clubs or school parties. But in villages the only chances for social interaction between the two sexes might be a wedding or village festival. Here dancing is more a collective practice that involves a large number of males and females. It is rare in a village setting to see a girl dancing with a boy alone: mingling is more acceptable if it is part of a group activity.

One form of entertainment that might be defined as specific to Turkey in comparison with other parts of Europe is the phenomenon of "beer houses" (*birahaneler*). Only men go to these places, something that is different from a typical bar setting with men socializing with women. Another type of socialization specific to Turkey is the get-togethers for women alone: women who are members of a circle of friends usually take turns hosting other women, and unlike potlucks in the United States, those invited are expected not to bring anything as gesture of appreciation for the hostess. The hostess is in charge of providing different types of foods and drinks to her guests.

Similarly to what happens on Halloween in the United States, Turkish kids get treats from neighbors on Bayram, a religious holiday that marks the end of the fasting month of Ramadan. Youngsters usually go from house to house knocking on doors and wishing "a happy Bayram" to residents, who are supposed to give either candies or money in return. This is not foreign to a common practice in Turkish families on major holidays, when parents and siblings give money to younger family member as an expression of good wishes. But this also refers to a willingness on the part of the adults in the family to treat youngsters as mature siblings who can decide for themselves how to spend the money given to them instead of deciding on a gift to give. However, these customs have started to disappear in urban parts of Turkey as observing and celebrating holidays take on more Western norms.

In the second half of the 1990s cybercafes became increasingly popular all over Turkey, especially for teenagers. Although coffee houses had always been very common for Turks as public spaces for socializations, the notion of Internet cafés was new, and soon teenagers started to frequent these places in their leisure time. Teenagers would mostly use the Internet access to play online or video games such as *Age of Empires*, *Max Payne*, *Counter Strike*, and so on.

RELIGIOUS PRACTICES AND CULTURAL CEREMONIES

Islam is the religion of the majority of the population in Turkey.[8] Among conservative families, religion is practiced by adults as well as teenagers. This includes performing prayers on a daily basis, observing the fasting month of Ramadan, and going to the mosque on Fridays. On the other hand, more urbanized parts of the population might not necessarily adhere to the teachings and rituals of religion in as strict a manner. But one interesting observation is that even for teenagers who might not be closely identify with Islam, on Fridays they might go to the mosque either with their friends or with other members of their families.

As has been explained above, religion plays a significant role in shaping the aspects of life for many in Turkey, such as in the areas of dress codes, mingling with the opposite sex, sexuality, and dating. But at the same time Turkey is the only country in the Islamic world where secularism is the constitutional character of the nation. Religious freedom is granted as a constitutional right to all Turks, and there is total separation between the state and religion.

One major religious and cultural celebration that marks the passage of young Turkish boys into the first stages of adulthood is circumcision. Circumcision is instructed by some Islamic teachings and is socially viewed as the marker of the transition a young male makes into early adulthood. Around the age of 10, a Turkish boy is typically perceived to be ready to make this passage into adulthood. A social ceremony usually accompanies this transition; typically the ceremony lasts for two days. The first day is a preparation for the actual carrying out of the circumcision. Family and friends gather either in the house of the boy to be circumcised or in a hotel hall especially reserved for the occasion. Music is played, people dance in honor of the boy to become a man, different foods and beverages are served, and some money is given to the boy to be circumcised as an expression of celebrating his passage to manhood. On the second day some religious rituals are performed before the operation of circumcision is carried out. Despite the considerable pain of the circumcision, family and friends conclude the ceremony by celebrating this special day when this younger sibling of theirs has made it into the very first stages of his manhood.

CONCLUSION

Trying to understand the life experiences of Turkish teenagers is not an easy journey. Teenagers in Turkey, like other members of the society at large, come from cultural, geographical, and socioeconomic conditions that influence their lifestyles, experiences, and daily choices. Youngsters from urban areas, ghetto neighborhoods, and rural parts of Turkey may share elements of life and experience other than belonging to one age group or speaking the same language. But they may also differ in many ways, as our exploration of family life, schooling experiences, entertainment, dating, premarital sex, recreational activities, marriage, dress codes and choices, and so on may show. The chance that two Turkish teenagers from two different social and geographical groups would have little in common is too great for them to be said to share a certain typical lifestyle or set of experiences. Differences among Turkish teenagers are the distinctive feature of teenage life and socialization in today's Turkey. In the parts of the country where economic factors and conditions of Westernization help establish a lifestyle that is similar to the Western lifestyle, teenagers might be seen as sharing some aspects of teenage life with U.S. youngsters, such as the way they dress, their musical preferences, and their choices in matters of dating and premarital sex. But the story is quite different and not that straightforward when we shift to other parts of Turkey where customs, religion, and socioeconomic factors interplay differently. This does not mean that you cannot, for example, see kids in different parts of Turkey who do things that are similar to other parts of the world, such as going to fast-food restaurants, enjoying a Disney film on TV or a VCR, or wanting to associate with some idols of U.S. and European popular culture. However, these alone do not make teenagers all the same or create typical conditions for them in general. After they eat their McDonald's meal, and finish seeing the Disney movie, teenagers have to deal with the realities of their family, social, and cultural lives. These different realities influence teenagers in different ways, and it becomes more difficult for one to be able to find unchangeable tendencies that can be described as typical. That is why instead of looking for generalizations and similarities that enable an identification of a typical teenage condition either within Turkey or in comparison to the United States, we may better understand the situation and experiences of teenagers if we look at how the different backgrounds create differences in how they live, love, entertain, and interact with their fellow teenagers, families, and the larger society.

NOTES

1. For detailed information, see Karpat, K. (2004), *Studies on Turkish Politics and Society: Selected Articles and Essays*, Brill, Leiden, Boston: Knoninklijke.

2. Every year on April 23 Turkish children celebrate their national day, with children coming from all over the world. These foreign children are housed in Turkish homes as long as they stay in Turkey. This day also has been recognized by UNICEF as International Children's Day.

3. For detailed information about the daily life practices of Turkish people before the foundation of the republic, see Lewis, R. (1971), *Everyday Life in Ottoman Turkey*, London, New York: B. T. Batsford Ltd. & G. P. Putnam's Sons.

4. On September 12, 1980, the military forces took control of the country due to political violence in the streets and the passivity of Parliament in handling the situation. All political parties were abolished. Soon after the coup, more than 30,000 people were arrested. Returning to civilian rule happened after the parliamentary elections of November 6, 1983.

5. In addition to this, Saktanber suggests that "the newly acquired images and characteristics that can be observed in Islamic youth in Turkey can not and should not be explained, of course, merely within the limits of a set of given political actions and ideological discourse. This is actually what has usually been done to understand both the Islamic and wider youth culture as a whole in Turkish society" (2002, p. 255).

6. The word *gecekondu* in Turkish means "built overnight." These are unregulated residential areas built on the outskirts of cities without obtaining proper construction permits. People who live there usually migrate from rural areas in seeking employment and better life in the city, but what they find is infrastructure deficiencies that reduce quality of life and economic productivity while increasing the vulnerability of the urban poor (Baharoglu & Leitmann, 1998). These can be described as ghetto neighborhoods mostly populated by poor migrants from the countryside.

7. *Simit* is a sort of bread that is circular in shape with sesame seeds. It is a common traditional fast food.

8. For different interpretations of Islam in Turkey, see Oktem, N. (2002), Religion in Turkey, *Brigham Law University Law Review*, from http://www.law2.byu.edu/lawreview/archives/2002/2/Okt10.pdf.

RESOURCE GUIDE

Baharoglu, D., & Leitmann, J. (1998). Informal Rules! Using Institutional Economics to Understand Service Provision in Turkey's Spontaneous Settlements. *Journal of Development Studies*, 34(5), p. 25.

Durakbasa, A., & Cindoglu, D. (2002). Encounters at the Counter: Gender and Shopping Experience. In D. Kandiyoti & A. Saktanber (Eds.), *Fragments of Culture: The Everyday of Modern Turkey*. New Jersey: Rutgers University Press.

European Union. (2003). *Annual Report 2003: The State of the Drugs Problem in the Acceding and Candidate Countries to the European Union: Turkey*. Brussels: European Union Commission.

Karpat, K. (2004). *Studies on Turkish Politics and Society: Selected Articles and Essays*. Brill, Leiden, Boston: Knoninklijke.

Kongar, E. (1976). A Survey of Familial Change in Two Turkish Gecekondu Areas. In J. G. Peristiany (Ed.), *Mediterranean Family Structures*. Cambridge: Cambridge University Press.

Lewis, R. (1971). *Everyday Life in Ottoman Turkey*. London, New York: B. T. Batsford Ltd. & G. P. Putnam's Sons.

Mardin, S. (1994). *Türk Modernlesmesi*. Istanbul: Iletisim Yayinlari.

Oktem, N. (2002). Religion in Turkey. *Brigham Law University Law Review*, from http://www.law2.byu.edu/lawreview/archives/2002/2/Okt10.pdf.

Saktanber, A. (2002). We Pray Like You Have Fun: New Islamic Youth in Turkey between Intellectualism and Popular Culture. In D. Kandiyoti &

A. Saktanber (Eds.), *Fragments of Culture: The Everyday of Modern Turkey*. New Jersey: Rutgers University Press.

State Institute of Statistics (SIS). (2001). *Turkiye'de Calisan Cocuklar (Child Labor in Turkey)*. Ankara: State Institute of Statistics.

Yurdadon, E. (2003). Sport in Turkey: Pre-Islamic Period. *Sport Journal*, 6(3).

Nonfiction

The Making of Modern Turkey (The Making of the Middle East Series), by Feroz Ahmad, New York: Routledge (1993).

Turkish Transformation: New Century, New Challenges, by Brian Beeley (Editor), Huntingdon, UK: Eothen Press (2002).

Children of Turkey (Through the Eyes of Children), by Connie Bickman, Edina, MN: Abdo & Daughters (1994).

Eyewitness Travel Guide to Istanbul, by Deni Brown, New York: DK Publishing (1998).

The Development of Turkish Democracy, by C. H. Dodd, *British Journal of Middle Eastern Studies*, Vol. 19, No. 1 (1992), pp. 16–30.

Sister Shako and Kolo the Goat: Memories of My Childhood in Turkey, by Vedat Dolakay, Guner Ener (Translator), New York: Lothrop Lee & Shepard (1994).

What Hath Rock Wrought?: Blues, Country Music, Rock 'n Roll and Istanbul, by Clifford Endress, *Journal of American Studies of Turkey*, Vol. 1 (1995), pp. 33–39.

Crescent and Star: Turkey between Two Worlds, by Stephen Kinzer, New York: Farrar Straus & Giroux (2002).

A Changing Turkey: Challenges to Europe and the United States, by Heinz Kramer, Washington, D.C.: Brookings Institution Press (2000).

Let's Go 2003: Turkey, by Let's Go, Let's Go Travel Publications, 5th edition (2002).

The Emergence of Modern Turkey (Studies in Middle Eastern History), by Bernard Lewis, Oxford, UK: Oxford Press, 3rd edition (2001).

Turkey and the European Union, by Ronnie Marguiles, *Middle East Report*, No. 199, Turkey: Insolvent Ideologies, Fractured State (April–June 1996), p. 27.

Blue Guide Turkey (Blue Guides), by Bernard McDonagh, 3rd edition, New York: W. W. Norton & Company, (2001).

Gender Relations in Agriculture: Women in Turkey, by Behrooz Morvaridi, *Economic Development and Cultural Change*, Vol. 40, No. 3 (April 1992), pp. 567–586.

Political Cartoons in the Middle East: Cultural Representation in the Middle East, by Fatma Muge Gokcek (Editor), Princeton, NJ: Markus Wiener Publishing (1997).

Faces of the State: Secularism and Public Life in Turkey, by Yael Navaro-Yashin, Princeton, NJ: Princeton University Press (2002).

Portrait of a Turkish Family, by Irfan Orga, Ates Orga (Afterword), London: Eland Books (2003).

Just Enough Turkish, by Passport Books, New York: McGraw-Hill (1990).

Turkey Unveiled: A History of Modern Turkey, by Nicole Pope, Hugh Pope, New York: Overlook Press (2000).

In Turkey, Women's Fertility Is Linked to Education, Employment and Freedom to Choose a Husband (in Digests), by L. Remez, *International Family Planning Perspectives*, Vol. 24, No. 2 (June 1998), pp. 97–98.

Photo Essay: Transsexuals and the Urban Landscape in Istanbul, by Mary Robert, Deniz Kandiyoti, *Middle East Report*, No. 206, Power and Sexuality in the Middle East (Spring 1998), pp. 20–25.

Turkey and the Middle East in the 1990s, by Sabri Sayari *Journal of Palestine Studies*, Vol. 26, No. 3 (Spring 1997), pp. 44–55.

Turkish Reflections: A Biography of a Place, by Mary Lee Settle, Carmichael, CA: Touchstone Books (1992).

Islam, the Turkish State and Arabesk, by Martin Stokes, *Popular Music*, Vol. 11, No. 2, A Changing Europe (May 1992), pp. 213–227.

Lonely Planet Turkey, by Pat Yale, Verity Campbell, Richard Plunkett, 8th edition, Oakland, CA: Lonely Planet (2003).

Europe in the Turkish Mirror, by M. E. Yapp, *Past and Present*, No. 137, The Cultural and Political Construction of Europe (November 1992), pp. 134–155.

Fiction

Night: A Novel (winner of the Pegasus Prize for Literature), by Bilge Karasu, Guneli Gun (Translator), Baton Rouge, LA: Louisiana State University Press, reprint edition (1994).

Anatolian Tales, by Yasar Kemal, London: Writers & Readers Publishing, Inc. (1983).

Memed My Hawk, by Yasar Kemal, Eduardo Roditi (Translator), London: Harvill Press (1998).

Salman the Solitary, by Yasar Kemal, Thilda Kemal (Translator), London: Harvill Press (1999).

Belshazzar's Daughter: A Novel of Istanbul, by Barbara Nadel, New York: St. Martin's Minotaur (2004).

The Black Book, by Orhan Pamuk, Guneli Gun (Translator), (2002).

My Name Is Red, by Orhan Pamuk, Erdag Goknar (Translator), London: Vintage (2002).

The New Life, by Orhan Pamuk, London: Vintage, reprint edition (1998).

Snow, by Orhan Pamuk, Toronto: Knopf (2004).

The White Castle: A Novel, by Orhan Pamuk, London: Vintage, reprint edition (1998).

Dear Shameless Death, by Latife Tekin, Saliha Paker (Translator), Mel Kenne (Translator), London: Marion Boyars Publishers, Ltd. (2001).

Web Sites

http://www.die.gov.tr/ (statistics about Turkey)

http://www.exploreturkey.com/ (history, culture, life, tourism)

http://www.gazeteler.com/ (newspapers—Turkish and English)

http://www.kultur.gov.tr/ (Turkish Ministry of Culture)

http://www.mfa.gov.tr/ (Turkish Ministry of Foreign Affairs)

http://www.odci.gov/cia/publications/factbook/geos/tu.html (CIA Factbook)

http://www.turizm.gov.tr/ (Turkish Ministry of Tourism)

http://www.tursab.org.tr/english/default.htm (tourism, information)

http://www.worldtrek.org/odyssey/mideast/timeturkey.html (cultural travel)

More Information

Abercrombie & Kent
1520 Kensington Road
Oak Brook, IL 60523
Tel: 800-323-7308, 630-954-2944
Fax: 630-954-3324
E-mail: info@abercrombiekent.com
Web site: http://www.aegeantours.com/

ALP Travel
1029 Main Street, Unit D
Paterson, NY 07503
Tel: 973-247-1622
Fax: 973-247-0777
E-mail: alptrv1@aol.com
Web site: http://www.alptravelusa.com/
ATC Anadolu Tours
420 Madison Avenue, 10th floor
New York, NY 10017
Tel: 1-888-ANADOLU, 212-755-6516
Fax: 212-486-4014
E-mail: alkanoral@hotmail.com
Web site: http://www.atc-anadolu.com/

New York Tourism Information Attaché
Office of the Turkish Tourism Information Attaché
821 United Nations Plaza
New York, NY 10017

Tel: 212-687-2194
Fax: 212-599-7568
E-mail: ny@tourismturkey.org
Web site: http://www.tourismturkey.org/

A Touch of Class Tours
21820 Burbank Boulevard, Suite 225
Woodland Hills, CA 91367
Tel: 800-203-0438
Fax: 818-883-4624
E-mail: sales@atoctours.com
Web site: http://www.atoctours.com/

Turkish Embassy
2525 Massachusetts Avenue NW
Washington, DC 20008
Tel: 202-612-6700
Fax: 202-612-6744
E-mail: contact@turkishembassy.org

American Turkish Council (ATC)
http://www.americanturkishcouncil.org/

Assembly of Turkish American Associations (ATAA),
http://www.ataa.org/

Assembly of Turkish Student Associations (ATSA-DC)
http://www.atsadc.org/

Ataturk Society of America (ASA)
http://www.ataturksociety.org/

Federation of Turkish American Associations (FTAA)
http://www.ftaa.org/

Institute of Turkish Studies (ITS),
http://www.turkishstudies.org/
Intercollegiate Turkish Students Society (ITSS)
http://www.itss.org/

Turkish American Business Forum
http://www.forum.org/

Pen Pal Information

http://www.polyglot-learn-language.com/recherche.php?country=Turkey

INDEX

ABOUT THE EDITOR
AND CONTRIBUTORS

Shirley R. Steinberg is the program head of graduate literacy at Brooklyn College and also teaches with the CUNY Graduate Center Urban Education Doctoral Program in New York City. She is the author and editor of many books and articles, as well as the senior and founding editor of *Taboo: The Journal of Culture and Education*. She is the series editor of many successful book series in education and cultural studies. Her most recent books are: *The Encyclopedia of Contemporary Youth Culture*, (with Priya Parmar and Birgit Richard): Greenwood Press, 2006; *Kinderculture: The Corporate Construction of Childhood*, Westview Press, 2004; *Things You Don't Know About Schools*, Palgrave Press, 2005; *19 Urban Questions: Teaching in the City*, Peter Lang, 2004; and *The Miseducation of the West: How Schools and the Media Distort Our Understanding of the Islamic World*, Praeger Press, 2004 (many with Joe L. Kincheloe). Her areas of research are youth culture, media studies, queer theory, and pedagogy. She is a devoted fan of rock and roll, and travels internationally with Joe Kincheloe, presenting on issues of youth and of education.

Anna-Maria Ahlén has an M.A. in international education and is working at the Department of Education, Uppsala University in Sweden as a Ph.D. student.

Anthony E. Azzopardi is a senior lecturer at the University of Malta. He coordinates the Youth Studies Programme and chairs the Extracurricular Credits Board. He is the chairperson of the Youth Research Network of the Council of Europe and a consultant on youth policy. He has published a number of articles and book chapters both in Malta and in Europe.

Françoise Bodone is an international scholar who received her Ph.D. in educational policy and leadership from the University of Oregon. Her interests include critical pedagogy as applied to research and classroom practices and cultural/social justice in education. She is the editor of *What difference does research make and for whom?* (Peter Lang Publishing).

Marilyn Clark is a social psychologist specializing in criminal behavior and addiction studies. She lectures full time with the Programme of Youth Studies and the Department of Psychology at the University of Malta. She is presently an assistant to the Magistrate on the Juvenile Court.

Vítor Sérgio Ferreira is a sociologist and junior researcher in the Institute of Social Sciences of Lisbon University.

Ainhoa Flecha is researcher at the Department of Sociological Theory, University of Barcelona. She teaches sociology of education and women in popular education. Her research interests focus on gender studies, particularly from the perspective of dialogic feminism and the inclusion of "otherized women."

Carme Garcia is assistant professor at the University of Lleida, where she teaches in communication studies. Among her research interests are learning communities and the study of active citizenship. She has worked close to the student movements in relation to the democratization of higher education.

Amanda Kluveld is assistant professor of cultural history at faculty of humanities of the University of Amsterdam. Her current research topic is the history of pain from the nineteenth century to the present.

Claire Lambe was born in Ireland. She taught high school art and art history in Dublin for many years. She moved to the United States in 1996 and now lives in Woodstock, New York. She is currently teaching English and art history to high school students at the Woodstock Day School.

José Machado Pais is a social scientist and is "Coordinator Researcher" at the University of Lisbon (Portugal) and has been visiting professor in several South American universities. He has conducted research in the fields of youth, culture, leisure and social structures and has been coordinating the Portuguese Youth Observatory since 1991.

Antonio Petrone has a Ph.D. in methodology of social sciences and is a lecturer in sociology at the University of Molise. He has published some articles and contributes about new media, youth, elderly and society and the environment.

Nicole Pfaff is a Ph.D. candidate at Martin Luther University in Wittenberg, Germany.

Mustafa Sever, born in Turkey, is currently Ph.D. candidate in Department of Educational Leadership and Policy, University at Buffalo, The State University of New York. A graduate of Ankara University, he earned his M.A. degree in social and historical foundations of education.

Gitte Stald is assistant professor of film and media studies at University of Copenhagen. She is working on three studies: media and mobility; online gaming cultures; and fascination of death and violence in computer games. She participated in the European comparative project *Children, Young People and the Changing Media Environment* 1995–1998, and in the research program *Global Media Cultures* 1999–2001. She is currently finishing the project *Global Media, Local Youth*. She is the editor (with T. Tufte) of *Global Encounters: Media and Cultural Transformation* (Luton Press 2002). She is local head of a cooperative research and development project on qualitative content for young Danes' mobile devices.

Michael Watts is a senior research associate at the Von Hugel Institute, St. Edmond's College, Cambridge. His main research focuses on global citizenship and widening participation in higher education.

Wiel Veuglers is a professor of education at the University for Humanistics in Utrecht and a teacher and researcher at the University of Amsterdam. He has published many articles and books on youth culture, moral and democratic education, and educational change.